KU-007-236

AS *If*

Blake Morrison was born in Skipton, Yorkshire. He is the author of two collections of poetry, *Dark Glasses* and *The Ballad of the Yorkshire Ripper*; of a children's book, *The Yellow House*; of critical studies of the Movement and Seamus Heaney; and is co-editor of *The Penguin Book of Contemporary British Poetry*. His bestselling memoir *And when did you last see your father?* won the Waterstone's/Esquire/Volvo Award for Non-Fiction, and the J.R. Ackerley Prize for Autobiography, in 1993. He lives in London.

'*As If* is the mature, considered and very personal response f one man to a tragic act. It is what our media should have given us . . . Morrison's voice is, as ever, eloquent with both passion and intelligence.' A.L. Kennedy, *Scotsman*

'Very finely written . . . supple, densely allusive, glittering prose.' Lucy Hughes-Hallett, *Sunday Times*

'Blake Morrison attended the trial and has written a lyrical, personal and intensely painful account of what he heard and felt . . . This is an important and, in the true sense of the word, dreadful book.' Beryl Bainbridge, *Evening Standard*

'Morrison brings to the case an uneasy conscience which insists that nothing is black and white . . . [he] exposes the inability of an adult tribunal to deal with such young defendants.' Joan Smith, *Financial Times*

'Blake Morrison is interested in the fundamental question of why the two young boys killed another child . . . [he] has contributed greatly to the debate and his thought-provoking book should be read by all those who have a serious interest in the vital process of reform.' *The Times*

'Honest, courageous and subtle.' *Independent*

AS *If*

BLAKE MORRISON

Granta Books

London

Granta Publications, 2/3 Hanover Yard, London N1 8BE

First published in Great Britain by Granta Books 1997
This edition published by Granta Books 1998

A CIP catalogue record for this book is available from the British Library.

1 3 5 7 9 10 8 6 4 2

Typeset in Janson by M Rules
Printed and bound in Great Britain by
Mackays of Chatham PLC

... from this instant,
There's nothing serious in mortality.
All is but toys, renown and grace is dead,
The wine of life is drawn ...

WILLIAM SHAKESPEARE, *Macbeth*

But never did Henry, as he thought he did,
end anyone and hacks her body up
and hide the pieces, where they may be found.
He knows: he went over everyone, & nobody's missing.
Often he reckons, in the dawn, them up.
Nobody is ever missing.

JOHN BERRYMAN, "Dream Song 29"

For the children

CONTENTS

1   *The Children's Crusade*   1

2   *Court*   25

3   *15:42:32*   44

4   *The Walk*   60

5   *Experts*   82

6   *Home*   102

7   *Lies, Tears*   120

8   *Weekend*   140

9   *Beatings*   159

10   *Sex Marks*   180

11   *No Defence*   207

12   *As If*   233

Acknowledgements   245

I

The Children's Crusade

Woe to the land that's governed by a child.

WILLIAM SHAKESPEARE, *Richard III*

"**A**s if this were the start of a dangerous adventure, the small boy puts his hand in the bigger boy's, and they follow a third boy through the square . . ."

When did I first hear the story of the Children's Crusade? Was it at home, in bed, from my mother, an anthology of classic legends perched in her hands? Was it at primary school, under the big window where we'd gather to hear The Famous Five or Dr Dolittle? At Sunday School, between singing "Onward Christian Soldiers" and receiving stars (gold and silver milk-bottle tops) for biblical knowhow? Did I pick up Henry Treece's *The Children's Crusade*, published in 1958, a novel for under-twelves, at some raffle or jumble sale? Or was it later, at big school, in a history lesson on the Middle Ages, something chalked up on the board, "read pp. 154–7 of your primer and describe in your own words the meaning of the Children's Crusade"? I don't know. I can't recall. But the story has stayed.

As if this were the start of a dangerous adventure, the small boy puts his hand in the bigger boy's, and they follow a third boy through the square. Stephen sees them coming. They're not the first children to approach but they move more purposefully than the others, threading through the adults to where he stands in the cathedral's midday shade. The sight of them cheers him – like a star, an omen, a sign his mission will succeed. Blond-haired, twelve or so, in a plain brown shepherd's smock, he stands on his straw-bale, by the cathedral of Saint-Denis, and raises his two hands, palm upwards, like the saviour in the stained-glass windows. The trio come forward, then sit on the ground in front of him and stare.

He takes a letter from his pocket, and unfolds it. It was given him by Jesus, he says – in the sheepfold, three nights ago. He reads the letter aloud: "Dear Stephen, I have chosen you to lead a crusade of children to the Holy Land. You must leave your work and abandon your home. Gather followers as quickly as you can, for time is short. Your pilgrimage must leave from Vendôme in two months. Have faith. Take strength. I will not appear to you again – see, I am gone already, as you read. But I will sit at your right shoulder and guide you safely to Palestine. Trust in God, our father. You must begin at once."

Stephen explains to the children: Christendom is in danger from the Infidel. They must take the cross and go on a long journey together, the sea will dry up before them, they will pass through the waves like Moses and recapture the Holy Sepulchre, Islam will be vanquished under their sword. It is hard work, preaching. Stephen's voice is like a stone cast down the side of a ravine. He waits for other stones to be caught in its wake, an army of stones cascading. Seeing the trio at his feet, other children have gathered now, a dozen, two dozen, more. They sit wide-eyed while he asks them to step up and pledge their troth. He begs them to have faith. No movement yet. Undaunted, he talks on.

The first to come forward is a boy his age, brightly dressed, like a jester. Pierre, he says he's called. He gives his hand, then takes out a wooden whistle and starts to play. The music seems to help. Stephen tosses his words into the air, and the pipe leaps up to pitch them further off. More converts. In dribs and drabs at first, brothers and sisters, two by two, into Stephen's ark. Then whole families, flocking. A priest watches suspiciously from the vestry window. Time, Stephen thinks, to move on. Already they are thirty, and by the time they reach the outskirts they have gathered twenty more.

At every village, he follows the same routine. By the church or pump, Stephen finds a place to stand, a step or bale or stool, something to raise him above the crowd. Then he casts the words of God, each time a little smoother, more persuasive, and Pierre pipes up to pitch them further off. Curious, spellbound, the children come. Sometimes adults come as well. They too are entranced. Didn't Christ himself appear in this way, out of the blue? Let the children have the fun of it while it lasts. Even a priest mutters approval: "These children are a reproach: they march to recover the Holy Land while we slumber." Some parents are less convinced. They stand at the edge, trying to wrest their children from the other children. One hard-faced apothecary drags his daughter off by the hair. Later, as the marchers leave town, she steps from behind a tree to join them. She has a small canvas bag, with provisions.

It is as much as anyone brings. Some come with nothing at all.

That first night, camped by the roadside, Stephen tries to talk to Pierre: he has plans, proposals, ideas to share. But Pierre's not one for words. He listens awhile, and for a reply gets out his pipe, its notes rising like stars to soothe the marchers off to sleep. Sweet May warmth, a late-darkening sky. Some children have blankets to lie on, others only the daisied grass. Next day the route goes north: Beauvais, Amiens, Abbeville, St-Omer. At Calais, they spend a day by the sea, over a thousand of them now, the little ones thinking these must be the waves they'll walk through, even the big ones not grasping how far they have still to go. Another week. Their route curls west, then south: Dieppe, Rouen, Elbeuf, Lisieux, Alençon, Bonnétable. Word goes ahead of them now. At the edge of one village, they are barred by fathers bearing scythes. Stephen turns away, across the fields, where a dozen village children wait to join them. Everywhere it's the same. At their head, Stephen seems to grow taller, blonder. He has his own pulpit now. A carpenter's boy knocked it up for him, a little dais to stand on, a lectern to read from, two supporting rails. Six of the bigger lads, hulking farmhands, make it their job to transport it between towns, bearing it on their shoulders like a coffin.

At Mortemer, as Stephen mounts the pulpit, an old priest steps forward to denounce him.

"You, boy," he shouts, "the false prophet, who are you to speak for God? Every word you say is blasphemy. Go back to your homes, children: do not listen to him. It is the Devil talking."

The priest brandishes a crucifix. Cross-legged, the children giggle. Stephen answers back.

"Is the church so corrupt it cannot hear God's word? I have

no tricks, no magic, no secret powers to make these children follow me. Only God."

"You claim to serve God, but you are wrong. In God's order, parents command, priests preach, knights crusade, and children obey. You are turning the world upside down. When children rule adults, Satan smiles."

This time, rather than speaking, Stephen slips his smock from his shoulders and shows his back to the crowd. Gasps, murmurs. The skin across the spine is striped with purple. A long pause, then Stephen turns:

"Other priests have spoken like you. Some have gone further, as you see. But no lash or whip can stop this mission. These children hear the Lord speaking through me. That is why they come."

And still they come, in thousands now, and tens of thousands. They spread like locusts across the plain, more and more and more of them. Leprosy, some call it – a festering plague. But Stephen speaks of water in the desert, and triumphal swelling progress: raindrop, runnel, rivulet, river, sea. Skirting Cloyes, his home and birthplace, the marchers reach Vendôme. Thousands more are waiting. Will those with special skills please make themselves known to him, Stephen asks, and they do: this one is the daughter of a cook, that one the son of a doctor – they will come in useful. Later he preaches to the multitude, reminding them of miracles: Daniel in the Lion's Den, the Voice from the Burning Bush, David and Goliath, the Parting of the Red Sea. A young priest says prayers. Local shopkeepers donate food: oranges, melons, bread, cakes, honey, wine. The mayor has given a donkey-cart, and volunteers are painting it sky-blue. A pipe band strikes up, led by Pierre. There are thirty thousand children, of all ages and sizes: fat and thin, toddling and lanky; the dark, the fair, and the ginger-freckled; a few who are blind, some who are deaf, and many with missing front teeth. They fall in behind. The great journey begins.

At the head of the march a boy in a borrowed surplice carries a cross, made of bronze. Flanking him, two other boys bear gold-tasselled banners that snake in the wind. Just behind, in the heaven-blue donkey cart, under a canopy improvised from grain-sacks, elevated yet safe from sunstroke, sits Stephen. Many walk barefoot. A song goes up, and another, along the miles: Latin hymns at first, then marching rhymes, later ballads and harvest love-spoons picked up from older siblings. Four and eight abreast, the procession stretches back a mile. Too excited still for tiredness, young children run beside Stephen's cart, touching the dusty wheels and bright-blue boards, eager to be close to their leader. He waves and smiles, and sometimes pulls the smallest up beside him, to ride a mile and rest those aching limbs,

They stop that evening in a grassy hollow by a wood. It looks too small to accommodate thirty thousand marchers, but they manage it, or Christ does on their behalf, a miracle. More miracles are wrought with supper, the spit-roast of a single roe-deer captured in the woods sufficient to feed them all. Afterwards, as dark comes on, the grassy hollow echoes with the crying of infants: mama, mama, mama. Older children try to calm them with lullabies:

> Sleep, little ones, sleep.
> Your father's in the mountains.
> Your mother's weaving baskets.
> The valley's full of lilies.
> The horse is eating lemon-leaves.
> Sleep, little ones, sleep.

Next morning, the children rise like mist from the fields, marching while half-asleep. Important to keep the pace up, while the weather's kind and legs are not too weary. Twenty miles a day, preferably thirty. Day on day, step after step, ditto, ditto, ditto. Deeper south, the little water they have runs out but Stephen, casting spells from his canopy, replenishes trickling becks and dried-up wells. No shortage of food, either. Old women in lonely villages, hearing the rustle of the army through the corn, come forth with trays of sweetmeats. A ram is found, its horns caught in a thicket. Flocks of geese flying north to cooler weather are brought down in hundreds by slingstones. In the mountains a snow shower meets them, with flakes that seem to taste of more than water. South of Lyons, they turn the corner of a sunken road and find a baker's cart on its side, its axle broken, bread spilling on the grass – neither baker nor horse is to be seen, but the loaves are still warm. Next day, by the Rhône, some boys rush back excitedly, saying they've dammed a shoal of fish, and would the girls prepare a grill. Manna from heaven. Loaves and fishes. Daily miracles.

But the days are long. How much longer? A group of peasants in the fields, getting wind of the coming army, drop their scythes and run across, clamouring for locks of Stephen's hair. Where are they going? they ask the children. To God, they're told, and in return are asked: How far to the sea? Three days, maybe four, they say, pointing to the horizon. Somewhere along the way a dog, a retriever, has attached itself to the march, and now it's hoisted up with Stephen, resting its head on the prow of the cart, black snout pointing ahead. Next morning, the dog seems excited, its damp nose sniffing something. Others do, too – salt in the air, a freshness. Then a wide gleam in the distance, not heat haze over vineyards but a sharp sliver of silver. Houses grow more numerous, clotting towards land's end. The children can see sails now, out in the bay, and then masts, unmoving, in the harbour. Finally, at sunset, the town square of Marseilles. The little army is fed and watered, spends the night curled up in doorways, then at dawn moves to the harbour, for the miracle. On his donkey-cart, Stephen stands like Moses, like Canute, raising his arm to the waves. Through the water lies the new Canaan. The sea is going to part for him, for everyone, a miracle.

Here the story peters out, on the brink, triumph just a walk between the waves away. What happened after that? More triumphs. More onward-marching Christian soldiers. So I thought then, or think I must have thought then, in the days of *as if*, when most things seemed possible – Santa Claus, the tooth-fairy, the Easter bunny, witches, ghosts, the virgin birth, heaven, God. Back then, the Children's Crusade felt like something out of the Bible, with a bit of Enid Blyton thrown in. Children, it seemed to be saying – if they're brave, deter-mined, trusting – can have the most amazing adventures. And beat the baddies as well.

I see myself listening, wide-eyed, an open book. It was a tale of Innocence, appropriate for the time, childhood, or my child-hood, the late 1950s and early 1960s. We were innocent then, or wanted to be – even the adults who'd had (and were trying to unlearn) the experience of war. The world was all right. We crusaders were going to make it even better. Or so it seemed, from where I was, in a small village surrounded by gentle hills. I lived in a sort of biblical haze. My parents – GPs – were healers. Tillers of the fields moved beyond the window, with their sheepdogs. The Jersey cow had a golden calf. The larder

ran with silverfish, like the Sea of Galilee. *As if* lay all
me. It wasn't hard to believe in the Children's Crusade.

But perhaps, even then, I grasped there must be m
the story – could sense it had been edited down. Chi
can be credulous, and I was more credulous than most
there were things about Stephen that didn't ring quite tr
story about a twelve-year-old set in 1212: it seemed too n
numerologically, to be convincing. There were myths of fr
birds, fish and dog packs travelling to the Holy Land: I kn
they couldn't be true – did this belong with them? I imagi
myself curled up in the window behind the *Encyclopaed
Britannica*, getting older and more distrustful. Was th
Crusade like all the other *as if*s, a lie told by parents? I saw
film at this time (saw it being filmed, in fact, on a nearby
farm): *Whistle Down the Wind*, with Alan Bates and Hayley
Mills, about a group of children who find a man in their barn
and take him for Jesus Christ. One of these children, a boy,
isn't fooled: he knows the man's not Jesus. I liked this boy. I
too was becoming suspicious. I'd begun to sense a world
beyond Sunday school and U-certificates. Adolescence had
started, my arms and legs sprouting hair like Esau's. I was
moving on – from birds' eggs and Dinky cars to girls and
Tamla Motown. The 1960s were also moving on, from
Innocence to Experience. Every age has its own story, or
rewrites the same story; every Age, too. I see myself getting
the atlas out and – jaded, disbelieving – following the child
Crusaders down through France. I play the film back, reviewing it through narrowed eyes.

Vendôme, the day of the great departure. Here are the parents, brave and tearful, waving their children goodbye. And

there's the donkey-cart, its wheels spoking up dust, with Stephen enthroned like a little emperor. The plain smock has gone: he has decked himself out in silk – also, in the process, refurbishing the cart with cushions and rugs. Beside the cart, with its stilled, revolving wheels, little children run excitedly, eager to be close to their leader. Stephen quickly tires of this – the relentless staring obeisance distracts him from his prayers, he says – and he asks his deputies, Jacques and Julien, a strapping pair of twins, to shoo the children off. The twins oblige, raising their stakes, biffing and prodding any intruders – a little blood, some tears, best set the right example from the start. Later, in the interests of security, curtains are drawn around the cart, and only those with permits allowed in its vicinity: the flag-bearer, the two deputies, the three body-guards, the four "sons of . . ." (chef, doctor, magician, pedicurist), and Pierre, the joker with the flute. Strictly no girls up front: the Crusade is a voyage to God; females on voyages bring bad luck.

By dusk on the first day, the procession is straggling back over the horizon, the little ones not keeping up. Three days, and already several thousand, bored, tired or losing faith, are heading home. Others – teen thieves, con-boys and baby-whores – joined up in Vendôme only for the prospect of roadside trade and now, disheartened by the lack of it, slip off to passing towns. Each day a little harder, each day a little hotter. No wells or streams to drink from, no vineyards to raid grapes from, only dust and endless roads. The little ones ask for bread, but mostly there is none to break. Now even older kids fall by the wayside, resting then dying there. Every procession leaves rubbish in its wake, and this one is littered with small corpses. Before they reach the mountains, ten thousand of the thirty thousand die.

In need of new recruits, Stephen stops off in towns to preach. Not easy: with the children at his side so lame and sick, sermons of milk and honey aren't enough. He has to perform: to display his martyr's scars (the purple weals painted on his back), and work the egg and scarf tricks learned from the magician's son (there had been a rabbit, earlier, but that had had to be eaten). Even then, the would-be recruits can be reluctant: they want to know what's in it for them. These southerners don't have the Faith. No one likes dragooning, but ways are found to rope in volunteers.

South and further south, worse and worse. In Lyons, an incident. Stephen and his henchmen visit the cathedral, to pray for help, and are given food by a young priest. Afterwards, a gold chalice is found to be missing. Four riders are despatched after the marchers, to secure its return. Stephen protests his innocence: a messiah, a man of God, surely they're not accusing him, or any of his followers . . . Unimpressed, the horsemen dismount and search the cart, under the cushions, all bags and knapsacks. Nothing. The four horsemen are angry – apoplectic. Stephen, they warn, has not heard the last of this. Once they've safely gone, Pierre pipes up from behind a boulder. He has a bag over his shoulder, and a gleam from inside it catches the light. He climbs beside Stephen, on the cart.

The journey continues. Step after sore step, dried-up source after dried-up source. From Lyons, word has passed ahead: in every town, the crusaders are greeted by closed blinds and empty streets. Only the priests will speak to them: they denounce Stephen as a leper, a locust, a louse. Lice are indeed a problem, and other vermin. Hard to sleep at night for the high whiff in the heat and the scuttle of rats. Grapes shrivel on the vine. There has been no hotter summer for a century. It is only God testing our mettle, says Stephen, from the shade. While his troops grow weaker, he looks bigger, stronger, less like twelve than fifteen. Good for the hormones, being a messiah. At night girls are escorted to his donkey-cart, some as young as ten. Strange screams in the darkness. The dwindling young cry for their parents. The older ones despair of reaching the sea.

But they do reach it, late one evening, a lift of spirits, hopes burnished by the low red sun. Weeks and weeks of walking towards this moment. They throw themselves in the waves, to wash away the dust of all those miles. To quench their thirsts, too, some of them: they are inland children, innocent of the bitter taste of sea. Grilled fish for supper and the sleep of the blessed. Next day, in the harbour, Stephen stands on his donkey cart, for the miracle. He raises his arms and bids it come. A pause, a delay, a wait for God to get His act together. Nothing. Stephen opens his hands and holds them palm-upward to the sky. The sea abides, unparted. Surprise, surprise, no miracle. A last try. He wades in, up to his thighs. The sea laps about him, unreacting. Empty-handed, Stephen turns to face his troops. Some are for lynching him there and then. Others begin mapping the journey home. The annalists have their pens poised: "thus deceived and confused, the children began to return; and those who had been earlier wont to traverse the lands in happy throngs, always singing to the heavens, now returned one at a time, the boys silent and hungry, the girls deflowered, fools in everyone's eyes".

So the story goes, the revisionist version. A Massacre of Innocents. Despair instead of faith. Not trust and goodness, but manipulation and evil. Disillusion, failure and death.

Children – *big* children – as devils, rather than angels. The *Lord of the Flies* view. A story for our century, or the end of it: religious cults, false messiahs, infants dying of disease and starvation, a long march ending in catastrophe. All of which makes it easier to believe.

The Crusade, in this version, has lost its magic – is short on hope and conviction. Disenchantment: something that happened to me at a certain age, in my teens; something that happened to the Age, too. The state seems widespread now, in the 1990s. You don't have to grow up to feel cynical. You don't even have to be a teenager. *As if*, my children say, as I used to say at their age, but the phrase doesn't mean what it did. We'll be sitting round the television together, *The Nine O'Clock News* on, with its cries of pain from other countries (Bosnia, Somalia, Rwanda), and every two minutes or so my son (who's twelve) will be there with his four letters, his two blunt words, coming down like a brick against anything that's wishful or implausible. Hopes are high that a peace agreement can be reached next week. *As if.* American scientists believe a new drug may provide a significant breakthrough in the treatment of cancer. *As if.* The England manager today named the squad which he is confident will bring home the next World Cup. *As if.* The trope used to be enlarging, wondrous, a means of seeing beyond our noses, an escape from the prison house of fact. *As if*: it was the sound the swing made as it scythed us upward through the air, the whisper of dreams and lovely promises. Much virtue in *as if*. Now, in kids' mouths, it means the opposite. Earthbound scepticism and diminution: tell me about it, dream on, get real. Not hope but the extinction of hope. *As if*: not a candle to light us to bed, but a chopper to chop off our heads.

As if. Doubt is addictive. Doubt is catching. I've doubts even about the doubting version of the Children's Crusade.

Maybe the story itself is a fantasy. But when I look it up in reference books, there it is, documented from fifty or more thirteenth-century sources. Stephen, it seems, wasn't the only boy visionary that year. From Cologne, between Easter and Whitsun, a twelve-year-old called Nicholas led another Crusade, his route taking him over the Alps, the expedition then breaking into different groups to reach Marseilles, Genoa, Pisa, Brindisi and Rome. Most histories of the Crusades carry a paragraph or two. Like the stories of Christ and Robin Hood, this one seems to have a basis in fact.

But the accounts vary. The interpretations are infinite. There are as many versions of the Crusade as there are sources. And even where there's agreement about the narrative, there are questions still to resolve. Motivation, for instance. What were the parents doing, letting their children go off? If they'd wanted to stop them, surely they could have, easily? So why did they consent? Innocence says they, too, had faith in Stephen's mission; experience that they found him useful. Times were hard, circa 1212: large families, poor harvests. A third of children died before they reached two, but that still left a nest of hungry mouths to feed. What to do? What had always been done. Abandonment – taking a child or two to the forest, or city, and leaving them there. "Exposure", as it was known – the nicest kind of infanticide, since it didn't always lead to death. The tradition went back to ancient times. Every language has a word for such children, or the lucky ones, the survivors: foundling, *enfant trouvé*, *gettatello*, *expósito*. Every culture has its legends of them: Oedipus, Romulus and Remus, Moses in his creel. Hence the allure of Stephen, salve to the adult conscience. Just when you thought you'd have to dump, strangle or sell your child, a Godsend, the Crusade.

And the children? Why were they so enthusiastic to go?

Did they hate the life they had? Was their Crusading a kind of mass hysteria? And how could they have walked so far? In those days, children had to grow up fast. Even so, a journey of such a distance: can we really be talking four-, six-, eight-, ten- and twelve-year-olds here? I'm perplexed. It doesn't feel right. I dig around, without success. Then a friend gives me an article, by a Dutch academic, Peter Raedts, published in the *Journal of Medieval History*. Raedts points out that the word used in contemporary accounts of the Crusade was *pueri*, which can mean children, but also meant, more generally, youngish persons (anything from seven to twenty-eight), and, more loosely still, farmhands, labourers, dependants, servants, and younger sons not due to inherit. In some mouths, *puer* seems to have been (as "puerile" is) a derogatory term, a put-down, more to do with social status than with age – much as US white Southerners once used "boy" to refer to blacks. The sources also say that some of the *pueri* were married, and that *pastores*, *mulieres*, *homines* and *pauperes* also joined in the march. It's only later, less reliable accounts that speak of twelve-year-olds. So the "children", it seems, were young people, most of them unemployed and without prospects. Stephen himself would have been twenty or so – an idealist or ideologue, an ascetic who hated the system and promised a better life overseas. His followers were the no-hopers of the feudal economy, a mob of disgruntled teenagers with nothing to lose, their Crusade a yobbos' outing to the Med.

The more I look at it, the less about children the Children's Crusade seems to be. The Crusaders themselves were adult, more or less. The chroniclers of the Crusade were also adult, but liked to leave adults out of the picture, as if absolving them of responsibility for what went on. Maybe that's why the tale seems modern, familiar, a story the present Age is also fond of, a story of kids being in control – or rather out of control, beyond all supervision. When adults talk about children these days, they seem to picture themselves as Gulliver among the Lilliputians, roped down by little people. We're powerless. Our hands are tied. The little sods ignore everything we say to them. There's nothing we can do.

But isn't this the most implausible story of all? For look how adults crowd the frame. Watch for their prints. Unmask them between the lines and in the margins. See them put their thumbs on the scales. Admit, when the verdict's passed, the inadmissible evidence. Listen again: to a story about grown-ups.

After his failure to part the waves, Stephen sits disconsolate on a capstan. He hadn't wanted this. He never planned to go it alone. Though he feels to have been singled out, as God's Elect, he knows he can't succeed without help. Many times along the march, he has prayed for some adult to intervene, to offer help and guidance, to share the burden. But the adults, if not actively hostile, have been indifferent. Now the Crusade has reached the sea, the dead end of Europe, and he's stuck in this rotting harbour, the tattered army sullen and mutinous at his back.

Enter two merchants, Hugh the Iron and William the Pig. Sitting down next to Stephen, among the ropes and corks and fishing nets, they introduce themselves, tell him they know about his mission and offer to sail the Crusaders to Palestine, free of charge. *As if.* Even Stephen is suspicious. Whoever heard of merchants doing something for nothing? But The Iron and The Pig have the next life to think of, and sins to atone for in this. Hands folded like monks' hands, they beg Stephen to let them perform this humble service for God. He accepts their offer. They shake on it. He goes off to face his gang.

In a quayside bar, there has been an earlier meeting: the Iron, the Pig, and Pierre. The jester, drunk, offguard, has been boasting of his exploits on the road – the sex, the drink, the scams. He mentions the gold chalice, acquired in Lyon, and they ask to see it: he flashes it at them, a million-franc gleam from his bag. Impressed, they buy him a drink and ask what he wants for the chalice. Its price is a thousand boarding cards to Palestine, he says, free passage for the Crusaders. They frown and hesitate and shake their heads: ships come expensive. But all right. Plus a thousand francs for him, says Pierre, upping the stakes. Five hundred, they say. Eight hundred. Seven. Seven fifty. Done. They shake hands on it, and go their separate ways. Afterwards, The Iron and The Pig talk to an Arab merchant: a Saracen, a Moslem, a cousin of the caliph, a trader in cattle and figs. He has seven ships leaving tomorrow, with room below decks for extra cargo. They have a proposal for him. Suppose . . . He listens. They haggle. A deal is struck. They hand him money – no, *he* hands *them* money. Why? Shhh. The Iron and the Pig come out smiling, several thousand francs the richer, and still with the chalice to sell.

Back on the quay, Stephen addresses his troops. A wave of enthusiasm. One thousand crusaders embark on seven ships. From the quayside, a pipe band – Pierre at its head – serenades them off. On board, Stephen offers up thanks to God: "Our faith in Him endures as a rock. It is for Him we must retake the Holy Sepulchre. We cannot fail with God watching over us. He will wipe away every tear from our eyes, and death shall be no more, neither shall there be mourning nor crying nor pain, for the former things have passed away."

The picture fades. The seas go dark. The pilgrims sleep in the cattle-hold. Mouldy bread and sips of water. In bad weather off Sardinia, two ships capsize, all crew and passengers drowned. Five ships sail on, and reach their haven, with half the cargo still alive. Dhows sail from the harbour to greet them: a welcome party of Saracens. Where have they been? What delayed them? Are they all here? Hugh the Iron and William the Pig promised seven ships, not five. And so many corpses below deck. The caliph may make trouble: when he buys a thousand slaves, he expects a thousand slaves. "Slaves? Is this not Palestine?" Stephen asks. Laughter from the beards. No, this is Bougie, Algeria.

The slave-market in Bougie, some days later. Blinding sun and camel shit. Lot 29, the caliph's Christians – the Christians the caliph has chosen not to keep, fewer than he'd hoped, but a bargain all the same. Bids are invited. Merchants, like doctors, walk among the *pueri*, in search of fat and muscle. The *pueri*, feeling fingers prod at their flesh, wonder if they will serve *at* dinner tables, or *on* them, as supper. The horror, either way. Frying-pan to fire. They'd like to settle with Stephen – if it weren't for these chains.

But Stephen isn't there. Though chained and guarded, he is spending the day with the governor of Egypt, Al-Adil, who is here in Bougie on business, and has heard about Stephen's mission. Al-Adil is joined by his son, Al-Kamil, a student of philosophy and French. Over sherbet and mint tea, they question the prisoner. Haggard and beatific, Stephen speaks of his faith, and describes his followers as "peace-loving pilgrims" – no word about a Crusade, or Palestine, or recapturing the Holy Sepulchre. Father and son are impressed, and make him an offer: a place in their palace as a tutor. And his disciples, Stephen asks, thirty thousand once, three hundred now, what of them? They reassure him: they have funds; they have merchant friends in need of workers; suitable arrangements will be made. Stephen accepts the offer, and returns, under guard, to bring his followers happy tidings. One day, when the time is right, they'll join forces in Palestine to take the Sepulchre. Till then they'll work as tutors and gardeners. Does he not mean as slaves? No, guarantees have been made – it will not be slavery. At least, he says, they'll have a bed and food now. At least they'll be doing useful work. At least they can stay true to their God.

Years pass. A long darkness. Gulls mew like the newborn. Back in Marseilles, the old man mending nets looks to the horizon and wonders: whatever happened to those young Crusaders? The town doctor on his evening stroll, the women leaving the shore with bundles of driftwood: all have heard rumours of catastrophe – can they be true? Parents from the north have made the long journey, wanting to know. But there is no one to ask. Hugh the Iron and William the Pig are long dead, whether stabbed in a brawl or hanged for treason no one seems sure. There is nothing firm to tell. There are only rumours. Then a priest disembarks from the East. He has a beard now, and a bald spot, but was once a Crusader – one of the *pueri*. He tells the tale: the voyage, the welcome committee in Bougie, the selling into slavery, as arranged by The Iron and The Pig. And then the dispersal to all parts of Islam. In Baghdad, he says, eighteen of the Crusaders became martyrs, executed for refusing to worship Mahomet. Others, like him, were luckier: they earned no money, were underfed, depised and mistreated, but were allowed to keep their Christian faith. And Stephen? No word of Stephen. That rumour of him going to work for the governor of Egypt? No truth in it, as far as he knows. The priest has heard another story but keeps it to himself. People crowd round, asking for details, but he will not tell.

Runs it through his head, though, constantly. And later, grown old in a Spanish monastery, sets it down, on parchment (the source now lost, but its spirit recuperable). The slave-market at Bougie. High sun. Blinding light. Lot 29, the caliph's Christians: sold to assorted bidders, to be collected in the morning, after prayers. The angry disciples round on Stephen. To have gone through hell and high water for this.

"What is it I've always told you to have," he asks, "even in adversity?"

"Faith."

"Right. And what is it you have now?"

Silence.

Then a voice. "Enough, that's what we've had, enough."

They demand to see Christ's letter, hand-delivered all those months ago when Stephen was a simple shepherd's boy. He will not show it, and crosses his arms over his chest. Though it's hard for them, in chains, they strip his clothes and find the letter sewn in the lining of his smock. It is torn and faded – also blank. Stephen, disbelieving, asks to see it: blank, blank, blank. He swears there was writing on it, Christ's signature. It must have faded in the salt or sun. Faith, they must have faith, he says. They move towards him, move in on him, as far as they can move, in chains. They've had enough. His time's up. And yet they hesitate. Suppose he is God's Chosen, and they kill him, what punishment will follow? Will they not roast in hell? They stare, not knowing what to do. Have Faith, Stephen says, see what tomorrow brings. They back off. Then one – a boy, dark-haired, the youngest of the party – picks up a stone and hurls it at Stephen's head. Stephen falls, gets up again. Another stone, and another. Have faith, he cries from the ground, God is testing our faith, the last trial, then freedom. *As if.* The stones rain harder. Then chains, and a blade from somewhere, and all the anger of months and years released at Stephen's head.

In February 1993, in Liverpool, two ten-year-old boys abducted a two-year-old called James Bulger from a shopping centre, walked with him for two and a half miles to a railway line and there, as darkness fell, with bricks and an iron bar, battered him to death. Some deaths are emblematic, tipping the scales, and little James's death – green fruit shaken from the bough, an ear of grain sown back in the earth – seemed like the murder of hope: the unthinkable thought of, the undoable done. If child-killings are the worst killings, then a child child-killing must be worse than worst, a new superlative in horror. In that spring of cold fear, it was as if there'd been a breach in nature: the tides frozen; stars nailed to the sky; the moon weeping far from sight. Those nameless boys had killed not just a child but the idea of childhood, all its happy first associations. No good could grow up from the earth. Ten-year-olds were looked at with a new suspicion, and toddlers kept on tight reins.

It was the video footage from a security camera, jumpy and poignant as a cine film, that made the case famous. The little boy could be seen at loose among shoppers, then following two older boys, then disappearing with them – the beginning of the long march to his death. Since then, there've been other killings by children. In France, as the Bulger trial opened, three boys, one of them only ten, kicked and beat a tramp to death. In Norway, a five-year-old girl was battered and left to die in the snow by three boys of six. In Chicago, two boys aged ten and eleven dropped a five-year-old boy fourteen storeys to his death, after he'd refused to give them sweets. There weren't public trials in those cases; the killers weren't treated as adults in an adult court: only the Bulger case has that distinction. But many papers have carried reports of child depravity: "Boys aged 10 and 11 are charged with rape", "Boy, 13, accused of killing 85-year-old woman", "Boy, 8, attempts armed robbery", "Boy, 13, denies rape in sandpit", "Boy, 12, beats pensioner with iron bar", "Boy burglar, 6, batters baby to death". It's the age of Bad Boys. And we're the Frankensteins who made them. From the spring of 1993 can be dated this new horror, of the monsters to whom we've given birth – dwarf killers, noon shadows of men complete.

In the autumn of that year, nine months after the killing, the boys accused of murdering James Bulger appeared in court in Preston. An American magazine invited me to go and write about the case; I said yes, like a shot. Friends found my enthusiasm difficult to understand; my wife did, too. I remember standing with her on the doorstep of our house, the night before the trial, waiting to go to Euston station. My bag was packed with shirts, trousers, razors, useful addresses, and copies of two books by Rousseau – *Émile*, his theory of childhood, and the *Confessions*, his story of him. It was a Sunday night, Hallowe'en, and the air was full of smoke from Guy Fawkes bonfires set off early. Our three children, black cloaks and scare-masks over their jeans and trainers, were tricking-and-treating down the street. The murder trial would be gruelling: why was I so keen on going, Kathy wanted to know? I think she suspected me of running away from work, or our children, or home, or her. None of which was true, or admissible. But what was the reason? I couldn't explain. I stood there holding her hand and twizzling her wedding ring between my finger and thumb, rotating it below the knuckle, as if to tighten a screw, or loosen it maybe, turning us back to a time before she wore it, before marriage and babies, back to childhood, before we met. Then the minicab was there, a kiss, a hug, a faraway shout to the kids, and off I went through the smoky night, like a man escaping the fire that will consume his house and family, guilty, lonely, exultant to be free.

I stayed in Preston for a month, coming back at weekends. I found the experience disturbing, even traumatic, but once my article was published, I thought – knowing the rhythms of journalism, and how quickly an assignment can be set aside – I would be able to forget it. The world moved on: war in Bosnia, peace in Bosnia, mad cow disease, the beginning and end of an IRA ceasefire, Fred and Rosemary West, Dunblane. The world moved on, but I didn't. I was still stuck in Preston, with the sights and sounds of that long month: the faces of the boys as their taped confessions were played over the public address system; the Bulger relations sitting in a row; the barristers, judge, jury, witnesses, psychiatrists, policemen, social workers, journalists and court ushers; the man with the slurpy geiger rod who used to search us as we entered court. I couldn't get rid of all this. I began to wonder if I wanted to. It was as if something important had happened there that still hadn't been faced or explained.

In truth, my difficulties started the moment the trial did, though I couldn't admit it at the time. I'd gone there expecting an answer to the question that everyone wanted answering: Why? What made two ten-year-old boys kill an innocent child? But murder trials are about Where and When and Who and How, not Why, and even during the case I found myself having to look for answers elsewhere – outside the court, not inside it. Increasingly, trying to answer Why seemed to require some leap of empathy, or speculation: from the churningly gruesome facts of the case into more general thoughts about what it is to be a child – and a parent. All roads lead inward, to the imagination. Perhaps that's why the Bulger case was and is so haunting, to me and a million others: it may have happened out there, at a safe distance, but it goes on happening here, in our hearts and minds.

Stephen, in his sky-blue donkey-cart, is as far from Bootle Strand shopping centre as the year 1212 is from 1993. Yet the Children's Crusade and the killing of James Bulger do have elements in common. Innocence and the loss of innocence. Faith and the betrayal of faith. Abduction: the blind leading the blind. A long walk. A desperate conclusion. The problem of allocating blame. The difficulty in interpreting the behaviour of the participants. Narrative multiplicity – how to decide which of several conflicting versions is true? Above all, there's the inadmissible but unmistakable presence of adults. Both these stories seem to have children as their subject. But really they're stories about grown-ups.

2

Court

"Piggy."

"Uh?"

"That was murder."

WILLIAM GOLDING, Lord of the Flies

November 1, bitter dawn-light, and I stand in a square in Preston, waiting for a transit van. Round the corner, in the covered Victorian market, traders are setting up their stalls: toys, children's clothes, discarded kitchenware, cheap videos, empty golf bags, local maps in dusty frames – but no one yet to buy. An encampment of outside broadcast vans, here for a snooker tournament, sprawls in the other direction – no signs of life there, either. But in the gloom of this cobbled square, under a sky smudged like newsprint, up from the monument to the massacred mill-workers, the first grey souls are flitting through.

Nine months ago, in Liverpool, a two-year-old was killed, and today his killers will stand trial. Half an hour back, in my hotel room, I flicked through the photocopied press cuttings, needing to remind myself what happened, and yet not needing to, since for me, as for everyone, it's there like a watermark on

the psyche, a shadow across the heart: the abduction of James
Bulger, the discovery of his body on a railway line, the week of
police investigation, the arrest of two primary school kids.
Features and editorials, documentaries and special reports
have worried away at the case and, beyond it, at a larger fear:
that kids are growing up too quickly, are brutalized and
beyond control. I've read the columns. Some of them use
words like "brutes" and "little animals". Some are written by
novelists: Anthony Burgess, Martin Amis, William Golding,
Alice Thomas Ellis, Piers Paul Read. They scatter the blame
at different targets – single mothers, absent fathers, schools,
the Church, the Pill, the sixties – but most seem to agree that
children, these days, are spoilt. There's a line about it in the
Bible: "Cocker thy child and he shall make thee afraid."
Cocker (I had to look it up), meaning pamper or indulge. By
sparing the rod we've bred a generation of hoodlums.
Cherub-faced muggers. Rapists who don't have pubic hair
yet. Pre-pubescents with glittering knives. What's childhood
coming to? Keep your kids well back. Childhood's not a place
for children.

I buy myself a cappuccino and lean against the window of a
toyshop in the shelter of the arcade. Behind the pane are the
leftovers of last night's Hallowe'en celebrations: horror-masks,
Dracula fangs, Devil forks, witches' broomsticks and capsules
of blood. Hallowe'en: it didn't seem to count for much, once.
In the north of England, thirty years ago, we had Mischief
Night instead – mild pranks with treacle and doorknockers.
Now the kids are into stronger stuff. Can I have a death's-
head, Dad, can I have a skeleton? I've seen the comics, full of
crucifixes and aliens. Last night, from the train, at every station on the way here, I watched the revellers with their black
cloaks and pumpkin skulls. The bones aren't under the skin

but fluorescent on the surface. The horror, the horror – give us more.

The coffee smokes in my hand. No sign yet of a transit van. Others are waiting, too, from all over the world. They stand with camera straps and notepads and high-poled furry mikes as big as carwash rollers, impatient for news. In Sefton, back in February, when the boys who killed James Bulger were first charged, several hundred people gathered outside court – grandparents, mothers, teenagers, children strapped in pushchairs. There's a photograph among my cuttings, a dozen would-be lynchers, young men mostly, a line of screams and angry fists. Retributive justice, the stony verdict of the mob, *communitas*, locals taking the law into their own hands. The men in the photograph had come wanting to kill the kids who'd killed the kid, because there's nothing worse than killing a kid. As the police vans with the boys inside drove away, or tried to, the crowd pushed through the cordon. Eggs were thrown, and rocks, until arrests were made. It's in the hope of similar trouble that journalists have come here, three hours before the trial begins. They're quite a crowd, but not the kind of crowd you see in photographs – rather, the kind of crowd you don't see in photographs, the ones laurelled with lenses and light meters, the snappers not the snapped.

A wind blows through the square, kicking up bits of paper. I chuck the empty cup away and stand in a cloud of my own breath. What if the rumour's untrue of the boys being driven here early? What if they were brought last night? Suddenly, commotion, a stretch of necks. Two white transit vans appear at the far side of the square. They come down past the Town Hall, past the library, towards the cenotaph, not at speed, not too inert and interceptable either, twenty miles an hour or so, making for a pair of high gates. Guiltily excited, I press forward. The entrance to the gate is protected by barriers, and these barriers are patrolled by policemen, in case a photographer should try to leap them, which could happen, which picture editors expect to happen if it means a better shot. When the vans reach the cenotaph, the gates begin to open, as if by magic, while the vans, still doing twenty, come steadily on. Zoom lenses are tracking the barred windows in their side, everyone's eyes trained there, hoping for eyes in return, or maybe a mouth foaming blood. But the panes are black, the windows tiny and meshed. It's as if these were zoo vans delivering dangerous animals, and maybe they are. In strict convoy still, the vans pass between the barriers. A machine gun of clicks, a lightshow of flash, and they disappear through the gates, which at once swing shut. The crowd outside loosens and drifts apart, unpenned now and untentacled – like a beast, after its kill, going back to sleep.

Disappointed and complicit, I, too, turn away. I didn't see the boys. I don't even know their names.

Three hours later, I do. In an oak-panelled, green-tiled courtroom, under a vast skylight, beneath the robed portraits of dead predecessors, the trial judge is speaking – Michael Morland, head of the northern circuit, though the north isn't evident in his voice. Gentle, greying, unlofty in his red-leather chair, he gives instructions to the press: until further notice, the defendants, Robert Thompson and Jon Venables, will be identified in all reporting of the trial as Boy A and Boy B. Thompson and Venables: now their names are out in the open, at least *in camera*, I feel a strange shock.

Then the great moment. From the dressing room in the pit below, up the stairs to the arena, through a hole in the middle of the court, into the dock, come the boys. They're not alone. A policeman like a referee walks ahead of them, and two social workers like linesmen sit down alongside. Carpenters have worked to raise the dock by three inches so the boys are high enough to see the judge and jury. They look tiny, all the same – the rails of the dock are like the bars of a cot or playpen. Which boy is which? One wears a navy suit and light-blue shirt, the other a black jumper, tie and white shirt; Venables, Thompson. As the court's arranged, with most of us sitting behind the boys, it's hard to see their faces, but it seems, from their furtive sideways glances, that they're podgy, double-chinned, *fat*, though also pasty and wan-cheeked. With their neat haircuts, they look like brothers, even twins. They seem uncomfortable in their clothes – stuffed into shirts intended to make them look older, cleaner and nicer than they are. However respectable, the clothes can't save them from being stared at. Being stared at is bad enough at the best of times, and this is the worst of times. Just because they're murderers, if they are murderers, doesn't make the staring easier to take. Even interrogation is preferable: how can you answer a look? Only with an answering stare, or by turning away. Thompson looks levelly back, Venables down at his lap, and in those postures, before even a word has been spoken, meanings are inferred: defiance in one case, penitence the other.

Now the boys are spoken to, directly. On this first morning of the trial, as again on the last day but never in between, they are, very briefly, addressed: this is how long the court sessions will be, this is where they will sit, and they've their barristers to talk to if they do not understand. Thompson, on the left, is cooler, less overawed than Venables, who puts his head in his hands and leans against his social worker's shoulder. Neither has the cool steel of a hardened offender. Neither looks like a murderer. What do murderers look like? What do *child* murderers look like? Mary Bell, twenty-five years ago: a sweet-faced child, smiling out serenely, who squeezed her victims' necks until they died. And now Jon Venables, who looks, as she did, rather pretty and vulnerable. Robert Thompson seems tougher and more self-possessed, but before his chins grew in custody neighbours called him "cherub-faced" and he was teased for looking like a girl. A and B, T and V: they look so innocent, if not of the crime. Maybe they are innocent, even of that. No one expects it, but let's see.

But the barristers for the boys don't want us to see. They ask for a stay, or deferral. The pre-publicity has been prejudicial, they say: the emotive language and saturation coverage can't help but have influenced the jury. David Turner, defending Thompson (each boy has his own pair of barristers), has assembled 247 press cuttings, which compare the accused to Myra Hindley and Saddam Hussein. As the pull-out quotes of doorstepped neighbours are read aloud – "One kid is like a girl but his pal is a brat" – I try to measure these words against what I see, the matching neat haircuts, the best-behaviour clothes and sticky-out ears. When people describe criminals, they always speak of eyes (as if eyes were a window to the soul's depravity), and sometimes noses, too (hooked, bent, beaked, broken). But ears: ears are always young and innocent; only their removal or disfigurement denotes criminality.

Thompson has taken his shoes off now, and his jacket, too, trying to stay cool, or trying to be cool, I'm not sure which, but there's a nerve and swagger about him. He yawns. The yawn isn't surprising: it's been a long morning (that early arrival, to avoid crowd scenes), and even the brightest eleven-year-old would find the legal arguments hard to follow. But I want to shake Robert Thompson and tell him: don't yawn even if you're tired; don't scratch even if the newly bought clothes are itchy. Yawning and scratching make you look cruel and unrepentant. But then, maybe he is.

Behind me, the door of the public gallery screams open: a flustered man with a notepad. To judge from the number of other notepads, nearly everyone in the gallery's a journalist. We've taken over the place – there are only a couple of bona fide members of the public here. David Turner's last cutting is from the *Sun* for October 7. I have it back in my hotel room – a report and photograph of the boys arriving in Preston for a familiarizing court visit, a dummy run. A tipped-off snapper saw them coming, and had his scoop: a shot of one of the boys with a lollipop. It was a gift: look, the killers of James Bulger, with their sugar-stick of callous disregard. The cutting describes the thinner of the two boys strolling "as though he did not have a care in the world", while the fatter one "casually walked along behind". There is more in the report about the "luxury" of the boys' secure units, and the pampered conditions they'll enjoy during the trial. No one could miss the subtext: the killers of James Bulger, spoilt, swaggering, unrepentant, with toys and computer games to soothe their idle tax-paid days.

For legal reasons, that photograph in the *Sun* was pixelated – the boys' faces were a mesh of Mondrian squares. Are they any more visible now, in the flesh, just feet away, listening to David Turner's representations? Physiognomy: a dubious art. Here we are, scrutinizing, in search of a sign. But it's hard to learn much from a face that's on guard (and under guard), among strangers. *Macbeth*: "There's no art/To find the mind's construction in the face". Can the press and public see the boys right? More important, can the jurors? Or has their vision been clouded by pre-publicity? That's what's at issue. The argument bats back and forth: David Turner (pale, fastidious, Modern) for Thompson, and Brian Walsh (hearty, big-nosed, a Restoration wit) for Venables, versus Richard Henriques (tall, solid, Victorian) for the Crown. It's like the sixth form again, the first whiff of adult life – lovely intellectual banter, free spirits talking themselves to death. Easy to forget that ten-year-olds are the object of this, and that they can't follow the debate. After two hours, the judge reaches his verdict "unhesitatingly": the application for a stay is refused; the trial will go ahead.

We stand like schoolboys as the judge rises for lunch, and peer at Thompson and Venables returning below. They look like brothers: Cain and Abel, little love lost between them, but joining together to murder Seth.

Afternoon and, murder trial or not, a feeling of languor has set in. Another application, another photograph – a police photograph, number 47, the battered head of James Bulger, "so emotive and distressing", claim the defence, that the accused won't get a fair hearing. There are others in court who aren't getting a fair hearing, who shouldn't have to listen to this. Immediately in front of me, in the first row of the gallery, with a good view of the boys (the rear of the boys), are the eight seats reserved for the Bulger family. This morning the seats were empty. Now five of them are filled. Denise, James's mother, seven months pregnant, has stayed away. But the dead boy's father, Ralph, chewing gum and wearing a light-brown calfskin jacket, is here with several relations and friends. They are a big clan, the Bulgers: Ralph was one of six, Denise the twelfth of thirteen. They are physically big, too: Ralph and his relations, Ralph and his mates, you wouldn't want to tangle with them. Lanky, thin-faced, a dad put through the wringer, Ralph reminds me of Liverpool FC's Ian Rush: someone to keep an eye on, a striker, a danger man. The Bulgers are trying hard to look unthreatening. Silent, dignified, they have the public's sympathy and they're not going to forfeit it by rowdiness. All the same, their eyes bore like Black and Deckers into the necks of Thompson and Venables. Have Ralph and Co. been searched for weapons, as the rest of us were on entering court? Even if they're weapon-free, it wouldn't need much to leap the rail of the gallery and mete out justice with their own hands. It has crossed my mind. It must have crossed their minds. They wouldn't be human if it hadn't. Ralph goes on chewing his gum.

The application to withhold the photograph is refused. The trial begins. A Manchester man and regular here, Richard Henriques outlines the case for the Crown. It takes him all afternoon, till 3.30, when the court must end prematurely, in deference to the child-defendants, whose hours can only be school hours, whose attention spans are short. As Henriques describes the events of that day back in February, and what became of James (a blood-stained scarf, hairs from an eyebrow on a brick), the neck muscles in Ralph Bulger's neck tighten. Ahead of him, the boys look interested at last. We are out of the greylands of legal nicety and home to a place they know: the shops they stole from in Bootle Strand, the people they met, the kicks and bricks. Jon Venables leans against his social worker and cries. He seems to have a good relationship with this social worker, who's chubby, cheery, cuddly, whereas Robert's social worker, lean, agonized and Strindbergian, never looks at his impassive charge. Robert takes his jacket off. He swings his legs. When the afternoon break comes, he carries his shoes out, having removed them earlier – as he didn't when (so the Crown claims) kicking James Bulger in the head. Only the first day of the trial and already an impression is being formed of Robert – "Bobby" – as ringleader, and Jon as hanger-on. The gallery and jury look stonily at both of them. I've heard of criminals so charismatic in court that they've charmed themselves off the hook. Not this pair: it's hard to warm to them, no matter how tender their years.

It doesn't help that they're fat. Robert always was (though he liked to describe himself as thin), but Jon has put on two stone in six months. Three solid meals a day and lack of exercise. It does them no good, in here, looking overweight. It feeds bad thoughts: that they're not too put out by what happened, that they're happy with their lot. Fatness: a measure of contentment, or slobbery (you don't get happy anorexics, you don't get thin slobs). At their age, I too was overweight: the Fat Controller in his last year at primary school. My sister Gillian was fat, too – fatter than me. The memory (slides to prove it) of a holiday in Majorca, when I was ten and she was eight, divebombing the swimming pool. Her jellywobbling splashes and a group of Germans, who guffawed each time she hit the water. My bit for the war effort, circa 1960. I took her hand and led her back to my parents, denying the nasty foreigners (maybe her, too) a bit of fun. Later, like me, she became self-conscious, and suffered from feeling overweight. Maybe Jon and Robert suffer the same – or, spared the teasing of the playground, maybe not. Why do we think fatness means feeling at ease with the world? Because *Angst* eats the soul, gnaws away at body fat ("What's eating him?")? The racked screwball, the pool-eyed widow, the pining lonely-heart, who eat by themselves and into themselves. But *Weltschmerz* is not a monopoly of the skinny. Fat people can be anguished, too. They usually are, if only about being fat.

3.20. Like T and V, I yawn and fidget. T and V: it's the shorthand I use in my notebook, less confusing than A and B. The clerk of the court uses it too. In all the relevant legal documents, this trial – Regina versus Robert Thompson and Jon Venables – is known as *R v T & V*.

Another point of nomenclature, to end the day. Richard Henriques says that he will refer to the victim throughout as James Bulger, not Jamie. James isn't just the formally correct Christian name but what the child was called by those who knew him. I wonder what Ralph and Denise felt last February, when their son, in all the headlines, became JAMIE. I wonder how they feel now seeing his name (or misname) in the headlines once again, hearing him always spoken of in diminutive, as if the media, in its intimate wisdom, knew better than they did who he was. Another kind of abduction, another kind of murder: his becoming someone else and someone else's, not him, not theirs. But maybe it will help them cope: their son is twice removed now, once in death, once by public appropriation. James died back in February. Now only Jamie is there.

At the hotel, I take the lift to my narrow cell: single bed, table, phone, chair. A newsreader is Jamie-ing on screen, over a photograph of that blondly angelic head. It's the only image viewers have of *R v T & V*, apart from the meshed police vans crossing the square and the Victorian-style artists' impressions of the courtroom – whereas in court James's is the one face that's missing. Hard for those outside to feel involved with the defendants, when they're nameless, faceless, rootless Boy A and Boy B; hard for those inside not to, now we're on first-name terms.

I switch channels to a drab, hoofing football game, and try

to remember how old Cain was when he killed Abel and was banished to the land of Nod. Probably about fourteen. Even if it was 100, in the Old Testament you have to divide by ten. And then the other fictional precedents for children killing children. *Lord of the Flies*: "Kill the pig, kill the pig" – and Piggy, too, the one with National Health specs who died like James, with a rock in his face, though he fell not on rails but in the sea. Teenies toting guns, toddlers tearing butterfly wings, babies gnawing crusts at two hours old. Original sin is enjoying a revival. Films showing children as little devils are now almost a genre – *Rosemary's Baby*, *The Omen*, *The Exorcist*. Children as inherently bad: I've had such thoughts myself. Easy enough, in the torture of sleeplessness, to imagine your baby as a devil – that cradle-cap the seedbed for Satan's horns, those screams straight out of hell. Easy enough, seeing strange, violent children in the streets, to think them capable of evil. Maybe psychopaths, like policemen, are getting younger: if they drive cars at ten, or take GCSEs in maths then, why can't children be murderers, too? But those boys in court today didn't appear evil or psychopathic: there are only looks to go on, but they didn't look the real thing.

Day 2, the first witnesses. They're women shop assistants, who noticed the boys hanging about that Friday morning in February, suspected them of wanting to nick things and wondered why they weren't at school. It was a Baker Day, the boys said, an Inset Day, a day off. This was a lie: the boys were "sagging", truanting. Robert, it seems, was an old hand at sagging. In many families, there's a tradition of siblings going to the same school. In Robert's family, the tradition was of siblings not going to the same school – his older brothers had all not gone to the same school as him. Jon was more of a novice at sagging, and had an incentive not to sag that day: a note for the teacher from his mother asking if he could take the school gerbils home with him, for half-term. But then he met Robert. And decided to bunk off. The gerbils would have to go home with someone else.

I look at Jon, and he reminds me a bit of a gerbil. A hamster, anyway: the bright, darting eyes; how, when he's upset, he beds down and disappears in the lapels of his jacket; his soft, hutched blinking at the noise and light. Robert is squatter, porkier, more of a guinea pig. An aggressive one at times. Jon flicks him nervous glances, seeking reassurance; Robert ignores them, putting the squirt in his place. Jon seems to be in thrall to Robert. I know the feeling. I see myself in Jon's black eyes, idolizing older or rougher boys, thinking the way to their affection is to emulate them at their worst. Jon flicks another nervous glance: what would he not have done to win Robert's admiration? These short, silent exchanges speak volumes: that Robert is the cool leader and Jon his enthusiastic sidekick; cunning fox, eager beaver. More animals. In some recent drawings for the *New Yorker*, the artist Sue Coe, never having seen the boys, represents them as hunch-shouldered, long-armed, ape-like. Everywhere animals. But then it's natural to think of animals, with the boys gawped at all day, as if in a cage.

Hamster, guinea pig, beaver, fox. Little animals. Until the nineteenth century, it was common for animals to be tried in courts of law. Throughout Europe, when crops failed or children were injured, pigs, weevils, cocks, caterpillars, termites, sparrows, locusts, dogs, moles, snails were tried and often executed for their offences. Some animals, like the boar, were considered the devil incarnate. Others, like dogs, because expressing recognizable human emotions like fear and joy, were thought free and intelligent agents. Either view, when something went amiss, justified a trial and execution. Watching the boys, I feel the spirit of medievalism working still in court: the dumb incomprehension and deep silence from the dock. Beneath the slow civility of this trial, the old retributive savagery persists.

Jon looks anxious this morning. Maybe his anxiety (including the anxiety to please) is to do with having his parents here. They sit just behind him: his mother, Susan, smart and brisk in a royal-blue dress and with a gold-chained handbag; his father, Neil, hunched in anguish in a thin suit. Mrs and Mr Venables. Mrs and Mrs Average. Your typical couple, no less typical for having separated several years ago and for her looking the stronger of the two. They seem well-matched, or complementary: Vamp, Wimp. Neil cries at times, whereas Susan toughs it out: beneath the neat make-up which she renews each tea-break, only a suppressed anger shows its face. Though they glance occasionally at Jon, they never look at Robert, the bad boy who dragged down their good. Robert's on his own, unaccompanied by parent or relation. The aloneness makes him seem more sinister – as if he cared for no one, and no one for him. I know little of his life yet, only that he's a fifth child, which makes me think of Doris Lessing's novel, *The Fifth Child*, about a child-ogre, a troll-hoodlum, born into an otherwise perfect family. Some of Lessing's descriptions of her boy-monster might fit how Robert looks in court. Already, there's a feeling against him – a feeling that he doesn't have feelings.

I look at T and V and try to see the court as they see it: the half-familiar witnesses; the stern-kindly judge; the silent, unreacting jury; the barristers so similar – robed in tradition under effacing wigs – you can't tell them apart. Nothing in their experience could have prepared them for this. Even the courtroom dramas they've seen on television will have been wigless, American, and no kind of precedent. Anonymous, synonymous, black-gowned unfamiliars, the judge and lawyers seem to be in with each other – whoever's side they're on, they look like the opposition. I'm struck, too, by the overwhelming maleness of the proceedings. The two accused; the judge, barristers, solicitors, social workers; most of the press; nine of the jury; all the police except Mandy Waller, the WPC whose job, after James went missing, was to comfort Denise. Is James's gender relevant, too? If T and V had taken a girl, might they have acted differently? Did it have to be a boy for them to act at all? Whatever, masculinity dominates the trial. The Roman arena aspect of it, the gladiatorialism, is quintessentially male. And I suspect that if the legal profession had more women in high places, these boys would not have been brought to trial in an adult court.

In the gents, during tea-break, I find myself next to Albert Kirby, head of the police investigation: lean, teetotal, late forties, bright-eyed as a young vicar. He nods at me from his stall. I nod back.

"How's it going, then?" I ask.

"Fine, fine," he says, "exactly to plan."

Small talk from our stalls. This is how it's supposed to be in the office gents, a chat with a colleague, him with his penis in his hand, you with yours, white porcelain in between.

"A good man, Henriques," he says. "Safe pair of hands."

"You think it's cut and dried, then?" I ask.

"It should be."

As we zip up, another journalist arrives in an adjoining stall, a local bod who seems to know Albert well, and next thing they are arranging a drink. I'd guess Albert is an eye-for-an-eye man, which means I won't see eye to eye with him. To him, the boys are a pair of cunning professionals, tracked down by a highly sophisticated police operation, and convicting them requires ruthless prosecution; to me, the trial has already begun to feel like a sledgehammer used against a nut.

Back in court, more witnesses. They're good witnesses, from the Crown's point of view, formidably attentive and with stunning recall. They remember it was dull and cold that Friday (39 degrees F, cloudy). They remember the papers carrying news of the Queen volunteering to pay tax for the first time, of Ranulph Fiennes on a polar odyssey, of a Home Alone girl of twelve left to fend for herself while her mother jetted off for a fortnight's holiday in Spain. They remember buying Valentine's cards (last chance to post them), paying the gas bill, going to the doctor, walking the dog, putting bets on horses, drinking tea, looking at magazines, driving home from work, passing the sign by the church that says "You don't have to be on your knees to pray", drawing their curtains against the dark. They remember all this. And they remember, as they performed these actions, seeing the boys who are now in front of them in the dock.

But how to put this into words? They find it hard. One by one they're led into the box. They swear their oath. They confirm their name, their employment, why they were where they say they were, what it was they saw. They know before they enter what it will be like to stand here. They have been coached, and are being coaxed. It isn't much to ask – more a yes–no interlude than a quiz. But they can't do it. They mumble, they stumble, they choke, they weep. They are requested to direct their words to the judge and jury. They are asked to speak up, over the noise of the air-conditioning. They are advised to hang on while the air-conditioning is turned off. They are offered tissues and drinks of water. They are invited to take as long as they like. They accept the invitation. But still no one can hear.

I feel for them, in their taciturnity. I, too, used to dry up and die. At school, during questions, I kept my hand down, not because I didn't know the answers but because I was afraid to say. At university, in tutorials, fearful of blushing, I tried to hide in the corner, not easy in a group of four. That fear of outing oneself: how I envied the fluent. I didn't know then that wordlessness has a power. "Even a fool who keeps silent is considered wise." Glib means untrustworthy; the stuttering are thought to be honest; the silent seem to *know*. A sign of strong emotion, too: the Bulger family in front of me do not exchange words, because of all they feel. But if you're a witness, whatever your feelings, you have to have your say. These witnesses are having trouble having theirs.

Class is part of the problem. The judge and barristers speak the same language – the language of the court, not the language of the tribe. It scares the witnesses, who're scared enough to begin with. Tongue-tied and trembling, they stand there in Sunday-best overcoats and special-occasion suits: shoppers, shop assistants, pedestrians, bus passengers, car drivers, schoolkids, pensioners, all with same story to tell, if you can hear it – the taller boy in the mustard jacket, the chubbier one in the dark jacket, the baby in the blue anorak, walking together, seemingly a family group. One by one they come forward, inaudibly corroborating each other, reliving the same terrible sequence of events.

No one doubts their sincerity, but why is it they all use the same adjective, "mustard", not a colour in most palettes, to describe Jon Venables's jacket? Why were so many of them wise after the event, wise after the after-event, the *Crimewatch* television programme, shown nearly a week after the crime? You could say those skippy Bootle Strand video pictures must have jerked their memory, but remembering and imagining aren't easily untwined. "I shouted out loud on the bus 'What the hell are those kids doing to that poor child?'" one woman tells the court, looking fiercely at Thompson and Venables. Yeah, sure. But no one on the bus heard her. And it was ten days before she went to the police.

Still, I mustn't blame them, these witnesses. They're only trying to help. They couldn't have known, when they came forward, that they'd be treated as the guilty ones, criticized for doing nothing at the time. They feel as though they're in the dock, not the witness box; the witness box *is* the dock. There's a new nervousness now: not just fear of speaking aloud in court, but fear of public condemnation. Witnesses against terrorists and ganglanders have been known to chicken out, in case of reprisals. The terror here is not of kneecappings but of headlines: We Name the Guilty. Laceration in print, flogging in 64-point: this is what's inhibiting them.

The boys, by contrast, look more confident. They're getting used to it here. Jon has begun to raise his head and look around. Robert, so journalists report, has taken to "staring them out". But while the boys sit tinily in the dock's cradle, the words still go over their heads. How many of these words do they catch? How much do they understand? They don't say, since their role is to be wordless. Wittgenstein: *Wovon man nicht sprechen kann, darüber muss man schweigen.* What we can't speak of, we must pass over in silence. How much is unsayable or inadmissible here? Everything but the sightings of witnesses, it seems. Already these witnesses have established beyond doubt that the boys abducted James Bulger and took him to the railway line, where – though no one saw this – he was killed. But what they witnessed doesn't help with the Why. Only the boys can help with that, and they can't speak yet, and perhaps won't speak even when the turn of the defence comes. I begin to wonder if it's worth being in court at all.

Another day gone, 3.30, and the hack pack shuffles out. The early dark seems like a kindness: sealing night, scarfing up the tender eye of day. In the square round the back of court, by the post office, a crowd of photographers has gathered, to watch the boys leave in their transit vans. A handful of shoppers and schoolchildren stand watching the photographers. No one could call them a crowd, let alone a furious crowd like that in Sefton, but a picture editor in London might try. Tomorrow these browsers back of court will appear in photographs as people who came to watch the boys – as *tricoteuses* in front of the guillotine, eager to see heads roll. But the public gallery has been almost empty today, except for journalists, and now there are just these casual shoppers, as if murder trials were losing their allure. Guilty, collusive, voyeuristic, I turn my back before the vans appear. Whatever the answers, I'm not going to find them here.

3

15:42:32

The childhood games are over,
The rest is over with youth –
The world, the good games, the good times,
The belief, and the love, and the truth.

ELIZABETH BARRETT BROWNING, "My Child"

On my narrow bed, I lie awake and think of Denise. I try to imagine where she is at this moment, what the room looks like, what she's wearing, how her voice sounds. But she never speaks, the room won't come into focus, I can't grasp what it's like to be her, or pretend to understand what she feels. Maybe none of us can, not even those who have lost a child. Everyone's pain is different. Everyone's child is, too. The nearest I come, which isn't near at all, is the memory of what it's like *nearly* losing a child, or the dread that I might do still. Most parents know these feelings. If they don't talk about them much, it's because they're too busy worrying. Worry can be very consuming. You can worry yourself to death worrying about your kids' deaths, but at least that way they don't predecease you. To be predeceased is the great dread, more dreadful than one's own death, and the one sure mark of parental failure. It isn't much to ask, to see your children safely through to adulthood. It's asking the earth, that's all.

Is there a worse thing than losing a child? Only losing two children, or three, or . . . All human lives are equal, it's said, but it can't be true. The small life, the hardly begun life: we hold this to be more precious than the life of the geriatric. Every child that dies dies before its time. Given the choice . . . there is no choice. Let the old die first. Even the old would agree.

But children die, all the time. The dark economy of heaven: so short the path from womb to cloistered tomb; so brief the dolorous stumble from rag-pallet to grave. How many ways? Let me count the ways: drowned, run over, strangled, mangled. Oh, the calamities in all the manuals: the overturned cradles and the livestock stuffing themselves with bits of baby; the crack in the ice, the drift towards the waterfall or millwheel, the goring by oxen; the pits, wells, water-barrels, fires, knives, horses, snakes, poisonous plants, dangerous tools, small swallowable objects; the homicidal fathers, the cannibal mothers, the sibling rivals; the diseases waiting in the wings . . . I could go on. I will go on. Sometimes it's all I think about. Sometimes it creeps up when I'm not thinking about it, or when I think I'm not thinking about it. I'll be sitting in an office or on a train and the shadow will pass over, a tune start up: "Ladybird, ladybird, fly away home, your house is on fire and your children are gone." Anyone who's ever let a child out of sight, or entrusted it to someone else, has thought the worst. If you're a parent, and have found a way to think about other things, let me know, will you? I need your tips, I need the Knowledge.

Denise, to whom the worst has happened, the nightmares all come true: what can I say, or anyone say, to console her?

There are no counsellors, no support groups, for women whose children have been killed by other children. However supportive Ralph is, and the family, and the empathizing grief of half the world, she feels alone still – alone with the spooling tape of little James's smile, alone back in the Strand and that first second of losing him. Again and again the tapes play, forward and back, forward and back, stop, rewind, review, pause, freeze. They play in her head. And now, in court and on the news, the video compilation of security stills plays in endless detail for us all. 15:38:55, James alone outside the butchers. 15:40:24, Denise searching. 15:41:29, James on the upper floor, close to two other boys. 15:42:10, Denise still searching. 15:42:32, the still that froze a million hearts, James's hand – raised in trust – in the hand of Jon Venables, Robert Thompson leading the way. 15:43:08, the three boys leaving the precinct. Forward and back, stop, rewind, review, pause, freeze. Forward and back, forward and back, as if we watched it often enough the picture might change and James be there again, safe by Denise's side.

She had got up late that day, as she did most days, as James did, too: having lost her first baby (stillborn), she needed to have him with her at all times, and he would go to bed when she and Ralph did, round midnight. She'd gone to Bootle Strand more for company than for shopping. When children are small but past the age of sleeping during the day, how do you fill the desert between lunch and teatime? There's television, videos, books, jigsaws. But they get bored. You get bored. You have to get out of the house. Denise had got out of the house and was round at her brother Paul's, with his girlfriend, Nicola, and the little daughter of one of her other brothers, a companion for James. Nicola needed to change some underwear at Bootle Strand, so they piled in the car, driving in past Walton Prison. At the Strand the two kids were given a 20p mechanical see-saw ride and a sausage roll each. James, happy not to be strapped in his pushchair for once, kept running away. He tried to get on an escalator and wailed when Denise pulled him off. In one shop he began throwing babysuits around. In another he helped himself to some Smarties and a carton of apple juice. Denise, flustered, seeing everyone thinking "Bad mother – no control of her child", gave James a slap. After, there was a bribe, a packet of Opal Fruits from Superdrug. They'd been shopping for an hour now. It was end-of-tether time. Only one more stop, the butchers A. R. Tyms, back where they'd started, next door to T. J. Hughes.

There weren't many customers: no queue. Denise went to the fresh counter and Nicola to the cooked. Afterwards, there were neighbours and relations who said, or who let her think they thought, that she had failed to keep an eye on James, that she must have lost her concentration and let him wander off. Hadn't she seen him, as Nicola did, playing in the doorway with a smouldering cigarette? Denise wanted lamb chops but the man brought her pork. That delayed things, slightly. Still, it could have been only a minute when she turned from the counter, dangling her white plastic meat-pack, and found that he was gone.

At Security, the guards, unfussed, followed the code. They asked where the boy had last been seen; they consulted their monitor screens; they announced James's name over the tannoy. Denise, panicky, wanted to believe them when they said not to worry, kids went missing in the Strand all the time, he was probably in Woolies, that's where they usually turned up, playing with toys. But none of this made her feel better. This wasn't any child, but her child. They were used to this happening, yeh, but it was happening to her, now. She gave them a description. A month short of three. Brown-blond hair ready for cutting, side-parted; when he runs about, it falls in his eyes. Blue eyes, with a brown streak in the right. A full set of baby teeth. Fair-skinned, with a reddish birth-mark on the back of his neck. Legs with small bruises where he'd knocked himself. A navy-blue anorak with patch-type pockets and press studs on the flap. A grey tracksuit. A white T-shirt with the word Noddy on it. White Puma trainers with black lettering. A blue woollen scarf with a white cat's face and white bobbles. Loves trains, planes, police cars, taxis, anything that moves really. No known allergies.

The tapes wind on, ushering James away past Mothercare, past his mother's care, beyond the care of all the world. The tapes have played in court, on television, in all our heads. What is it that's so distressing about them? The waveriness, like early Disney or a home cine, the quivering old 8mm. The boys jerky as puppets. The mucky colour (because the lenses were mucky), the soupy black and white. The silence under the whirr, as if in need of commentary: "Here's James walking, and the big lad's got his hand." The pain of seeing what Denise couldn't see at the time. History frozen at 15:42:32. Knowing what will happen. Being planted in this moment before it did happen, when it wouldn't have been too late to stop it. You don't often see kidnaps and killings, in life. There aren't the cameras there to catch them. But here's one unfolding before our eyes. And nothing we can do.

Forward and back, forward and back, in whirring silence. No words so hurtful. No evidence so bleakly unforgiving. Review, rewind, redress, resuscitate, reincarnate, reprieve.

*

In the Harris Art Gallery, round the corner from court, I search for a picture to replace the pictures in my head. There it is straight away: *Going to Bed* by William Dring (1946), a girl's raised hand in the hand of her mother, a cardigan over her nightdress, as they stand together by the cot. Up the stairs, around the walls, are other happy tableaux, mostly Victorian: children picnicking in dappled shade; straw-hatted, basket-wielding girls in pinafores; boy-gleaners resting against haystacks; mothers leaning adoringly over their sleeping babes; a father sitting exhausted at a table, while his wife and eldest daughter organize the family for prayers. Children as angels, under frisbee haloes and sprouting wings. Children by picket fences, playing piccolos. A mother doting on a daughter, who in turn dotes on a doll. All things bright and beautiful. Every baby a blessing, with hand raised. Every baby a God, worshipped by kneeling adults. Heaven lying about us in our infancy.

Or adults lying about our infancy, sentimentalizing it? *Going to Bed*: perhaps the smile on the mother's face is the prospect of peace, her daughter soon to be asleep and out of the way. Victorian paintings and photographs like to show children dressed as angels. It could mean that Victorians saw children as angelic. But if they loved children as deeply as these images suggest, how could they have let them be factory hands or mine-slaves or chimney sweeps? Perhaps these paintings of white-laced cherubs were there for encouragement, to set an example: not what Victorian parents believed their children were but how they wanted them to be, *putti* from which to mould them. Or perhaps these paintings were a way of making it up to children: down here, on earth, life might be shit for them, but up there, in frames, they could be wafted to heaven on wings – like the chimney sweeps in

Charles Kingsley's *The Water Babies* cleansed of their grime.
Either way, the image pixelates and blurs. Art: not to be
trusted. How adults have treated and felt about children: not
deducible from these frames.

And yet my heart shrivels at these blondly smiling infants,
these Jamies of an earlier age. I stand in front of *Going to
Bed* again, the girl's hand in her mother's, that picture of
perfect trust. It makes me think of other protective gestures,
other claspings of tiny hands. Hansel and Gretel following the
pebbles back to safety by moonlight. The Startrite shoe ad,
two bright-shod children stepping out on a long and winding
road. A documentary from 1945, war at an end, a girl and
boy walking through bomb-ruins to the brow of a hill, the
green future beyond – "the new world is theirs". The old
Barnardo's logo, three arm-linked orphans in a circle. The
new Mothercare sign, a child sheltered under the right arch of
the letter M. Charmed circles. Fairy rings. Children in croc-
odile lines, on school outings. Little people in the care of
bigger people. Emblems of perfect trust.

But the small hand in the larger can be an image of abduction, too. The winged lions bearing Dorothy in *The Wizard of
Oz*. The pouncing monkeys in Little Black Sambo, carrying
off Little Woof and Moof. The Pied Piper, beckoning to the
children with his music, leading them under the hill. Ducks
and hens, baby goats and baby rabbits bundled into sacks by
hungry foxes. Old men up lanes, bogeymen and goblins waiting in hedges. The coalmen who used to call when I was a
child, their black-goggled eyes and the glistening bodybags
they carried on their backs. And now poor James, on video,
tiny among shoppers' legs, his hand in the hand of Jon
Venables, a little boy lost though he does not know it yet, as in
a poem by William Blake:

The weeping child could not be heard . . .
The weeping parents wept in vain.
Are such things done on Albion's shore?

Blake also offered happier resolutions, innocence not experience, illustrations of children regained. After seven days' searching, the distraught parents – "famished, weeping, weak" – find their lost daughter, asleep among tigers. Also found, the little boy lost in the lonely fen. Most art is kindly: the lost children all turn up – "I believe", goes that schmaltzy pop song, "I believe for every child that goes astray/someone will come to show the way". No such luck in life. No miracle for James. No innocent endings here.

A bell goes: the gallery closing. I descend the stairs, into the street. Darkness falling from the air, an hour to kill. In the bus station, over the road, a woman stands with shopping bags in her left hand while reining in a toddler with her right. Reins, harnesses, leads to stop your toddler getting away: there'd been a run on them after James's death, when abduction followed by death was "every mother's nightmare". The trial just up the road is proof that there's another mother's nightmare – having a murderer for a son. If for every murderee there is a murderer, then this nightmare should be as common. Only the logic of the heart ensures it's not. Gently, fearfully, as a double-decker bus swings past, the mother over the road reins in her baby, the most precious child (as every child is) in the world.

When my son was small, I used to hover over his cot, holding my breath to hear him breathe, unable to believe that just because he'd done it these last few weeks he would carry on doing it now. Easy as breathing, but what was easy about breathing? What was in it for him, who knew nothing of life yet, who didn't even know he was alive yet, to keep up the habit? I'd listen for ten minutes or so, start to creep from the room, then detect some change – like thinking someone has finally answered just as you put the phone down. I'd read about cot deaths. If I left the room, he'd certainly stop breathing: only my being there could guarantee his staying alive.

Then he got meningitis and I knew I'd been right. It happened the day we moved house, just so we wouldn't notice. He'd been sick the day before and run a temperature, and we took him to the doctor who said it must be flu, he'd sleep it off, no worries. In the night I found his forehead beaded with tears and his body hot as bread from the oven and his heart thrashing about like a blackbird in a fruitcage. Calpol settled him, brought him down. Through all the move next morning, he was still out: "Good," I said to Kathy, "He's sleeping it off." Lunchtime, early afternoon: he slept on, dead to the world. Round teatime, his carrycot among chairs and packing cases, we began to worry. We called the doctor, another one: it was Saturday, no surgery, but yes, he'd come to the new address. Temperature, pulse, a listen to the chest, a prod about: nothing alarming there, only the unreactingness. Then a lift of the neck: response, a cry of pain. An outside chance of meningitis, the doctor said – best be on the safe side and get tests done. An ambulance arrived, a blue light swimming round the house we'd been in just six hours, intriguing the neighbours we hadn't met yet, who, as our son was carried out by ambulancemen, must have wondered what they were in for, a nice new family on the block. Kathy disappeared inside the white doors, under the pulsing blue. I drove behind, thinking: the new house is hubris, my baby is going to die.

The test results, two hours later, confirmed meningitis. His sleep became deeper, a coma; by his bedside neither of us slept at all. He stayed out cold next morning, and on into the afternoon, further from us than he'd been the day before. There was a drip in his arm, and blood, but he did not stir. He had gone from the world he'd only lately come into, unlearnt the skills – babbling, smiling, sitting up – the little skills he knew. Kathy cried and I held her. A doctor passed and looked at us with bemusement and faint contempt: the illness was being treated, the danger had passed, what was our problem? Next day our child began to move. It took a week, but he came back to life, undamaged but for a terror of needles and white coats.

The terror – my terror – never left. As my son grew bigger, so the terror grew bigger. The chief meaning of his life was the likelihood of his losing it. Danger was all I saw, and I could see it everywhere. He'd wake and want to climb out of his cot, but get his head stuck in the bars, strangling himself, or fall awkwardly over the side, breaking his neck. We'd have forgotten to flick the switch up on one of the plug sockets, and he'd dip his wet finger in. He'd squeeze under a bedroom sash window, and plummet onto the concrete below. He'd drown headfirst in the nappy bucket. He'd find his way to the bottles and packets under the kitchen sink, the bleach, the mouse poison, that unlabelled bottle from who knows where, the contents of which turn out, at the inquest, to be paraquat. Now he's out the back door, face down in the garden pond, or being stung by a bee (that allergy we didn't know about), or climbing inside the chest in the garage, the disused freezer with the self-locking lid. No, it's the front door he's through, on to the road, beneath the reversing furniture van, the refuse lorry, in pursuit of his merrily bouncing ball. I pull him clear and teach him to stay on the pavement, a safe place until the day a careering joyrider, or police car in pursuit, mounting the kerb . . .

Time to eat: what shall it be? A fishbone in his gullet, the chip-pan whose handle he reaches for (boiling oil, 80 per cent first-degree burns), or the Brazil nuts (*another* allergy we didn't know about) swelling his throat? Now he is playing safely in his bedroom, the worst place to be when fire breaks out downstairs or when the giant elm we meant to show the tree surgeon topples on that part of the house. A drive after lunch? A pity I didn't remember the safety belt or the child-protection lock on the offside rear door; a pity I let him lie on the shelf in the Range Rover, beside the paneless window (broken by thieves last week, meant to get it fixed), never thinking that at eighty on the motorway the force, as in an aeroplane, would suck him out.

Holidays now: the wardrobe in the rented villa that topples as he tries to climb inside, the rapids, the windy cliff edge, the bull, the snake, the offshore breeze dragging off his rubber dinghy, the collapsing sand tunnel on the beach. Phew, September again, his eleventh September, he's made it through primary and now it's big school – the tragic head injury on the rugby field, the knife-carrying nutter walking in off the street, or the choice of schooltrips: which will it be, the minibus crash, the avalanche while skiing, or the canoes swept out on a hypothermic sea? But it's all right, he's a teenager now, he graduates from being drowned, set alight or hanged from a tie by schoolmates, the "prank that went horribly wrong". He remembers from last time that the Rottweiler behind the warehouse fence has the jaw, when you get too close to the wire, to scalp you through the mesh. He knows from previous incarnations how quickly a pothole fills with water, how fast fog comes down on the mountain. When policemen tell him there's a bomb alert, will he step this way please, he knows from bitter experience to move quickly and never risk the cordoned-off streets. He is growing up now, he reads the papers, he is coming into new powers as a citizen. At sixteen he can die legally on a motorbike, at seventeen in a car (or under a car: a puncture on the bypass, that cranky old jack I told him never to use), at eighteen from alcohol poisoning. He develops a drug habit, a heroin habit. He's HIV-positive. He commits suicide (from a bridge, off a towerblock, under a tube) just before Finals. He takes up hang-gliding, rock-climbing; a rope snaps, a chute fails to open, we get the call in the middle of the night, the I'm-sorry-to-have-to-tell-you knock at the door. He is in a bar, a bank, a shopping mall, the innocent bystander caught in a robber's crossfire – or maybe he is the robber, the bullet a police bullet. No, he is a shy, unworldly, shoulder-against-the-wall kind of boy, who likes to be helpful about the place, who wants to surprise me by Flymoing the lawn even though the grass is wet, who severs the electric cable, can't grasp why the machine has stopped, stoops down, bemused, picks up the power line . . .

So many ways, let me count the ways, bizarre, banal, by fire or water, in the air or under the earth. And all this supposes we are kind to our son – haven't beaten him overmuch about the head, starved him, locked him in a room in his own shit, abandoned him after birth in the grass by a river or down a rubbish chute. And supposes we've let him be born in the first place, not plucked him out, or sucked him out, untimely ripped, from the womb. Many of us have a death like this on our conscience: the children that might have been, the embryos. A murdered foetus: not to be equated with a murdered child.

And yet, and yet. There are no weighing-scales for the guilty heart.

I've been gathering cuttings lately of accidents and infanticides. I have a blue folder in the third drawer down in my desk. Most days, there's something to add to it. On a bad day, or a good day, when there's nothing, I dream up new deaths instead. Often, before these deaths, there's torture, as if death were not punishment enough. It's torture even to have these dreams, but I can't help it: they sing out of my night like rooks – the irrepressible, black, cawing *as if*s.

The worst involves a baby of eight months, whose mother is about to put him in the bath when the doorbell goes. The men on the step push her inside, demanding money, jewellery, credit cards, her body. She gives them all she can: let them take anything but her baby, let them take everything. She gives them all she can but it's not enough. The men turn ugly. A knife comes out, a clawhammer – yards of blood. They're about to leave when they notice the child. He has got himself from flat to sitting upright, he is (a first! if only she could see it) bottomshuffling from the bathroom to the hall. Jesus, what to do with the baby? These men are rapists, thieves, muggers, murderers, but they cannot kill a child. The taller man picks up the baby and carries him back to the bathroom. He notices the bath, with its nine-inch lining of water: tepid, safe. He sits the baby among a fleet of sponge shapes, boats, ducks, plastic submarines. A fighting chance: if only the baby can stay upright, soon surely his daddy will be home. And normally the daddy would have been home, but he has chosen today to work on at the office. There he is, looking like me, finally – too late – showing up.

Ah, the dreams, and the refinement of dreams. To put them through it like this, a woman and child who might be my wife and child: I tell you, I resent my subconscious, I want to shove it in a dark cave and tell it never to come out. I resent my consciousness, too, the shrink in my ear explaining my dreams for me, planting the thought – thanks, pal – that what I fear and most desire are joined like melted plastic. This is not what I want, right? This is what I dread.

I know others dread it, too – losing a child: the worst thing – and have always done, even in ages when kids dying was commonplace. George Orwell, on the Victorians: "In a family of ten or twelve it was almost inevitable that one or two should die in infancy, and though these deaths were sad, of course, they were soon forgotten, as there were nearly always more children coming along." Sad? Devastating. Soon forgotten? Never forgotten. Mothers usually take it harder, having put in more of the care. Fathers used to be spared the worst – Herodotus, in the fifth century BC: "until their fifth year [children] are not allowed to come into the sight of their father, but pass their lives with the women. This is done so that, if the child die young, the father may not be afflicted by its loss." Ralph Bulger, chewing gum in court, doesn't look as afflicted as Denise, but he must be, inside. Soon forgotten? Never forgotten. A myth, too, that a murder like James Bulger's, if there was ever a murder like James Bulger's, would once have been more "accepted", less of a sensation. In the rare ancient cases of children killed by children, the outcry and repugnance were the same.

I lie awake in my bed. In their beds, Ralph and Denise are surely awake, too. James is always beside them: there's the pain of that, as well as the pain of him not being beside them. Those who have lost a child are the only ones not to lose a child. Most children, the survivors, grow up, suffer the changes of age, become adult and disappointing, like ourselves; only the dead

kids are immortal, frozen in an ever-smilingness, pretty pages
waiting on the imagination. James laughing under his blond
locks – it's the only image we have of him, or want to have. We
don't want the image from the courtroom, exhibit 47, James in
bloodstains on the tracks.

Will what's happening in that courtroom help Denise and
Ralph come to terms with James's death? There's an idea it
will – that justice (meaning a murder verdict) will ease their
pain. You see the bereaved on television, the families of
murder victims filmed on the court steps after the verdict,
solemnly jubilant if the sentence "goes their way". But is a
verdict which goes the Bulgers' way any way to make them
feel better? The trial itself can be doing them no good at all –
the witnesses, the details, the having to relive James ceasing to
live. Nor will the verdict, whatever it is, bring appeasement.
Appeasement? There can be no appeasement. I fear for Ralph
and Denise. Somewhere, because they're human, is the
thought that, with justice done, their son will walk back into
the room: an illusion to break their hearts all over again.

I want to see Denise, and tell her this, and offer what comfort I can. It's naff, I know: do I think I'm a fairy godmother,
or what? Intrusive, too: best leave her alone with her grief. But
she has already allowed *Hello!* magazine into her house, over
the summer, before the trial, to talk about her new pregnancy
and James's death – so why not me? She'll answer the door,
heavily pregnant, wearing the floral dress and dangly earrings
she wore when interviewed by *Hello!* She'll have put the ket-
tle on, and spoon the coffee into the mugs, one for each of us,
milk and no sugar for me. She'll invite me through to the living-room, to see the cache of soft toys sent by well-wishers
after James's death, cuddly bears mainly, and Thumper, a flop-
haired bunny. She'll be controlled at first, then angry, then

weep her heart out on the meadow-green sofa. And all the while, under the swoosh of her silky dress, the new baby awash inside her: life, tenderness, hope . . .

On my narrow bed, I try to imagine Denise, where she is, what she's wearing, how her voice sounds. But she never speaks, the room won't come into focus, I can't grasp what it's like to be her, or pretend to understand what she feels.

4

The Walk

I wanted to go home; I wanted to be good; I wanted to
study and never do any mischief; but Lampwick said, "Why
should you bother about studying? Why do you want to go
to school? Instead come with me to Playland."

CARLO COLLODI, *Pinocchio*

I sit on a bench in Bootle Strand shopping centre, notebook
in hand. There's a pain in my guts and I'm hyper, trembly. I've
heard so much about the place it's become a kind of Babylon
for me, a twin-towned Gomorrah, a ninth circle of hell.
Already, I've lost my bearings: some of the shops have several
entrances; others are located on two floors; the place is as
maze-like as a medina. I search the passing faces: were they
here that day? Did they hear Robert and Jon plotting abduction? Did they see them leave with James? I know it's mad, that
they're only shoppers going about their business. I can feel the
place is friendly, cheerful, not a soulless out-of-town drive-in
but a bazaar on the high street, with a whiff of the corner
shop, a place to stop and talk. On any other day, I'd appreciate
the fusion of old and new, the skin-deep modernity: ceramic-
tiled floors, glass pillars, aluminium-ribbed ceilings, circular
wooden benches (like this one I'm sitting on) enclosing fuzzy

plants. But my visions's clouded, my body's rumbling, I'm sore with the memory of what happened here. And nervous of what I'll find following in the boys' footsteps: the killing route, the pilgrimage, the two-and-a-half-mile walk to death.

When T and V came here that morning they were sagging – as I am from court, now. Time on their hands, a day to kill, there was hardly a shop they failed to visit, which meant rob. Among the objects they took, or were suspected of taking, were: a pen, a packet of batteries, Humbrol enamel paint tins, sausage rolls, party poppers, a clockwork toy soldier, a pencil, a tube of PrittStick, a troll, two yellow felt tips, a chocolate dip, a packet of iced gems, a balloon, a plum, a pear, a banana, Roses sweets, a Mars bar, a hamburger-lookalike candy, a lipstick tube, an eyeliner, a yoghurt, a milkshake, two cartons of Ambrosia rice, some wallpaper borders and a large tin of paint from Fads. Later, to police interviewers, they cheerfully confessed – and maybe exaggerated – their thieving, as if it were an index of their good character, a guarantee that they couldn't have done something really bad. Their more conspicuous thefts, and hyperactivity, had them ejected from a couple of shops, but mostly they went unchallenged. Just here where I'm sitting, near Toymaster (toyless now, out of business, its windows gone to white), they dropped one of the Humbrol tins and kicked it skidding across the floor – where it was picked up by a passing gentleman, who, seeing it was Antique Bronze, took it home to touch up a broken Toby jug.

If there was one item the boys might have planned to nick, it was the troll. Robert collected trolls: there was one he had snitched from Kwiksave just for its eyes, which lit up red and green. Little horrors. Nordic goblins. Fluorescent hair the length of a corpse. In my day trolls weren't collectable. There was only the one in the Ladybird book, who stuck his warty face up from the river at the three billy-goats gruff: "Who's that trip-trapping across my bridge?" The troll wanted to get a kid away, to gobble him up, but the little and middle billy goats outwitted him and the great big billy goat butted him to kingdom come. A happy ending, the three kids gambolling in a sweet meadow, not like this. The troll was forgotten once James was nicked. Robert said he dumped it behind the freezers in Iceland.

Nervy and nauseous still, I walk through Bootle Strand, feeling as if I'm being watched. I *am* being watched. Perched above my head are little nests of cameras, their lenses poking all-ways like the beaks of hungry nestlings. The eyes of the Lord are in every place. No man, since surveillance, is an island. But who is surveillance for? For security – not the same thing as safety. The monitors were installed to protect shops, not people. They caught the kids on film, walking smartly from the butchers out of the precinct. But it was hours after the killing before the images of the abduction could be found.

I walk under the lenses as the boys did, past the Mothercare sign and outside to the canal. The duo was a trio now. According to Robert, Jon had said: "Let's get a kid, I haven't hit one for ages." According to Jon, Robert had said: "Let's get this kid lost, let's get him lost outside so when he goes into the road he'll get knocked over". But having walked James safely round the corner, T and V told him to kneel by the mucky water, in the hope he'd fall in and drown. When the ruse didn't work (ruses in kids' games rarely do), they dropped him on his head. It left a graze, a "speckly mark" – like the shiny bruise the Witch of the North left on Dorothy in *The Wizard of Oz*, "a bump as big as a young cockerel's stone". Tormenting James some more, the boys shut the latchgate on him as he tried to follow them back up from the canal. They might have left him there; if only they had. But in the end they picked him up and carried him over the road – the beginning of the walk to Walton.

I cross as they did, pass the JobCentre, and enter the local library. It's National Children's Week, and a member of the local fire brigade, Fireman Sid, is instructing a class of five-year-olds in personal safety. I feel I've strayed into a storybook. Fireman Sid is a part-time author, and is reading from his work. There's one story about a crying brontosaurus and another about a duck called Josephine, and the moral of both is: never go off alone. "What should you do if you go out to play?" Fireman Sid asks his rapt, grey-jumpered listeners. "Tell your mam, else she'll be worried." Denise Bulger would have been worrying by this point. The boys didn't stop here with James, though Robert claimed they'd come earlier to look at some fairy stories (itself a fairy story), and Jon said they'd planned to find a *Where's Wally* book, also probably a lie but a comically appropriate one (searching for *Where's Wally* in a big and unfamiliar library: as difficult as searching for Wally in one of his pictures). I wonder: if Robert and Jon *had* been in the habit of coming here, instead of the Strand, would it have made a difference? Matthew Arnold's on the shelves, and Leavis: their big idea, that books humanize. But what's the evidence that children who read grow up less violent than their peers? How can you know? All you know is: you never know.

I leave the library, turn left and right, pass a pub called the Jawbone Tavern, and reach the roundabout by Christ Church. It was eventful at this roundabout. This is where a woman on the top of a bus cried out at a boy being mistreated, where a cyclist ran into the rear of a parked Nissan hatchback, where a second set of security cameras picked up the trail. Mark Pimblett came up to the roundabout in his dry-cleaning van around 4.15 and saw two big boys dragging a puffed-face smaller one whose heels scraped the pavement. Pimblett also noticed three teenage schoolgirls, wearing black stockings, and thought them "fit". It took some time for him to get on to the roundabout, what with the heavy traffic and the distracting girls. But finally, driving around it, he glanced in his rear-view mirror, and saw the lad in the black jacket kick the little lad high up on the body, in the ribs, under the armpit, "not a full-blast kick, more like a kick to persuade him to come on . . . a persuading kick". In court yesterday the defence had a bit of fun with Mark Pimblett. How could he judge the force of the kick while also driving and eyeing up schoolgirls? And why did he not stop? His story doesn't hang together, except for that fine detail, the distinction between ways of kicking toddlers, the persuading and the full-blooded. Persuading kicks, you get them all the time: it's a tough world, boys have to grow up hard, being bashed about never did me no harm. Kicking and beating kids: part of the culture, always has been. That lullaby about Bonaparte, sung by English nannies of the last century to scare the young ones off to sleep:

> And he'll beat you, beat you, beat you
> And he'll beat you all to pap,
> And he'll eat you, eat you, eat you,
> Every morsel snap, snap, snap.

Perhaps there's still some idea that infants, because smaller than adults, are less than human. That, however hard you drop them, they always bounce back. It must be some persisting Calvinist prejudice, that children are mere lumps of flesh:

if they're to become estimable (meaning adult), they need to be disciplined, beaten, knocked into shape. A *dog* kicked in the street, now that might have been worth stopping for, that would have given Mark Pimblett pause. Still, there's no point feeling angry with him. His priorities are those of his nation, my nation, a nation where the RSPCA does better for donations than the NSPCC. That news item the other day: a month-old baby was savaged in its bouncy chair by the family dog, a bull terrier. The baby died in hospital. The dog was put down some days later – but not before twenty people had rung the police station offering it a home.

I walk up Oxford Road, and in my Liverpool A-Z find a Cambridge Road, too, and a flurry of streets named after Oxbridge colleges: Merton, Balliol, Exeter, Gonville, Downing, Trinity, Magdalen, Keble, Wadham, Clare. Was this Oxbridgeizing the fancy of someone new to the area? Or of a local boy made good, having hopes for the place, wanting it to come up? Someone, either way, nostalgic for his three years in an Oxbridge quad. It could have been the same man who got the adjacent streets named after Shakespearian characters: Beatrice, Benedict, Orlando, Falstaff, Glendower, Hotspur, Miranda, Hector, Portia, Macbeth, Othello. Macbeth! Othello! Fancy living in streets called after murderers. But people do.

I walk up Breeze Hill, past a low, monstrous, anonymous slab of a pub called The Mons (Bootle is twinned with the Belgian town of Mons). James had walked a mile now, was tired, kept crying and saying "I want my mum," to which the boys replied "Come on: she's this way." I'd imagined their route as furtive, secluded. But for half a mile they walked along one of the busiest roads in Liverpool, with the traffic, between four and five on a Friday, at its peak. At the throbbing junction of Southport Road and Breeze Hill, six lanes up and down the hill, four lanes across, the traffic was stalled and watchful. The boys crossed at the lights, an awkward manoeuvre which several drivers noticed, just as they also noticed a crying child. So what? Kids cry. What was special about this kid crying? Weren't the two older kids looking after him? They were. The let's-get-a-kid-run-over plan had been abandoned, if ever truly entertained. By the lights, one driver noticed James entering a coned-off area at the edge of the road: dangerous, worrying, but the chubby boy picked him up and carried him to the pavement, the toddler bawling, it seemed, because he'd lost the chance to run around. The lights changed, and the cars drove on.

The lights change, and I walk on, along the pavement then up steps past the plaque saying Breeze Hill Services Reservoir, opened 24 March 1897. The top of the reservoir's grassed over, the one bit of green on the journey. Up here the police found a white fluffy lamb, a toy, and wondered if T and V had used it as a lure: everywhere the lamb went, James would walk behind. It's a bit like a hill-croft here: you can see for miles. But the view isn't enticing: pebbledash prefabs, turn-of-the-century terraces, blackened, redbrick back-to-backs, mock-Tudor semis, low high-rises, unsmoking industrial chimneys. The sea and rivermouth are less than a mile away – relief, escape – but they're hidden behind the roofs, only stilled cranes to show for them. It's the better end of town, but Coketown all over again: the school could be a factory, the pub could be an old people's home, the reservoir could be a playing field, the only foliage is the moss under broken gutters and leaking gable-ends. In the distance, the spire of Walton church and a hint of unhoused hills: otherwise, a vista drained of purpose, a blot of a landscape. It must have an effect.

There's a passage in *The Road to Wigan Pier* where Orwell says that industrial landscapes "go on being largely ugly because the Northerners have got used to that kind of thing and do not notice it." Robert and Jon had never known anything else. But not noticing doesn't mean a landscape such as this has no influence. Is my finding it ugly a rural boy's prejudice? I don't know. But I wouldn't want to live here. Would you want to live here? People live here.

Irene Hitman lives here, gentle, auburn, seventyish, belying her name. I remember her from the witness box: out with her dog for a walk, she saw two little boys dragging an injured toddler up the grass slope. She worried about this, and went on worrying until the television news report of James's disappearance that same evening; at which point she went round to her friend Jean Francis, who had also seen the boys, and then called the police at Walton Lane, the first witness to ring in. At the time, she made the following statement: "I asked if they knew the toddler and they both said no, they didn't. I told them that he should get some attention for his injuries and they both said they would take him to the police station. I wish now I had done something." In court, yesterday, she recalled a different conversation.

"What's the matter?" she had asked.

"He fell down there."

"Where are you going now?"

"We're going home."

"Hurry up then. And when you get home let his mum see his head."

The defence lawyers were interested in the discrepancy between these two stories. Originally she'd seen a lost boy with two strangers and had worried she should have done something; now she was saying she took them for three brothers and had encouraged them to go home to their mum. Which story was right? The latter. She must have made a false statement back in February, then? Awkwardness. Silence. Rather than words, just one word, perjury, waiting to be said. But at this point the defence lawyers backed off: no more questions; nothing to be gained from persecuting the witness. Perhaps they sensed what it's like to be Irene Hitman, living with it every day – how bad she feels whenever she takes the dog out, how guilty, self-castigating, terrible. But will never admit it in public. Has changed her story, and will even perjure herself, to bury these feelings and be absolved.

There were others along the way who saw the big boys hitting the little boy but failed to intervene. The Liverpool 38, the papers are calling them now, the ones Who Saw But Didn't Act. "Everyone is guilty of the good they do not do," said Voltaire. True up to a point, but too severe. These people weren't peasants working near Auschwitz. This wasn't complicity with known atrocities. They couldn't have known what would happen next. Even if they had their suspicions, even if some felt premonitions of harm, you can't blame them for choosing to stay clear. The streets are dangerous places. You don't get involved unless you have to, do you? In the subway, at the bottom of Breeze Hill, I see two boys of about twelve, smoking, skulking, mucking about. Saggers, for sure. I ought to go up to them, the scallies with fags, and ask their names and schools. But I pretend not to see and pass on the other side.

This is the subway where Jon dumped his satchel that morning. It's the pits, some 1960s dream of what the 1990s would look like, and now it is the 1990s and the future's come to pass. An expressway built in shouting distance, in sermon distance, of a sandstone church. A concrete pillar, daubed with flowers, holding up a flyover. Tunnels spoking out from a use-less patch of grass. Once, some architect was happy with this, or more than. Once, this subway was a plan on the drawing-board of high intentions – wide spaces, funnelled walkways, white concrete and northern light. It must have sat, in minia-ture, in a glass case at the town hall, with green felt and fuzzy trees and someone's dreams invested in it. Look at it now. A palimpsest of graffiti. Deafening traffic. Dogshit and frankly pissing kids. It would be hard to feel at home here, but for Robert and Jon it was home, almost. To the left is Neil Venables's flat, where Jon spent most weekends (Susan's house is further off, in Norris Green, a sixties semi on a raw, subur-ban estate). To the right is the school the boys attended, off and on. Straight ahead, through the graveyard, is the road to Robert's home.

A furlong of brown cassette tape spools around my leg as I come up from the subway. I bend to unmanacle myself, then walk past Cropper's Garage and a row of rundown stores: a florist, a pet shop, a DIY, awful but human. For the nearly two miles to here, T and V had moved with mixed purpose, half in deadly earnest, half a game. The abduction, first, and the surprise of getting away with it. The vague attempt at drowning, the callow boasts of getting James knocked over in the road. Now they faced three choices: to unload the grizzly mite on a passing adult; to take him to the police station; to leave him where no one would see. Hand over, report or dump: which was it to be? It hadn't mattered up till here. But now they were almost home it began to matter a lot.

It must be why they ambled in County Road, playing for time, wanting the choice to be taken from their hands. Here's the pet shop, Animate, where Robert stood looking at a fish, a Weather Loach, in the bottom of a tank. "It's dead," he told the assistant, who replied that it was only resting and, to prove the point, prodded it into life. Here's the DIY shop, where the owner watched the boys hawkishly: you had to, there were always pre-pubescent sniffers nicking tins of glue and paint. Here's the bookmakers that caught fire, bringing engines and sirens, a distraction for James. Here's the junction of Bedford Road, where Robert and Jon went to school, sometimes. Here's Walton church, here its steeple, here the mouldering graves of people.

Here, too, James was nearly saved. Going home with her daughter, and her shopping (two peach custards, butter, dog food, cheese slices, pears, two glass parrots, milk, eggs, biscuits and a bag of mixed crisps), Elizabeth McCarrick overheard three boys being given directions to Walton Lane police station by a woman with a dog. The little boy, she noticed, looked distressed and tired; the two older boys told her that they'd found him at Bootle Strand. She asked why they hadn't gone to the police station there. They said they didn't know there was one. Nervous, shifty, Robert let go of James's hand for a moment and looked ready to walk off. (He later claimed he was uneasy because he'd been "told never to talk to strangers".) Mrs McCarrick ordered her daughter to take James's hand. But then Jon assumed control, reassuring Mrs McCarrick and the other lady that they would pass Walton Lane police station on their way home. "Are you all right, son?" Mrs McCarrick asked little James, worrying about them crossing the busy road or maybe about the oddness of their story. Finally, she offered to help them cross over, if the other woman, with the dog, would watch her daughter a minute. The woman refused: the dog didn't like children, see. The boys moved off, across the road, beyond recall. It must have crossed Mrs McCarrick's mind that she might have persisted, done more, herself taken the little boy to the police station. It must have since crossed the minds of her tight-lipped friends. But she's not the one who killed James. As well blame the dog that didn't like children: if the dog had liked children, Mrs McCarrick might have taken James's hand and the story might have had a happy ending. But you can't expect dogs to like children if adults don't.

I turn the corner into Church Road West, as if in pursuit of three ghosts. The houses look jollier here, bright-painted, every door different, cheerful and Penny Lane-ish: the people who come and go stop and say hello, and there's even a place (Kenny's) to get your hair cut, as Robert, who liked his short, often did. But the barber shaving another customer is hidden behind a wire-meshed window. There are alarms on the houses that can afford them. And at Mersey Joinery, a plaintive signboard pleads with would-be intruders: "Because of Burglaries No Tools or Valuables Are Left in This Yard Overnight." Two boys who knew Robert saw him walking here. They had a pair of plastic handcuffs and planned to use them on him – a trick. They noticed the little boy with the grazed head. He was Jon's brother, they were told. He had fallen over. They were taking him home. "If you don't take him home I'll batter you," one of the boys with the handcuffs said. Or told the police he said. Perhaps the threat to "batter" was intended, after the event, to make himself look good.

Further up the street, by the railway, there's a JobCentre. The boys had begun their journey by a JobCentre and now they were going to finish it by a JobCentre. This one looks new, fenced in behind high red railings. In time Jon and Robert might have become familiar with it, if they hadn't improved their educational prospects by killing James. In Liverpool the JobCentre is where you go not to find work but to confirm there is none to find: in the month of the murder, unemployment was 15.2 per cent, 4.4 points above the national average; around 30 per cent of eighteen- to twenty-four-year-olds here are without jobs. None of the boys' parents had jobs, though Ralph Bulger had been on seventeen training schemes. From JobCentre to JobCentre: coming from where they did, the boys were trekking a route they could expect to walk again later. What effect does it have to grow up in such a place, where the one thing promised you is failure? I remember a piece of graffiti from the 1970s: I DON'T BELIEVE IN NOTHING. I'D LIKE TO SEE THEM BURN THE WHOLE WORLD DOWN, JUST LET IT BURN DOWN BABY. The author, I thought, must be some druggy, disaffected twenty-eight-year-old, a nihilist philosopher-poet of the streets. These days I'd put him younger. There are kids of fifteen, thirteen, maybe even ten who think that way.

I cross over the railway bridge to the "entry", or alley, that runs beside the line. Several more witnesses saw the boys here, and one of them, a man who knew the Thompson family, overheard Jon saying, in words calculated to defuse suspicion: "I'm fed up with having my little brother. I have him from school all the time. I'm going to tell my mum I'm not going to mind him no more." Or was it Robert who said this? The tall boy in the mustard jacket or the chubby one in the dark jacket? It could have been either. Both had brothers, and both were fed up with them. Jon was fed up with his older brother Mark because he'd been born with a cleft palate, was mocked as a "divvie", and consumed too much parental attention. Robert was fed up with the youngest of his six brothers, the new baby, Ben, who took up all his mother's time and was, besides, another man's child. And then there was Ryan, eight, who Robert had to cart around with him – on one recent truanting spree, resenting the burden, he'd left Ryan weeping at the canal by Bootle Strand. "I'm fed up with my brother" was a white lie and a black truth. "If I wanted to kill a baby, I'd kill my own, wouldn't I?" said Robert when questioned about James's death, self-exculpating and self-condemning at once.

Fraternity is an important notion in the north, or used to be, in the days of industry and trade unions. An area like this would have considered itself a brotherhood, a community, poorer in wealth but stronger on family values than the spivvy, lounge-lizard south-east. These streets by the railway are called Groves, an urban pastoral: Elphin Grove, Rymer Grove, Golden Grove. Their names and shapes evoke Lowry paintings, or *The Uses of Literacy*, or early *Coronation Street*: cramped but cosy, with father by the fire reading the racing finals, mother peacefully sewing, and the children with their penn'orth of mint humbugs playing hopscotch in the street. The smell of Woodbines, and fish and chips, and smoke rising from the chimney pots. That's how it was once, or fancied itself, a picture of mutual trust: the back door always open, people minding each other's business, friends who would give you their last shilling. Whereas now . . . A ten-foot wiremesh fence sealing off the railway; backyards topped with broken glass; barbed wire coiled around each climbable post; burglar alarms and guard dogs; dogshit and cartons and dented drinks cans; dead quiet; no one in the streets. Not neighbourliness, but Neighbourhood Watch. Not brotherhood, but the *stumm*, useless, unpreventing cameras of Big Brother. NYE BEVAN IS DEAD it says on a wall just up the road.

Are things worse in Liverpool than in the rest of Britain? The city has had its share of troubles recently – Heysel, Hillsborough, Toxteth, Derek Hatton, a corrupt City

Council – and of hostile reporting from London-based foreigners like me. The *Daily Mirror*, 1982: "They should build a fence around [Liverpool] and charge admission. For sadly, it has become a 'showcase' of everything that has gone wrong in Britain's major cities." An earlier hostile foreigner was Nathaniel Hawthorne, arriving to take up the post of US Consul: "I should not have conceived it possible," he wrote of Liverpool in 1853, "that so many children could have been collected together, without a single trace of beauty, or scarcely of intelligence, in so much as one individual: such mean, coarse, vulgar features and figures, betraying an unmistakeably low origin, and ignorant and brutal parents. They did not appear wicked, but only stupid, animal and soulless. It must require many generations of better life to elicit a soul in them. All America could not show the like." Maybe Hawthorne was on to something: generations later, the better life for children still hasn't come. The city suffers the same economic and social deprivation as other parts of the post-industrial north, but suffers them worse. It must have an effect. Yet I don't exactly blame Liverpool for the killing of James Bulger. Nor does Ralph Bulger, who thinks it "a great place, full of warm people". What happened here might have happened anywhere. There are streets near me in London no less a Slough of Despond. And were a child to be abducted there, it's even less likely someone would notice and intervene.

At the end of this entry, a witness could remember James laughing. It wasn't that he was happy leaving the alley – though I feel happy leaving the alley – but that Robert was playing a game with him, maybe a nice game or maybe a game of trying to push him into the road. James had been kicked and punched along the route; he had a sore head; he had reason to hate his abductors. And now he was laughing. His laughter offends both narrative propriety and adult psychology, but there's nothing odd about it. Children of three have short-term memories. They are distractable. Even a medieval writer could understand this: "if a child has just been beaten, should the person who beat him offer him a pretty flower or a red apple, he will forget what was just done to him and run to him with open arms to please him." How often, how easily, I've lifted my own children from the well of terminal misery with a funny face or stupid game. Part of the attraction of infants: that they forget so quickly. (Or seem to: some part of them is not forgetting at all.) To James, at the kerbside, Robert and Jon had stopped being torturers and were once more big, exciting friends.

The alley opens on to a road, but Robert and Jon must have felt to be in a cul-de-sac. To the right, a hundred yards away, is the Walton Lane police station; to the left, a little further, Robert's home in Walton Village. Either way meant trouble. The police, seeing the graze on James's head, might doubt the story of "finding" the boy. Ann Thompson certainly would. She'd know by now of Robert's truanting, and would be angry – as would Susan Venables, who was already looking for Jon and only minutes later would be trawling this same alley. The mischief of the abduction had turned sour. The kid was a pain, and – like young parents exhausted by a crying baby – the boys felt aggressive towards him (back up the alley, Jon had thrown the hood of James's anorak up into a tree). It's why they turned not left or right but chose a third route, a scramble up the earth-bank on to the railway. That way they'd not get into trouble. They'd simply lose the kid instead.

There may have been other reasons, or wonky self-justifications. A train might come, and that would be exciting (though Robert, a connoisseur of train times, must have known that none was scheduled). They could go to Robert's den (if Robert had a den: Jon said he did, but no one has ever found it). They could deliver James unobserved into the back compound of the police station, directly below the tracks. Up they went. I'd follow them if I could, but the gap in the fence has been mended now, and I turn left under the bridge instead. Up Cherry Lane there's a six-foot wall holding back the grassed embankment, easy but conspicuous to climb. I wait for a gap in the traffic, then clamber up, fast, furtive, my shoes showering soft brick fragments as I go. The grass is rough here, clumpy, brambled. I weave along a course of flattened blades, boys' paths, dogs' paths, rabbits' paths, to the white shale at the top, close to where James Bulger died.

It's safe up here, two tracks only, not electrified, and just a handful of trains each week, easily audible, easily visible, long straight runs either way. It's safe, I know it's safe, but a childlike fear overtakes me: that I'm trespassing, that a train will materialize from nowhere, that this is a terrible place. Fear in a handful of shale. 5.20, an hour or so after lighting-up time, just as it was then. In my head it always happens in daylight, blows struck under a cold sun. Wrong: it was after dusk. And yet the boys would have seen what they were doing. Glare comes off the white shale. There are streetlights shining from the distant bridge. It isn't dim here: my eyes adjust to it, as their eyes must have done. This wasn't murder in the dark.

I walk towards the bridge, with its high metal sides. The game, the dare, the impossible scam had escalated now towards reality. Did T and V think of pushing James off the bridge on to the road below? On the other side, there are trees but no leaves (none that day, either), and I can see through the windows of the police station. Beyond the tracks is a low wall, an old railway platform, with yellow rings on it where the police marked baby blood stains. Here the attack began, not with bricks and bars but with a tin of Humbrol paint, Azure Blue. Later, the police theorized the tin had been stolen for sniffing, though it would be hard to get high on Humbrol. More likely, the boys used the tin to violate and dehumanize James, to wipe him of his normal features. Splashed in sky-colour, he looked like something else – a troll or doll or alien – and was less conscience-troubling to kill. Who threw the paint? No saying. Who threw the first stone? No telling that, either, since each boy said – and maybe believed – it was the other. Between the wooden sleepers are shale-stones, big enough to hurt, but not damaging. The damage was done by the bricks. Brick after brick, and then an iron bar. "He just kept getting up," the boys said, "he wouldn't stay down." But finally he did stay down. Five minutes would have been enough.

On the railway, between shadow and streetlight. The frenzy of it. Or just the need for James to lie still. Bricks and bars: the crudity of the implements, the barbarism of the act. So *primitive*: dawn breaks in the head of early man and he stoops to pick a stone. So childish, too: the adult killer is sophisticated, carries a gun, a knife, an axe; whereas T and V, in the heat of the moment, used what lay to hand. A crime of passion, then; the police say the boys planned it, but they had brought no weapons with them. Not passion, more an end-of-tether anger, the kid crying for his mother, and they not knowing how to shut him up. Perhaps they thought of James, grown huge in his distress, as a Goliath. Afterwards they left a shrine of bricks around his head. Why? To cover up their crime? To stop the blood pouring out? Or as homage? Natural to use stones as part of worship: the blocks at Stonehenge; the slab in the mouth of Christ's tomb; Jews leaving flints and pebbles – memorial cairns – to honour their dead. Natural for

children to be seen with stones: the little Palestinian libera-
tors, mainsprings of the *intifada*, sanctified by history,
praised by Yasser Arafat. Or were T and V just thugs with
bricks?

Stone-throwing: an emblem of boyhood. I can remember it
from my own: crosslegged on the shingle, aiming at a Tango
can, one point for hitting, three for knocking it over; hanging
from a five-barred gate, throwing stones at the cowpats in
Dixon's field, the squelch when you hit, the halo of horseflies,
the stone like a yolk in the middle; vandalizing that wasps'
nest, which hung like a turban in the fir at the bottom of our
lawn – bolder and bolder we got, until one stone scythed the
basement off and the wasps came sirening out like firemen in
their yellow and black. Harmless stuff, but we threw snowballs
with pebbles inside at passing cars; we knew the lovely sound
of panes shattering in cold frames; tempers would get frayed
and stones were thrown in anger; someone would run home
with a bleeding head. It can't have taken much to hit on this
method of killing. The bricks were all around.

Traffic grumbles in the distance, below the bridge. Up here,
on the silver tracks, in the half light, I feel odd, not myself.
Perhaps T and V had a similar feeling – felt as if they were in
a dream, or nightmare, or film, or video, and became transcendent, something other than themselves: *as if*. They'd
never battered a child before. They hadn't much of a reputation as bullies. They weren't thought wild or dangerous. Not
even the cruelties inflicted *en route* were any real preparation
for a killing. A vague intention is not an act. Ibsen, *Peer Gynt*:
"I might think of it – wish for it – want it badly/But to do it . . .
That's something I can't understand." To kill is different. This
was different. Robert and Jon were different, playing at being
someone other, something worse. Though they'd never have

reached this point without each other, they were not themselves. They had moved beyond themselves. The past had been obliterated. So, too, almost, had little James.

I look up from the glare of the shale to the cemetery behind the police station. Vague figures, like ghosts, are carrying flowers along the paths between graves. It's cold, and a deeper night is coming on. To my right the embankment drops to the black shadow of a factory or warehouse. It was from here the boys descended – two boys now, not three; two boys coming down off the high of a dream – and crossed the road to the video store. The woman there knew Robert well, and asked him to run an errand round the corner – an overdue tape, a pound for him if he'd collect. Jon went with him, and when they came back there was Jon's mother, pouncing, hitting them both, then dragging Jon off to the nick. From here on the bridge, I can see the short walk she took in the hope the police at Walton Lane would teach him a lesson – and the short walk Ann Thompson took minutes later, also to the police station, to report Susan for hitting Robert in the face. Stranger than fiction. Within an hour of the killing, hauled there by their mothers, both boys were in the police station with blood on their hands – the same station to which they were afraid to take the toddler alive.

I think of James, lying up here, and I wonder if anyone heard anything (a breach in nature, lamentings in the air and strange sounds of death); and how the boys could leave him; and what they felt down in the video shop and police station knowing he might be breathing still; and whether they thought of going back to see. I picture him lying up here, taking an hour or more to die, and of his killers crossing and recrossing under the bridge, under his little death. And if he wasn't the one thought on their mind, if they managed to think of something else, I want to bring them back here and take the bricks from the wall, rip the sleepers from the tracks, and teach them to be human. If I were Ralph Bulger, I'd be up here, mad and useless, every night. The policemen, solicitors, barristers, counsellors, psychiatrists, journalists, social workers: surely they've come, too, to stand with a dull pain in the stomach, between the silver tracks and white shalestone where it happened, as if by being here they might begin to understand. It would be less than human not to come, and less than human, having done so, not to shudder in the nightlights and cry.

I clamber down again, furtive through grass and bracken, a man leaving the scene of a crime. I pass the Taxi-Drivers' Social Club, and the butcher's (now flogging antiques). FOR SALE and NO BALL GAMES say the signs between the boarded-up shops. Walton Village was decent, once, respectable, a cut above. Robert's house, 236, is a solid terrace, no slum. Amityville House of Horror, someone scrawled on it after his arrest. Tonight a bulb is burning behind the net curtains, and another family's there, unafraid of its troubled past. I buy a Murphys in Top House, the pub just up the street where Ann Thompson used to come drinking, and where Robert once, the summer before he killed, not finding her there, ran off taunting the barmaid: "Fuck off, you twat. You cunt, you slag." For a time this street was home to Robert and even, more or less, to Jon. For a time, they had the run of the place. For a time, they scamped and scallied. Never again. Yet somewhere, even now, in houses much like these, there must be boys not so different. What is the difference? Why did it go wrong for T and V?

I walk back to the railway, listening for trains – like the one that passed while James's body was lying there, cutting his torso in two. They call it The How, this grass embankment by the bridge. It was here, after the body was found, that flowers were heaped in memory. An act of love and piety, like the 1,086 memorial notices placed in the *Liverpool Echo* – "BUL-GER, JAMES – DEEPEST SYMPATHY" – in the week after the death. Very Liverpudlian. Heysel, Hillsborough: after deep horror, the quiet of flowers. Decent, saddened people, ashamed it could have happened in their city and wanting to pay respects to little James – and others playing to the cameras, and a few, more dubious still, like Milton's night-hag "lured with the smell of infant blood". Among those who came, the day before his arrest, was Robert. He had a single red rose, the colour of blood, and laid it down, just as he'd done on his grandmother's coffin. As perhaps he meant, a television crew captured him in the act, giving him (he thought) a solid alibi, a brick to throw back at the police: why, if he'd killed James, would he have come to lay a flower? Today, there are no flowers, only dew and scraps of paper under the streetlight. Passers-by look at me oddly, curious about my curiosity. It's only a slope of grass. It's just The How.

I turn back, no nearer understanding the Why.

5

Experts

Before the age of reason we do good and bad without knowing it, and there is no morality in our actions . . . A child wants to upset everything he sees; he smashes, breaks everything he can reach. He grabs a bird as he would grab a stone, and he strangles it without knowing what he does.

JEAN JACQUES ROUSSEAU, *Émile*

"**Y**es, yes, yes and yes." The ninth day of the trial, the boys' teachers and psychiatrists are due to speak, and – excitement in the aisles – Robert's mother, Ann, turns up for the first time. Short, stumpy, in a dark suit and with dark hair, she sits big-eyed and traumatized three rows behind her son. It's not that he has been alone till now: there are solicitors, barristers, a social worker, people he knows. But he has *looked* to be on his own, a dangerous loner, an oddball, and stories have begun to circulate – that his dad fled years ago, and his mum has disowned him. It hasn't looked good. It hasn't felt good. She's not been there for him. When he's stressed, he gets asthma attacks. Oh mother, I'm choking and my mouth is full of stars.

Jon's parents, by contrast, have been here every day: Susan smart and brisk with her gold-chained handbag, Neil hunched in anguish, the weepy one, not exactly an advert for family values, but a family of sorts, parents sticking by their kid. Both of them wear an air of disbelief – that such a thing could have happened to them! – as if they belonged up in the gallery, not down near the dock with their son. They keep their distance from the press, but make no secret of what they feel – that Jon is a loving, caring little boy, always has been, with plenty of friends, bottom of the league table for something like this, and never a truant, until he met Robert. But also easily led, or mis-led: if you told him to put his hand in the fire, he'd do it. Where did they go wrong as parents? They don't think they have gone wrong. He's had more love and attention than most children. He's had holidays, Christmas presents, an older brother and younger sister to play with, an education. Now they don't know what to do with the memories. Ever to laugh or smile seems inappropriate, even in private. They mourn the fun they had with him and may never have again: table tennis, snooker, holidays at Butlins . . . It's what Susan and Neil would say, if they could. It's what they will say, later. But for now they keep their heads down and try not to show too much. She doesn't want her make-up running; he doesn't like to be thought a weed. It's a working-class version of the stiff upper lip, a dignity that has won them sympathy in court. Robert's lawyers can see this. It's one of the reasons they've encouraged Ann to come.

But Ann's not much help to Robert. She behaves as if this is *her* tragedy, not his: Look what's been done to Me. She stares ahead, into empty space, wanting to become empty space, not this object of curiosity to the world. Robert turns round to see how she is: he's the protective one, worrying about her, the *puer senex*, old and wise before his time – the child as mother to his mum. She doesn't reciprocate, in public: she's too inhib-ited by the attention paid to her to pay him any, except downstairs, below the court, alone together, out of sight.

Where Susan, with her perfect make-up, determinedly conveys that she is coping, Ann's message is that she isn't, life's rotten, she has never felt worse. There's a deep passivity in her, as if she were the victim, and I find myself angry, wanting to shake her. Two women counsellors, one on each side, don't shake but stroke her, holding hands and murmuring sympathy. (One of them works for Aftermath, a charity which helps the families of killers.) They know what she is going through, she will be all right, just stay calm, nothing else terrible can happen, the worst is past. Ann needs some reassuring. She feels everyone in court is watching her, the woman who gave birth to a murderer, the Bad Mother. She's weepy and heavily tranquillized and she wants to be swallowed up.

But Robert's teachers are here, and – however bad she feels – she has a bone to pick. In Ann's mind, it's these teachers, not her son, who should be carrying the can for that poor baby. Hadn't she suggested, at a crisis meeting about Robert's truancy ten days before the killing, that he be moved from the school, and hadn't they refused to consider it? They said she could have done more to stop him sagging. But hadn't she hidden his shoes, shut him in his room, padlocked the back door, screwed the windows down, taken him to the local police station to show him the cells where he'd end up if he carried on like this? What more could a mother do? The only sure way to get Robert to school was for her to take him, which meant leaving the house early and walking half a mile, not easy with baby Ben. No, it was the school's fault. She's ready to do battle, to shout out if need be, should the teachers say anything unpleasant or untrue.

The teachers will be called as expert witnesses. They aren't the first expert witnesses. The brickdust specialist, the paint splash specialist, the fabric specialist, the shoe specialist, the skin scrapings specialist: they, too, have given evidence. For two days, through their parade of neutral science, I've listened with my eyes shut, unable to close off the subtext, the body of James Bulger on a slab. Some in the press and public gallery have truanted during these experts. I don't blame anyone for sagging. I've sagged, in a different way, myself – shrivelled and sunk when the pathologist, Alan Williams, enumerated every wound: the transected torso, the hanging lip, the torn eyelid, the scalp reddened by brick dust, the leaf stuck by blood to a naked foot. "Transected": a gentle euphemism – not gentle enough – for a body cut in two. After the horrors James suffered in his last hours of life, this other horror in the first hours of his death. "Transected": it makes me think of the Bible story told to exemplify the wisdom of Solomon. Two women have given birth in the same house, one of the babies has died, and each mother claims the surviving baby is hers. Solomon calls for a sword, and proposes to cut the infant in half – an equal share for each. The false mother agrees. The true mother protests, no, no, she'll let the other woman have the child rather than it be harmed. Thus Solomon learns what's what and who is who. Justice: the baby goes home with its mum, alive, unsundered. If only life were like this. But, even with kindly euphemisms, life is not.

Such a multitude of experts in death: I didn't know it employed so many. But today should bring us different experts, other kinds of knowledge. Psychology not physiology; motive rather than post-mortem; not How James died, but Why. A chance for insights into character. A chance to fill the gap in the story. Is one of the boys violent by nature? Are they both? Could they be deeply disturbed in some way – even psychopathic? Was it some pressure at school or home that drove them to do what they did?

Yes, yes, yes and yes, Eileen Vizard is saying. On the balance of probabilities, yes. Lean, earnest, fittingly cerebral, she
is a consultant child and adolescent psychiatrist, and saw
Robert Thompson, on a single occasion, one month ago. In
her view, he is suffering from post-traumatic stress disorder:
haunted by thoughts, memories, nightmares, flashbacks, he
sleeps badly, eats badly and has a high level of anxiety. She is
concerned, she says, when cross-examined, about the lack of
"skilled therapeutic input" he's had in the nine months since
the crime. She would like Robert to have been receiving therapy, and though she knows that under the law such treatment
is not allowed before a trial, she hopes, after the verdict, therapy can begin at once. Whatever happens, Robert should be
moved from the secure unit he has been put in, which isn't
intended for ten-year-olds: he needs appropriate help.

Ann Thompson stares suspiciously. She doesn't like this
talk of her son needing help. He isn't a nutter, and she doesn't
believe people should say he is, even if saying it could get him
off. Robert also stares at Eileen Vizard. He has seen her just
the once before today. Resistant, he didn't see the point of
the meeting: why try to make out he was mad at the time he
killed James when he didn't kill him anyway? Why plead
diminished responsibility when he wasn't responsible for anything? He still feels the same: that he's sane, normal, *ordinary*.
Hearing the lady-shrink speak of his stress disorder, he holds
a white tissue over his face.

Eileen Vizard looks nervous. In murder trials psychiatrists
are often the fall-guys, and she's wary of saying something
which a barrister or journalist might mock. She's also nervous because she knows there are some who think she
shouldn't be standing here at all, that she's a dirty turncoat. It
was Robert's defence team who commissioned her report. But

she also sent a copy to the lawyers for the Crown, who – since the defence don't intend to call her – have now persuaded her to speak for them. Robert's lawyers are incandescent. How could she take money from them and then appear for the other side? If she's so worried about Robert's stress disorder, what about the traumatic effects of her testifying against him, after he'd been persuaded to trust her? What the fuck does she think she's up to? It hasn't been pleasant for Eileen Vizard. She doesn't like the adversarial climate of court. Forget sides. Forget verdicts. Whatever the outcome, Robert will need psychiatric help. Healing is what's at issue. Her reason for coming here is to plead for therapy – and question the legal process which has prevented it till now. Quietly messianic, she'd like the lawyers to hear her out. But they don't seem much interested. What they want is her informed opinion, not a crusade. To reiterate. Did Robert Thompson, when he killed James, know what he was doing? Yes, yes, yes and yes.

Eileen Vizard steps down. She has spoken for, at most, five minutes. What I'd hoped she speak about – the kind of boy Robert is, the kind of family the Thompsons are, his relation to his peers, his character, his conduct, his intelligence, his mental stability, his manifestations (if any) of violent behaviour – has not been spoken of at all. Not that she doesn't have opinions about all this. But it's inadmissible evidence. All she can address, all Jon Venables's psychiatrist can address, all the two teachers can, is the following set of questions: on February 12 1993, the day of the killing, did T and V know the difference between right and wrong? Would they have known it was wrong to take a young child from its mother? Would they have known it was wrong to cause injury to a child? To leave an injured child on a railway line? To which, it seems, there is only one answer: yes, yes, yes and yes.

As If

It's what Susan Bailey says, when she takes the stand, also on behalf of the Crown. Blander, prettier, less nervous than Eileen Vizard, she stresses Jon's co-operativeness, and the co-operativeness of his parents. In all, she saw Jon eight times, and though she found him unable to talk about the crime "in any useful way", she is confident he understood its gravity. Like Robert, Jon is now suffering from post-traumatic stress disorder. But he wouldn't haven't been on February 12? No. So he knew what he was doing that day? Yes. There are some tangles in Susan Bailey's account. If Jon's defence lawyers didn't fear making things worse for him than they already are, they might try entangling her some more. They have their own report, commisioned from Arnon Bentovim, and might use it to challenge her. But she escapes without questions. "Yes, yes, yes and yes." Five minutes, and it's all over. Susan Bailey steps down.

I'm beginning to grasp the point. The psychiatrists are here to give evidence about intellectual maturity, not mental disturbance. This is what the Crown requires of them: if the defence can show the boys weren't mature enough to understand what they were doing, the prosecution for murder will fail. The name for what's at issue is *doli incapax*, the presumption that children of T and V's age are too young knowingly to kill. Under English law, no child under ten can be held accountable for a crime. Between ten and fourteen, children can be held accountable for crimes, so long as they know they're committing them (though only for rape and murder will they be tried in adult courts). T and V just creep into this category of the knowing. On February 12, both were ten and a half. And, say the psychiatrists, of normal intelligence.

I look at Susan and Neil Venables, and wonder if they regret co-operating with the Crown psychiatrist, now that she has done for their son. It was put to them that a plea of diminished responsibility might get the murder charge reduced to manslaughter; for this there had to be psychiatric reports. Like Ann, though, Susan and Neil felt nervous at the prospect. "It's all right, son, we're going to tell the judge you were mad when you did it," Laurence Lee, Jon's solicitor, is supposed to have said. It can't have gone down well. Still clinging to the idea of Jon as a "happy, ordinary little boy", Susan and Neil worried about the nutter stigma. If Jon's murderous impulses could be traced to inherited traits, or family tensions, what would that say about his parents and siblings? Where would it leave them? Suppose a jury were somehow persuaded Jon was insane – that it was found (following the old McNaghten Rules, which saved many a murderer from hanging) he did "not know the nature and quality of the act he was doing or, if he did know it, that he did not know he was doing what was wrong"? Such a defence was unthinkable. To "win" in this way would mean consigning Jon to a mental institution – a fate worse than prison.

Fear of the nuthouse. Susan and Neil have it. Ann Thompson has it. Most of us do. It's why psychiatrists still terrify: because, it's imagined, they want to invade – to incriminate and incarcerate, not cure. Fear of the loony bin: greater than the fear of jail. Menston was our nearest, when I was T & V's age: we'd pass it on the way to Leeds, a wall too high to see over. What lay behind it I'd no idea, and that was part of the horror. A grinning mouth behind a grille. A solitary light bulb dangling from flex. Cutlery drumming on a mile-long refectory table. Straitjackets. Foaming mouths. Staring eyes. Though ours was a hamlet, too small to boast a village idiot, we didn't lack the imagery. The wings of the madhouse had passed over us, we'd been brushed by its shadow and were afraid. "Menston, Menston, you'll end up in Menston" was the taunt for all silly, uncoordinated or just spontaneous behaviour. I dreamt of being admitted, victim of a misdiagnosis, condemned never to re-emerge. School doctors and nurses frightened me: I was healthy, wasn't I, so what were they getting at, with their tests? Had I a squint? No. A stammer? Not that either. Was I nail-biter? Yes, but not excessively so. Was I insomniac? No. Lacking in concentration? Not especially. Was I enuretic, a bedwetter? No. Encopretic, then, a pants-shitter? Please, do we have to go into this. Cause for concern, it seemed. They felt my scrotum and jotted surreptitious notes. My testicles ought to have descended by now. This way madness lay, and Menston.

Though grown-up now, and not insane, I understand the fear of shrinks. Ann Thompson and the Venables agreed to have their sons assessed in the hope it might do their case good, not because they thought psychiatric help was needed. The opposite was true. The boys needed psychiatric help, but the assessments have done their case no good at all. They will need help all the more when convicted of murder, an outcome which the psychiatrists have helped to ensure.

"Yes, yes, yes and yes." Irene Slack is in the box now, Robert and Jon's headmistress, eleven years at their school, and with personal knowledge of the boys. Like all children at Walton Primary, she says, they received a moral education, were taught about right and wrong: in RE, only recently, they learnt about the Good Shepherd. She would say that from the moment they enter school, at the age of four and five, children have a moral sense – know that it's wrong to strike another child, for instance – so, of course, yes, these two knew what they were doing. She stares into empty air, eager not to catch the eyes of her old pupils and their parents.

It's hard for Irene Slack, a dedicated and conscientious head teacher, who must wonder if she made a mistake when she kept the two boys down a year the previous September. At the time it looked a sensible decision: they were young in their year (both had August birthdays) and struggling in lessons (in Robert's case, because he usually wasn't there for them). But it was humiliating for them, all the same, and one of the reasons they teamed up together. It made them allies, inseparable. In the term up to Christmas, Jon truanted for forty half days, and Robert for forty-nine, out of 140. Robert's truanting, even worse after Christmas, had become such an issue that Irene Slack had promised him a present that week (a folder with Mickey Mouse on the front) if he could make it to Friday without bunking off; from Monday to Thursday he hadn't missed a class, but on the fifth day Irene Slack was away from school at a meeting, and in her absence the boys were absent too. It's said she has taken it badly for that reason: if only . . . There may be other reasons, too. Truancy on Robert's scale is unusual in primary schools, and raises questions about the effectiveness of the educational welfare officers and teachers concerned, not least the head teacher. It must be stressful for Irene Slack worrying if this will come up in court, and whether there'll be a slanging-match with Ann Thompson.

It's difficult for her in other ways. Her school's in a poor area, and she has worked very hard at raising standards. Stand outside the gates, with the kids running around in their yellow and blue ties, their yellow and blue jumpers, and you can see it's a place that cares, a Church of England school that's eager to disseminate Christian values. On the wall outside is a plaque to the Glory of God unveiled by the Bishop of

Liverpool in 1894, and the school still has a sense of religious mission or social calling. But February was a cataclysm. The danger now is of the place being remembered as the first British primary school with two murderers on its register. It's been unpleasant for Mrs Slack, mixing with other primary heads at conferences and so on, knowing that they know. And today must feel even worse, as if her school (though it can't yet be named by the press) were on trial in front of the nation. She might like, in her heart, to support and defend the boys, but in the name of the school she must distance herself, disown them. And so she has, in her statements to the police. "He is a liar and cunning," she has said of Robert. "Even when we had evidence against him he would continue to lie." Jon is "very different", more open, but with "an aggressive nature" and "short temper".

She is pressed a little by the defence. She is asked what sanctions there are at school, to punish bad behaviour. First, the class teacher will tell the child off, she says. And then? If further action is required the head will become involved and speak to the child. And then? Privileges will be denied – playtime and treats. That's the ultimate level of sanction? No, that's just the initial stage; the next stage means asking the parents to come to school, for a meeting, which generally does the job. But are there no other forms of sanction? Aside from suspension, or exclusion, no. Thirty years ago, the head would have used a cane, wouldn't he? Yes. But that's all gone? Indeed – and a good thing. For a moment, liberal education is in the dock: here were pupils with no reason to fear the consequences of doing wrong, since there were none. But the defence can't force this issue of strictness, or its lack. Strictly speaking, it's not relevant. Irene Slack is allowed to leave the box. Next witness.

Yes, yes, yes and yes, says Michael Dwyer, the boys' former class teacher, a man who has spent thirty years in education, some with maladjusted boys: certainly T & V would have known right from wrong. In class last year there'd been discussion of cruelty to animals – pulling the wings off insects, etc – and this led on to talk of human cruelty: bullying, teasing, fighting in the playground. Would Mr Dwyer say he considered it his job as a teacher to counteract certain influences stemming from videos and television? Yes. Would it be true to say that children these days are exposed to many more violent images than they were thirty years ago? Yes – but this doesn't mean they confuse right and wrong. Michael Dwyer stands there like Irene Slack, staring blankly, resisting the temptation to nod at his former pupils. Like her, he's been careful to detach himself, to show that the school's values of truth and goodness were not, despite all efforts, imbibed by these two boys. Robert, he told the police, "lied as naturally as he breathed" and was fond of "making bullets for others to shoot"; Jon, too, "lied easily", though when pressured he would cry and was more likely to tell the truth than Robert. Today in court Mr Dwyer isn't asked to repeat these statements. The only issue is knowing right from wrong. Which the boys did, no doubt about it. Yes, yes, yes and yes. Thank you, no more questions.

Mr Dwyer steps down, the last of the experts: this part of the trial has taken about half an hour. It's a terrible let-down: no insights into the boys' minds, only rebuttals of *doli incapax*, an ancient statute, a rusty precept, which many lawyers would like to see removed. A month-long trial, and this, the Why part, or what should have been the Why part, is over in thirty minutes. I feel angry, frustrated and naive for having expected more. Yet there are other countries where all the material we

couldn't hear today – the boys' family backgrounds, their relations with teachers and peers, their psycho-socio-sexual
make-up – would be allowed as evidence in court. And other
countries where these two kids, as *kids*, would never have been
put on trial in the first place. In theory, *doli incapax* was there,
like an old friend, to protect T & V. But *doli* is discredited.
These days, the nation's moral fabric is woven from a different
cloth: the belief that children grow up fast and know what's
what. T & V, the experts have decided, acted with adult consciousness. End of story.

Inadmissible evidence. Wasted knowledge. What's known but
can't be said. All those experts, not allowed to use their exper-
tise. Inadmissible because a court must investigate only
Whether: did these two boys kill James Bulger, or not? Pure
judgement: clean and clear as a mountain lake. The river Why
runs underneath but can't be permitted to muddy the waters.
A child has been killed and a verdict's wanted. The nation
must be purged and cleansed.

Inadmissible evidence. I sit on my bed and fish for it.
Courts are leaky ships, and the boys' psychiatric reports have
floated to me on the tide, like messages in a bottle. I read the
inadmissible, the stories that couldn't be told.

Eileen Vizard saw Robert just once, on October 16, a special day in his life, the fifth anniversary of his father's
disappearance from home. The meeting blazes off the page.
She had come up from the Tavistock to his secure unit, and
found him deeply apprehensive. Could she close the windows,
he asked, in case their conversation might be overheard? He
knew why she had come to visit: "to see if I am a nutter . . . to
see if anything was playing in my head when it happened". He

faced her across the table, drumming on the chair when the questions got difficult. They talked about the forthcoming trial, and his fear of "all the crowds": a good thing that the windows of the police van would be opaque. They talked about his family, how everything had changed the day his father left: "I couldn't make any sense of it." They talked about his mother's drinking habit afterwards, which he said wasn't that bad, "only three nights a week". They talked about his weight gain since coming to the unit: "I was like a matchstick compared with what I am now." They talked about a dream he'd had of chasing someone down the street, then being hit by a car. They talked about the murder – or rather, didn't, for the moment he was asked about it he put his hands over his eyes and began to cry. It was natural to cry, said Dr Vizard, he should let himself, it would help: "How does this help me?" said Robert angrily, through the tears.

Dr Vizard tried to reconstruct the crime, with dolls and a railway. He was more responsive to this. He moved the dolls around to show what had happened: the paint, the stones, the body laid across the tracks. His account was exactly that given to the police: Jon had done it all. What about the blood on his shoes, where had that come from? It must have come from James, mustn't it? Irritation: "Yes, it's not just started raining blood, has it?" What kind of little boy had James been? "All little boys are nice until they get older" said Robert. Why would Jon have wanted to steal a baby? "Jon doesn't like being around babies, I do." How did Robert think his involvement in the death would affect him later in life? "People will want to keep their children out of sight from me, in case they disappear." Was it possible Robert had bad thoughts about small children? "No." Because if so, it would be best to let these thoughts out. Robert pulled his legs up on his seat, sighed heavily, began to suck his thumb and banged the doll he was holding against the side of his chair. How angry did Robert feel with Jon? "I'd like to give him a slap." Not angrier than that? Robert chuckled. "I'd like to kick his face in." He picked up the Jon doll and began to kick it with the Bobby doll. And what would he say to James, if he could? "What, to the baby? I don't know." He became tearful. "I feel sorry for him."

In court Eileen Vizard had to verify "beyond reasonable doubt" that Robert knowingly killed James. Her report is less emphatic, using the phrase "balance of probabilities" and ending, even more tentatively: "it is not possible to reach a reliable conclusion about Robert's state of mind at the time of the alleged offence". Here might be a basis for reducing the charge of murder to manslaughter. The report is not without loose ends. But in court Eileen Vizard stitched them up. All she wanted was for the legal charade to be over. She hopes, once it is over, to play a part in the rehabilitation of the boys.

And Susan Bailey? When she came to Jon's secure unit, she found a boy deep in denial, trying, like the furry beasts he lined his bed with, "to keep the bad things away". Jon denied having bad feelings towards any member of his family. He denied that there were ever difficulties or disagreements: invited to reconstruct his family (Self, Mum, Dad, Mark, Michelle, Nan, Nobody), he had Nobody scoring very high – Nobody, that's to say, scolded, disliked, frightened or thought badly of him. He denied having wanted to murder James: he was forced into it, he said, by Robert. He'd even been denying (on advice from his solicitor) the nature of his offence: to his peers at the secure placement, he was a TWOCer, a taker-away of cars. What kind of bad thoughts did he have? A fear of being stung by wasps or bees; flashbacks to James with blood coming out of his mouth. What kind of wishes or fantasies? He would like to turn the world into a chocolate factory; to time-travel to last February 12; to snatch James back and return him to his mum. About the crime itself, he wouldn't speak. Surely there were things he could recall? No, no, no, no: if you've killed a kid, you want to forget it, don't you? And forgetting meant remaking the world.

In court, Susan Bailey said she was confident Jon knew what he was doing that day in February. Her report seems less confident. How easily, for instance, could Jon separate the real from the made-up? Watching 15-certificate videos, she writes, "he would make-believe it was only acting when he saw 'naughty things', by which he meant blood and fighting. During *Rocky* films he would turn his face away and put his fingers in his ears if somebody was punched and blood came out. Jon told me he also watched other adventure films, by which he meant kung fu videos which his father would get out. When he watched them he thought they were real and would cry." A grown-up man who cries at films because he thinks they're real, or who has to make-believe that actors are acting, might be considered pretty screwed-up – and for the purposes of this trial Jon must be considered a grown-up. What about his understanding of death? "Jon tells me," writes Susan Bailey, "that good people go to heaven where there is Jesus, Mary, God and disciples all in white, and naughty people go to hell." Is this immature, since it's childish nonsense? Or mature, since many adults think the same? A tangled web – unlike the straight line followed in court today. Had Arnon Bentovim, the defence team's psychiatrist, been called to speak, he would have added to the confusion. He thinks Jon knows right from wrong. But he has no doubt that Jon is "less mature than ten, psychologically and emotionally".

Right and wrong, right and wrong. I lie on the bed and think of Irene Slack's four-year-olds, who know the difference. I have a four-year-old at home. And if I asked him if it was right to hit a friend he'd say, no, it's wrong. Why would he say that? Because of the tone of my voice. Because he's picked up enough about parents and teachers to know how to give appropriate answers. Because he goes to nursery school and watches children's television. Because he wants to earn approval. Not because he possesses a mature moral understanding, but because he wants to say the right thing.

He says some funny things, this four-year-old of mine, who doesn't know the meaning of the word tomorrow, yet allegedly knows right from wrong. He ~~tells me he wants to~~ marry his friend Charles, and if he can't marry him he wants to marry a Ghostbuster. He asks me if God has a second name, and says he knows how God sees us, it's like Jack and the Beanstalk, He drills a hole in the sky and looks down. He says he doesn't like going to Granny's because one of the trees there talks, and he doesn't like talking trees. He says there are witches in the true world, but not at the bottom of Jonathan's garden. He thinks everything is male or female, including cutlery, crockery, furniture and cars. He calls his poos after his family – points at a bunch of plops in the lavatory and says: "That's Mummy and that's Daddy and that's me." He says what scares him most in the world is clowns. He watches clouds skimming across the night sky and tells me the moon has a beard, and asks: "If we say hello to the moon will he hear us? Will we hear him if he says hello back?"

I have a four-year-old who believes the man in the moon is real – who believes the moon *is* a man. Other four-year-olds have similar beliefs. They think the manikins in shop windows are dead people. They think the sea's there because someone left the tap running. They wonder who the sun belongs to, and whether heaven has a floor, and why people aren't in two all the way up. I know seven-year-olds who believe in the Easter Bunny and the tooth fairy. I know nine-year-olds who believe in Father Christmas. (I know forty-year-olds who think God lives in the sky and wears a white gown.) Long may it live, this belief in magic. More power to *as if*. But don't tell me four-year-olds know the difference between right and wrong.

And eight-year-olds, ten-year-olds? They understand the difference better, but can they act on that understanding? Did I? At ten I stole a Ferrari – a Dinky toy belonging to my cousin Richard. It was old and battered, but I thought that, by owning it, some part of Richard – who was bigger, older, more confident – would become part of me: that I could be *him*. I knew I was doing wrong but desire – such a good feeling, which as a child I hadn't learnt to distrust – made it feel right. "Want doesn't get" my parents used to say, determined not to spoil me. And (though they did spoil me), they were right: want can't get, want can never fulfil its desire. Richard's Ferrari could never have filled my lack. But I thought it would, and so I had taken it. I had moral sense but not moral conviction. How could I have conviction? I was a child.

Rousseau writes of a boy killing a bird *without knowing what he does*. The phrase is reminiscent of Christ's: "Forgive them father, for they know not what they do." Special pleading from the cross: that people sometimes kill in ignorance, even innocence, and should not be eternally punished for their sin.

The basis of *doli incapax* is similar: that before the age of reason, children can't be held responsible. When does the age of reason begin? Every country has its own answer, its own baseline: it's eight in Scotland, ten in England, Wales and Northern Ireland, twelve in Canada, thirteen in Israel, fifteen in Norway, sixteen in Cuba – and in Romania eighteen. The mad arbitrariness. And see how low the British come. Low is the word. Maybe Rousseau was right, or no less wrong than we are, to measure reason in inches rather than years: "Childhood has its ways of seeing, thinking and feeling which are proper to it. Nothing is less sensible than to want to substitute ours for theirs, and I would like as little to insist that a ten-year-old be five feet tall as that he possess judgment." Robert is four foot six, Jon four foot eight.

I doze on the bed, and think of Irene Slack on four-year-olds, and recall the movie *Bugsy Malone* and television ads I've seen of children dressed in grown-up clothes. I try to imagine what it would be like if the jury at this trial were composed not of middle-aged men and women but of infants in dark suits. The day is dragging. They are having trouble weighing the evidence. Frankly, they are not paying attention at all, and have begun fidgeting, fighting, drawing stick figures on their doodle-pads, throwing paper aeroplanes at the judge, giggling, asking can they go wee-wees . . . Why not such a jury, in reality? If children of four know the difference between right and wrong, let them be jurors. Let ten-year-olds, for sure. Wouldn't it be more appropriate for T & V to be tried by ten-year-olds, rather than adults, since this would mean, as juries are supposed to mean, judgement by one's peers? I try this question out, saying it aloud to the hotel room, but the answer comes back: of course not. Ten-year-olds as jurors? I wouldn't trust their maturity, judgement, intelligence – the qualities said to be present in T & V when they killed James.

I lie and stare at the blank ceiling, the neutral walls, the null air. God knows, adults find it hard enough to act on their knowledge of right and wrong. Can children, whose sense of right and wrong is newer but dimmer, fresher but fuzzier, act with the same clear moral sense? Do they grasp that badly hurting someone is much more wrong than stealing and truanting (which T & V had got away with for months)? Do they have a sense of the awful irreversibility of battering a child to death with bricks? Can death have the same meaning for them as it has for an adult? I submit, your Honour, that the answer to these questions is no, no, no and no.

6

Home

He loved no other place, and yet
Home was no home to him.

SAMUEL TAYLOR COLERIDGE, "The Three Graves"

For a while now, I've had this man in my head. He's a decent, quiet, thoughtful sort of chap – fiftyish, professional, with two late-teenage sons – who goes up for his mother's funeral, his father long since dead, and finds himself staying on, to clear the house and tidy up loose ends. That's what he tells his wife, that's the pretext. But standing at the window, looking out through the rain at the familiar trees and fields, he feels his past coming back to him. An L. P. Hartleyish sort of scene, sweetly sad, full of bicycles, long skirts and innocence. The *frisson* of rediscovering childhood textures: the gouged-out, bird-shaped hole at one end of the dining table; the yellowing sheep-rug, scorched at one corner, by the hearth; the folding wooden children's picnic chair, unearthed from the attic, with one slat missing – these are his watermarks, each with its own tale, rooting him to the spot. He tells his wife, his boss, he needs another week, then another. There are ultimatums.

From work he gets phone calls, then a letter, special delivery, a final warning, a suspiciously hasty final warning: they value his contribution over the years, but the firm's having a hard time of it, his portfolio needs attending to, there are other, younger, colleagues in the wings. His wife drives up one Friday evening, a surprise, a surprise to her, too, to see him looking so thin and vacant. She is kind, then angry, and goes back without him: he has asked for another week; she knows it will be longer.

I wanted to write the story of this man, but I could see where it would lead, the curve of disenchantment as he looks up old friends and finds they've moved away or are horribly altered, the grungy recognition that the old life, which he'd vaguely thought might be the new life, is dead and irrecoverable, the final scene back in London, on his own doorstep, the home he now accepts is home, pleading with his wife – who has secretly begun to enjoy living without him – to please, please, let him back in. I didn't write the story because I didn't want that for him, or for me. It felt too close – and what's the point of fiction when it's your own life in disguise? But I haven't quite got this man out of my head yet. Here I am, full of loss and going home again, just like him.

"Home," I told the woman in the car-hire place, when she asked me where I was off to. Home: meaning my mother's house, not the place where I now live. Home: where the heart, or heartbreak, is. Home: the place, said Robert Frost, where, when you have to go, they have to take you in. It used to be said of certain women – I remember my father saying it – "she's a good little home-maker". But can you *make* a home? Or even make yourself at home? Isn't home some place you have as a child, and spend the rest of your life running from or failing to get back?

As If

The road to childhood begins with a city-centre underpass, threads out past redbrick terraces, eases on to a ring-road through suburbs, descends a hill, crosses a motorway, becomes fields. The road to childhood – *my* childhood – is the A59 east from Preston, and, as the car-hire woman warned it would be, foggy. A marked field goes by with its facing Hs. A man by lock gates turning a set of wheels. A horse beyond a fence, its mane like a feathery shawl. The fog's not so bad here, but then it clots again, and the traffic slows in its half-light. Towards Whalley, or what I think must be Whalley (where's Whalley?), the fog comes in mile-long swirls and banks, emulsion-thick and impenetrable. Even where it thins to turpentine, it's clear only for a moment and then I'm in the dark, clinging to tail-lights. I peer through the m of the wipers. The fog's flooding the whole plain and valley, the Trough of Bowland and beyond, and I'm fording the bottom, sploshing through to the other side.

I'm going home to be reminded what childhood feels like, in the hope of understanding T & V. I'm going home to remember what it is to be a child. That's where the Why is, the missing chromosome, the vital clue. I'm also going home, I tell myself, for sanity (I need a break from murder), and out of duty (it's time I saw my mother), and from nostalgia for the place I grew up. I'm going home because, unlike most people, I'm able to – my mother's still there, my sister too, next door to each other and next door to our old house. But I may just be sagging, or digressing. In truth, I'm not sure why I'm going home – if it's an interlude or *The Prelude*. All I know is: this is the road leading back.

Can I get where I want to be? How easy is it, recovering childhood? Most people seem to have no problem. Speak, memory, and it does, volubly. I remember, I remember, in every last detail. Windfall light of morning. The mill race, dragonflies skimming the water, the blue whip of a kingfisher, the long bathing of an August day. Pussy willow in sunken lanes. Mother on her knees as she weeds between the goblets of tulip. Father's hands stained green by the mower box. A row of icicles like a new case of pencils. A laughing schoolboy riding the springy branches of an elm. The birthday kite, high among fleecy clouds, tugging like a greyhound at its leash. The hush of spiderwebs. The underglow from coals. Blanket-dens, tree-houses, egg hunts and paper chases, the spitfiring of boys down a meadow. Fair seedtime. An infirmity of love for the bygone.

As if. I'm distrustful. I think people misremember their childhoods. The images are always summer, and pastoral: no streets, or dog-shit, or piss-smelling eighteenth-floor walk-ways; never a town or city at all. I have an excuse. I grew up in the countryside. My childhood was (truly) surrounded by green. But I distrust my own memories, too. The reality is tangled with a dream compiled through fantasy and books. That's why I'm driving home. The value of revisiting a place is that memories are triggered by being there, and you know what's triggered can be no one's but yours. Just here, past Clitheroe, along the by-pass (the bends all straightened since my day), I'm climbing the hill to Slaidburn, where the local point-to-point races used to be held (still are, says the sign-board). Gisburn Races, circa 1960: the car park a churn of mud; the sign language of tick-tack men; mill-crowds packed against the white spectator rail, brushwood fences twice as high as me; thunderclouds of hooves and divots; the horses in the paddock afterwards, smoking from their nostrils and the saddle-shaped lather on their backs. Gisburn Races: clear as day, though it'll soon be forty years since I went.

As If

Most of my past is blank and foggy but other bits are brightly coloured in. Does recalling a particular episode mean that it matters? Which recollections count, when for every six that seem significant there are sixty that could as well be chosen, and six hundred, maybe no less significant, that lie just out of reach, and six million which share this status of having happened to one person once and of seeming to matter at the time? What if the important things, those that did most to shape you, you can't remember at all? The days and years disowned by memory. There are photographs, yes, but the shot taken at 125th of a second misses the other 124 125ths of that second, let alone the minutes, hours, days, weeks, months when the camera isn't there. How little we keep of when we're little. A cycle ride in Dunwich Woods the year after my son was born, he in his plastic child-seat behind me, pheasants in the verges, pale-lemon rings of primrose, sweet resin of pine, the heathered common to the sea. He'll remember none of it. It will be lost like Dunwich itself, a bustling city in the Middle Ages, now buried under the sea. The same for me, the same for everyone: a scattering of images, but almost nothing to show of what we did and thought and felt when we were small, only a blank tape or a roll of overexposed film.

Maybe the less retained, the better: happiness writes white. Was I happy as a child? Most children seemed to be then, spoilt by parents who had wondered during the war if they'd survive (or the world would) for families to be started at all. Not trailing clouds of glory we came, but the memory of Hiroshima and Auschwitz and bodies stacked like cars in wreckers' yards. Peace, consolidation, and the Age of Never-Had-It-So-Good – *as if* becoming reality. Year by year, more toys (Meccano, Bayko and Scalextric), more gadgets (a freezer, a television), more cars (a second one for my mother), more holidays (in 1959 our first abroad). It wasn't all Blytonish innocence. Boredom; *un*happiness; regimes of washing and bedtime; things we weren't allowed to do; how it was always somehow time to turn the light out – they were there, too. It wasn't all wholesome, either. The belief that children back then were "nice" and "good", unlike their progeny today: not a belief I share. As a country child, middle-class too, I grew up with advantages. Our village school had eighteen pupils, three in my year – if I'd truanted at Jon and Robert's age, it would have meant a third of the eleven-plus candidates going missing. There were fights, but nothing more than skinned shins and bloody noses. There was bullying, but no one boasted that they were going to kill a kid. And yet . . . Didn't we steal sweets from the village shop – didn't even Simon join in, whose father ran the shop? Didn't we torment younger children? Didn't my cousin and I airgun starlings from the telegraph wire outside my bedroom window, picking them off at three yards' range, the oily rainbow corpses piling up on the stone flags below? And other cruelties, dimly summoned: frogs squashed with bricks, fledgling swallows outed from their mudpacks and dropped to a swiping cricket bat below. Nothing like murder (nothing is like), but not particularly nice or good.

But there does seem to have been a nursery excitement and kindergarten optimism to the times. At school, I pored over a William Blake drawing of an angel-winged child, perched like a backpack on its father's shoulders, a beacon to show the way ahead. Later I read of Silas Marner finding Effie, who brightened his life for him, her hair like a hoard of gold coins: "In old days, there were angels who came and took men by the hand and led them away from the city of destruction. We see no white-winged angels now. But yet men are led away from threatening destruction; a hand is put into theirs which leads them forth . . . and the hand may be a little child's." Children leading adults away from destruction: that was us, after 1945. Whereas now, in 1993, after James Bulger, the image of a child led or leading by the hand . . .

The fog has cleared a bit. Nearly home now. The Stirk House Hotel, where I worked one summer in the garden, hoeing lettuces for a pittance, to learn about hotel management in case that should be my career. The Ribblesdale Arms, where four of us camped by arrangement next to some girls we knew, drinks up at the pub, then a switch of sleeping bags, a cold night of furtive, opportunist teenage sex. The lane end to Barnoldswick, one of whose football teams I played for and whose success one season meant a trial for six of us at Preston North End. And now the humpback canal bridge at West Marton, the airy-stomach, in-love feel of taking it at speed, as my father did, the extra lurch once when cousin Richard and I lay in the boot, the lid flipping open as we lay among the towropes and the jack. So many might-have-beens. What if I'd fallen out of the boot, or the girl in the tent had become pregnant, or the summer job (or soccer trial) had led to a career. What if . . .? Have these roads taken and not taken made any difference to the person I've become? What has me now to do with me then? Graham Greene said (or was it J. M. Barrie?) that nothing much matters after twelve. Psychoanalysts agree that the early years are the most important. But in other respects, surely they're the least important, since we're children then, under someone else's control.

I pass the church and almshouses, and turn left into my mother's drive. When I ring the bell there's the usual cyclone of yapping from Nikki, the dachshund. I can see him through the glass, rushing at the door, jumping up, retreating to the hall to call someone, anyone, to come answer, there's a stranger. My mother would normally be there in his wake, the calm after the storm, unchaining the chain. But today she takes a good minute: she's expecting me, but it's hard manoeuvring the wheelchair over the carpet. She leans forward, turning the Yale, and I'm in beside her, stooping to kiss her rippled cheek.

"How you doing, Mum?"

"All right," she says, slapping her arms on the wheelchair's arms. "All right but for this. I suppose I'll get used to it."

Not that she wants to, not that she will. She hates the indignity, and intends to be walking by Christmas. When I mention the possibility of hiring a motorized version – "electric chair" is what I say, actually – so as to make her progress round these rooms easier, faster, she says, brusquely: "Not worth it. They cost a fortune, I'm sure. And by the time they've fixed one up for me, I'll not need it."

I hand her her gin and tonic, hand her mine, too, while I wheel her along the carpet. It's unnatural how natural it feels, how settled I feel as my hands settle on the handles, pushing her forward, steering from behind her head. "I have a Zimmer frame, too," she says, laughing at the ridiculousness of the idea: to have come to this. But it *is* only weeks since it happened. Triumphant at shedding the arm-sling from her previous break, to her upper left arm, eight months before, she had begun to drive again, which with the pins in her arms caused some "discomfort" (her word for agony), but meant she was no longer at the mercy of friends to get her out. For the meeting at the Women's Institute, though, it didn't seem worth using the car: easier to walk the 100 yards. The night was frosty and by the front gate she skeetered on the glistening tarmac: just a tumble on her bum but enough for her to know she'd broken something. An ankle, she thought, and sat there in shock, cold, "discomfort", till a neighbour caught her in his headlights: there was blood on the ground and a bone sticking through paper. He called my sister, and they sat with her, a rug and thermos, till the ambulance came. Her main feeling wasn't pain but stupidity. Osteoporosis is cruel like that: most of us are plastic beakers bouncing back from flagstones, but my mother is best crystal.

I pull the curtains against the fog, and stoke and poke the smoggy coal-fire, our drinks set down on two of her set-of-three wooden stacking tables, her "collections" all about the room: the Wedgwood figures (simpering goose girls, flower-sellers, dogs), the snuff boxes, the paperweights with their amber implosions of flower – objects that haven't moved in years except to be dusted, whose breakage is much to be feared but which offer permanence while lives shatter around them. I help my mother from wheelchair to armchair, a standing-on-one-leg-and-turning movement which she's perfected already, requiring me only to be there *just in case*. Her face is as creased as late Auden's, a crumpled map of worries. In middle age she used to keep these worries under the surface; at sixty, in retirement, the days newly empty, they broke through. The depression came and went until my father's death, to be replaced by mourning. She's been told that after two years the bereaved begin to feel better. Now the second anniversary of his death is approaching, like a heavy black goods train which, having passed, will lighten her load.

"So what's been happening?" I ask.

"The usual. A couple of funerals, not much. Oh, and the house. There've been vandals in. Bloody kids smashing the place up for fun. If we'd not had him cremated, your Dad would be turning in his grave."

The house is our old house, which my father sold to a PR man called Stephen sometime in the 1980s, and at the back of which he built the new house, where we now sit. Close by as he was, my father couldn't help but feel proprietorial, more landlord than neighbour. It was hard for him not to keep an eye on things, and the things his eyes kept noticing – Stephen's "improvements" – were not at all good. Stephen had sold off the outbuildings and some land, "at a vast profit, so it's like a bloody housing estate now with all the flats and houses". The profit could not have been that vast, or there'd have been carpets in the house, which there weren't, another of my Dad's grumbles: "What was wrong with the old carpets, anyway? Not that tatty. Better than bare boards." As the 1980s ran out, so did Stephen: his pleasant, long-suffering wife held the fort, while he was less and less to be seen at home. His business was said to be in trouble, his mortgage payments had fallen behind, local tradesmen muttered about not having their bills paid. Letters went back and forth from solicitors – mainly forth, since Stephen was elusive. Finally, his wife came to say she was having to move, the house had been repossessed. She looked worn out – the six kids and running them about between teaching, which she'd had to take up again to make ends meet – but she didn't speak of Stephen. She didn't need to. Everyone knew he'd gone for good.

My mother passes a cutting from the local paper, the *Craven Herald*. A boy fined £100 (plus £35 costs) after causing £70,000 worth of damage to the Old Rectory, Thornton-in-Craven. I skim through, wondering (it doesn't say) how the boy was apprehended, and how many others were with him (ditto), and how you could do £70,000 worth of damage to an empty house without actually burning it down. The tone of the newspaper report is sternly neutral, but I can imagine the local reaction: Bloody kids. Little horrors. Animals.

"Who's got the key then?" I ask my mother.

"The building society. But you don't need a key. Gill says there's a door open. Kids are still getting in. Something should be done. All this vandalism will bring the price down."

I pull the curtains aside to look, but the old house is hidden in dark and mist.

"How's the fog?" my mother asks.

"Bad," I say.

"Stay then, love. I'd worry. You can enjoy your meal."

Which is her way of saying I've already had three gin and tonics, and there's wine to come.

"All right. Court's not till 10.30. If I leave by 9.00 I'll still be in good time."

"And you can see the house before you go."

I lie on the bed against the headboard, a child's headboard, but a bed I last slept in as an adult, more adult than I wanted to be, my father dying below. The place feels empty without him (the world does, life does), and now here's this other thing, my mother so much less than herself. The solidity of those who raise us, so quickly destructible and easily dispersed. At least my father wasn't young when he went. What if he had been, or had gone at the age I am now – speeding into a brick wall and dying instantly, or clearing off somewhere to start a second family, alive but not to us? How differently would I have turned out?

Fathers, or lack of fathers. A factor in the Bulger case, another Why. And when did Robert Thompson last see his?

Two years ago, it seems, among the mourners at his grand-mother's funeral – the only time they've clapped eyes on each other in half a decade. Robert and his brothers: fathered they are, yet fatherless. It's been hard on them – hard on their mother, too, abandoned for another (older) woman. I imagine her pouring her heart out like the wife of Macduff:

> To leave his wife, to leave his babes,
> His mansion, and his titles, in a place
> From whence himself does fly? He loves us not.
> He wants the natural touch; for the poor wren,
> The most diminutive of birds, will fight,
> Her young ones in her nest, against the owl.

Robert Senior left his chicks to fend for themselves. It hasn't been easy for them to forgive. They felt betrayed, dumped, and angry on behalf of Ann. Perhaps what Robert Junior did on the railway was a way of punishing his father – and a cry for attention or help.

The Venables: a split family, too. But when Neil went, two years ahead of Robert Senior, he moved nearby and stayed in touch. The family still spends weekends together. There's been an understanding with Susan, a *modus vivendi*. Jon's grudge against his dad, if he has one, can't have been his leaving, but his not being a dad to admire. Jon's into movie strong men, heroes and Stallones; whereas Neil's a softie, henpecked, less manly than Jon's mum. Maybe the attack on James was a desperate attempt at machismo, Jon's bid to show he needn't be a mouse like Neil.

Absence of fathers, absence of fatherliness. Rousseau, no reactionary, says: "A father, when he engenders and feeds children, does with that only a third of his task. He owes to his species men; he owes to society sociable men; he owes to the state citizens. Every man who can pay this triple debt and does not do so is culpable . . . I predict to whoever has vitals and neglects such holy duties that he will shed long bitter tears . . ." Is Robert Thompson Senior, wherever he is, shedding tears? Can he be happy with his new woman, having left such misery in his wake? Even now, the tabloids are trying to track him down: the absent father (the absence doing the fathering) of a murderer. And whether they find him or not, they'll columnize against the fallen world he's ushered in: loss of discipline, authority, the strong paternal hand. Bad dads: a phenomenon of the age. The theory is that fathers were more fatherly in the past. Too easy to be nostalgic, though. Those solid fifties patriarchs – the good dads – saw little of their children: domesticity wasn't in their nature; they left all nurture to the wife. More is expected of fathers now: that they do their bit at home as well. But not everyone's up to the job. A man has his own needs (a woman, too). There's only the one life. Sticking it out for the kids isn't healthy. Not every abandoned child ends up a murderer. All the shits running out on their families. Yes, but then the shits who stay, inflicting their tempers, their work frustrations (or out-of-work frustrations), their depressions, binges, urges, hangovers, fists. To be absent, mourned, despised, or present, feared, detested: that seems to be the choice.

And the mothers, Susan and Ann? They've stayed. They've tried. They've given their kids their youth. No tabloid can accuse them of going out to work. In court, Jon looks nervous of Susan, Robert protective of Ann. But neither relationship seems lacking in closeness. Above the television in Neil's flat was a framed plaque, in praise of the archetypal mother: "She works for you, loves you, forgives you anything you do."

Maternal love: if children don't have it, something feels to be missing; having had it, they shrink if it's withdrawn. But even mothers who do love their children can fail to give the right amount: there's cold neglect (starving them of affection), but also smothering attentiveness (loving them to death). So many ways to get it wrong. Yet the myth of the perfect mother dies hard. "A family man" it's said (mostly approvingly) of certain fathers; there's no equivalent phrase for mothers – it's just assumed.

Restless, wandering, I open the wardrobe door. Old familiar smells: mothballs and mustiness and mother. It was her wardrobe, once. When I was small I used to climb in and snoozle down among the scents from her furs and ballgowns. Or I'd sit at her dressing table, splaying the legs of a kirbygrip and rescuing strands of hair from the spongy hedgehog of her brush. Or she'd soap me in the bath and sing "Smoke Gets in Your Eyes". My love for her was purely physical then; later came platonic love. In between was infatuation – at the time I was fourteen or fifteen, the years when boys feel closest to their mothers, or when certain kinds of boy do, those frightened of their fathers. I had my first girlfriends then, and I'd talk to her about them, feeling sexually excited by doing so, and also faintly treacherous, knowing they fell far short of her. In time – no avoiding it – I grew away from her. In time – no one's fault – she was plain mother. But inhaling the wardrobe, I remember and mourn the intimacy we had, all that's aged and changed, and the impossibility of it not changing, and yet the thought that, somehow, if I'd been different, or my mother had, we mightn't have ended out of synch like this, besieged by losses and griefs.

I inhale the wardrobe for a last time, and feel along the shelf that once held lipstick, perfume, powder puffs, mascara brushes, eyelashes – empty now, but for a polythene bag of name-tags, my name and my sister's in scarlet thread. I tip them out, a handful of leftovers, and run them through my fingers, imagining my mother after work, the fire blazing, us in bed, a heap of new socks and jumpers in her lap. I think of her now, in bed downstairs, fraying and creased with age, and of these stitches in lost time, the name-tags she sewed. Ann Thompson and Susan Venables must have done it too, or something like, for their sons – must have labelled their shirts and jumpers, may even have felt a little jab in the heart seeing the names in bright red under the collar, Robert and Jon, names chosen and written on birth certificates while their newborn sons lay on cot mattresses, all a mother's hope and ambition vested in those names. Whatever Ann's and Susan's failings as parents, whatever Neil's and Robert Senior's, they must have loved their boys and wanted the best for them and dreamt of what they might come to. Murder is what they came to. I pour the tags back inside the bag and shut the wardrobe door.

I get up round eight, a fog still clinging around the house, but thinning now, without the billowy menace of yesterday. A mug of tea, my mother in bed with the *Mail*, and the mail. The dog pat-padding behind me, I walk down the Yorkstone path, through a gateway (the gate, unhinged, leaning against a wall), over the long grass to the house where I grew up.

I try the front door: locked. I walk round to the kitchen, past the living room (neat, starred holes, like bullet holes, in its windows), past the greenhouse (paneless, open to the elements), past a blue, upended children's slide, a skinned tennis ball, a racquet twisted in the rain. I try the back door: bolted.

Next to it is the old washhouse, now a children's playroom, toys still scattered as if the occupants had left in a hurry (which may, with the bailiffs, have been how it was). I try the playroom's sliding door: open. I step inside.

The floorboards are bare but for sharp-toothed strips of carpetgrip. Wires hang bulblessly from ceiling roses. There are bright, unfaded patches on the wallpaper where paintings and mirrors kept off the bleaching sun. Small fires have been started. In the kitchen there's a smoke-blackened oblong where the Aga used to be – the Aga to which we once brought a shivery thrush-chick we'd rescued from the cat, feeding it from a milk dish till it died. Plaster leaks from laths. Black mildew furs the cornices. The dried-up lavatories are stuffed with last year's papers. In the bottom of a cupboard is a frayed shuttlecock. Broken bottle glass is scattered across the billiard-room floor. Light shines down its length, as if this were a gallery. I feel as if I'm looking at an allegory: The Desecration of the House of Childhood.

I climb the stairs, here but not here, at home among ghosts. A walnut wardrobe once stood in this bedroom: I remember the day it toppled like an oak-tree on my sister, who lay beneath it (luckily unbroken), while the crash brought my mother screaming upstairs. That plaster-square on the ceiling was a loft ladder, which I climbed to the train set in the attic, or to learn about sexual diseases from my parents' damp, secreted tomes. And this is my own room, where I lay when sick, fancying myself to be Colin in *The Secret Garden*, a wimpy won't-get-up, the weak-eyed bat no sun would tempt out of his grange. Children seemed to be sicklier then. Flat out with flu or tonsilitis, I used to stare up at the aeroplane which hung by Sylko threads from the ceiling. Its fuselage was battleship grey, with dabs of white Humbrol and transfers to denote windows, doors and Britishness, BOAC. Other boys – dab hands at model-making – had whole fleets of planes. But this one had taken me all summer, and it turned in the wind alone.

Sunlit from Embsay Moor, my parents' bedroom is smaller than I remember, and disproportionate, its 20×20 transected (one of Stephen's improvements) by an ensuite shower. In one of the drawers of the built-in wardrobe I find a box of colour transparencies: shots of a naked woman, bravely smiling for the partner who must have taken them. I hold the slides up against the light of the sash window – to judge from the thumbprints, the kids who broke in must have done the same. Here she kneels on the bed, there she drapes herself against a window. The photos are too amateurish to be pornographic, too enthusiastic. But I feel shocked coming across them, in broad daylight. They feel like an intrusion on sacred ground. I stuff them back inside their box.

I call to Nikki, but he doesn't appear. I call again and go to the bannister, half its rods ripped out, and look down. Nikki's trembling on the stair, he won't come past the landing, something is spooking him. Before we moved in, there were stories of headless knights, laughing girls in white dresses, dragging chains, inexplicable cries, overturned objects, "presences". But we never had ghosts ourselves. Is it my father, come back against his better judgement, against his best atheistic convictions, in an afterlife of protest at what's been done to his home? The dog feels something. You should trust dogs when they're like this. But I can't sense anything. Plenty of feelings, but not that feeling.

What *do* I feel? Dereliction and dismay. As if my childhood's been taken from me, as if it's been violated, as if the efforts of a lifetime (my father's lifetime) had been in vain. Yes, but to see the house occupied – someone else's stuff rather than mine – might have been even worse. Dog in the manger, part of me feels grateful for the vandalism: if I can't live here, I'm damned if anyone else will. The house was ruined when my father bought it, and it's ruined now, again. I like the circularity. Gone to pot, it seems restored, the 1950s version, in need of work, not the 1980s version, ripped out and tarted up. Its decay is like my father on his deathbed: the lath bones showing through plaster, the ruined innards, the boarded-up eyes. Even its emptiness seems apt: room for imagining, for projecting memory's cine on the blank walls.

I walk down beside the toothless bannisters, like a ghost of my own past. All gone now, my childhood; all gone, the idea of childhood: a clean slate; a wiped-over blackboard. I should have known. It couldn't have been otherwise. Being grown-up means that I can't think as a ten-year-old thinks any more than I can fit in a ninety cm vest or crawl under a nursery chair. I see faces, remember details. But I can't find the texture, the feel of what I thought, the feel of what I felt. As you get older, as you recede from it, childhood becomes strange and unknowable. Once left behind, it's a country you can't visit in person, a place of exile, mourned and misremembered by the adults at its gates. This house, my home, was once the sum of my knowledge of the world. Now it adds up to minus, to less than nothing, to a sense of something taken away. I shouldn't have tried to come back.

I call to Nikki, sliding the playroom door shut with a thwack. Home: the best spot in the world, but no place to live. At the door of the new house, I bend to kiss my mother, and she stares from her wheelchair as I steer the car into the fog.

7

Lies, Tears

"Lies, my dear boy, can be easily recognised. There are two kinds of them: those with short legs, and those with long noses."

CARLO COLLODI, *Pinocchio*

Today we have taped confessions: the soundtrack of the accused. For nearly two weeks, Robert Thompson and Jon Venables have been silent as their victim, as if already punished, their tongues lopped at the stem and rooted out. Now the spell of stony silence is broken, and their voices fill the court – what they said nine months ago, when interviewed by the police, blooming and billowing about the room. Silent still, in the flesh, they listen like the rest of us, looped in on themselves. They're wearing headsets. So are the judge and jury – not Walkmans, but machines which dangle below the chin. Loudspeakers play to the gallery. The sun's in the skylight. And today we have the tapes.

There are eleven T tapes and nine of V, over twelve hours, and to play them will take the best part of a week. The scale is epic, Tolstoyan. Do we have to hear the tapes unexpurgated?

Couldn't they provide a synopsis, omit the boring bits, play only the highlights? By now, thanks to witnesses and experts, it's been established beyond reasonable doubt that T & V killed James. It's difficult to see what difference playing the tapes will make. Maybe they're being played for another reason, to give an insight, to help us with Why.

Robert Thompson first. There were five in the room during his interviews: him, DC Phil Roberts, DC Bob Jacobs, a lawyer from Paul Rooney & Co (Jason Lee at first, later Dominic Lloyd), and Robert's mother, Ann – here she is at the very beginning, announcing she has a terrible headache, doubtless from all the crying she's done since her son's arrest. And now here's Robert, a tiny, couldn't-hurt-a-fly voice, telling how he truanted last Friday and went to Bootle Strand. The library, where they sat in the corner; McDonalds, where they didn't eat: a banal day of sagging. He mentions seeing James in Bootle Strand, out with his mum and dressed in a blue jacket – even that sounds banal, though surely it's a weird piece of invention, and to Phil Roberts the first sign they're on to something. But Robert gives little away, yet. The only thing that stirs him is recalling being hit by Jon's mum when she caught them at the video shop: his eye was up, his cheek was bleeding, she was dragging him about in a fury. How could he feel hard done by when half an hour earlier he'd battered James to death? But he did. He does. He isn't putting it on. This is what children are like.

Buzzer. End of first tape. An admission he'd been in the Strand. A story about noticing James. Not much. On to the second interview, more relaxed, two hours later that evening. There is some camaraderie now: the police call the boy Bobby and tell him he can call them Bob and Phil. They lark about. They fall into laddish banter:

Q: What's your hobby, then?
A: Skipping school. [laughs]
Q: That's not a hobby, that's a profession, Bobby.

Bobby and the bobbies, one of them called Bob, the other Roberts. It's a battle of wits, a fight among equals, almost. Bob and Phil explain that trying to solve a crime is like fitting together the pieces of a jigsaw puzzle, and the image appeals to Robert – he has that kind of mind. He's good at remembering what he's said so far, at "sticking to his story", or – if tripped up – at weaving in new details to account for apparent inconsistencies. Whatever he gives away, he snatches back and controls. Jon Venables *might* have made baby James follow them, but he, Robert, didn't see because he didn't look back. Jon definitely did take the baby's hand, but then he let him loose again inside the Strand. Or outside. Or maybe by the church – certainly no further than that: "Jon said: I'm leaving him here. And I said: Don't, take him back." Robert's jacket looks like the jacket on one of the boys caught by the video camera, doesn't it? "Lots of people in our school have got the same." What about the paint on the jacket? "We've got paint all over our house." Robert treats the interview like a chess match, assessing how much his interrogators know and what more to concede without blowing his cover, trying to keep a step ahead. But he is only ten. Suddenly tired and exasperated, he bursts into tears. "I'm getting all the blame . . . With youse, we always get the blame." "We" means him and his brothers. He has the family honour to uphold, and it's not going well. He cries again.

The tape thins out towards its buzzer, the end of another round. Enough, it's more than enough for one day, but no, not quite, there is a third tape, only 24 minutes, the last interview that first evening, ending round ten. This takes us to the reservoir, Robert's new choice of venue for James's abandonment, the place where he might indeed have been abandoned, if Mrs Hitman, the woman with the dog, had, as she considered doing, intervened. The police aren't convinced by the reservoir story: would Robert leave his baby brother on the hill like that, alone? "No, cos he's my brother. He [James] isn't, though: he's not any relation to us." Deadly logic and further denials, until at last, James still in tow, Robert admits to walking over Breeze Hill. He didn't say that earlier, did he? They wish he would tell the truth. They can tell when he is telling it because "you fill up with your eyes". *In lacrimis, veritas.*

I sit back in the hotel room and fill up with my eyes. I know it doesn't mean much, crying. I know my tears are undiscriminating. I fill up when British athletes receive their bronze medals at the Olympics, when Stevie Wonder sings "Isn't She Lovely?", when the families of *Gladiators* contestants know their son or wife or sister or boyfriend has lost. I fill up at old cine films and national anthems (even *other people's* cine films, *other people's* national anthems). I've cried at adverts with animals and children in. I cried at my twenty-first birthday party – or after it, drunk, in the small hours, feeling life was over – because my best friend, or the man who I'd thought was my best friend, had failed to show. The things that have really moved me – the birth of my children, the death of a friend, heartbreak – don't seem to have moved me, not outwardly, visibly: they're too deep for tears. The naffer the occasion, the cheaper the music, the crappier the film, the better I blub. Spontaneous overflow. Tears, idle tears. It seems we're programmed. We go with the flow, and the more others are flowing round us, the leakier we get. Not that tears are merely manipulated; they can be manipulative, too. "The first tears of children are prayers," says Rousseau. Soon prayers become pleas, then orders. The loss of control can be very controlling. I remember a girl I'd never fancied until she brimmed and became beautiful. A welling eye is irresistible. Unless you have yourself caused the distress.

Distrusting my tears, I wipe them away. But I mustn't be too hard on myself. I've just heard a boy on a murder rap crumble, crumple. They should play the tapes on television: it would stop the boys being seen as demons. One of the signs of psychopathy is lack of remorse, lack of "normal feelings" for others. Now Robert has betrayed such feelings, the notion that he's a psychopath doesn't fit.

Unless he was acting. It's what the prosecution say: that because the police were on to him he *used* tears in the hope they might lay off. The crying is all part of the lying. And the lying – crucially – proves he knew right from wrong: if he hadn't known the difference, he wouldn't have bothered to lie, would he? Playing the tapes is a kind of character assassination: hearing Robert tell whoppers makes him seem capable of much worse. The logic goes like this: he lied, therefore he's a cunning little bastard, therefore he planned the whole thing and has to be found guilty of murder, not manslaughter.

The flaw in this is that Robert's crying sounds genuine, and his lying an act of desperation. It's true he can also sound cocky. But self-possession under interrogation reveals nothing of his psyche at the time of James's death. And there's no direct route from lying to murder; if there were, we'd all be inside for life. I imagine catching the Crown barrister, Richard Henriques, in the corridor and confronting him.

"Most lying", I'll say, "is just a way of trying to save your skin. We all do it, don't we?"

And he'll say: "Speak for yourself, mate."

Speaking for myself: yes, I tell lies. I used to lie to my parents, to escape them. I used to lie to teachers, to get myself off the hook. I grew up among lies (my father's kindly meant "fibs") and I've lived among lies as an adult. I have a truth problem. I've committed and omitted. I've thrilled to philosophers who argue truth is relative, and I've relished novels which have themselves relished their own inventiveness. Truth: who needs it? Is there a duller-looking flower than Honesty?

It's only lately I've become unhappy about this. I reproach myself, as others have reproached me: if you lie to someone once, or rather if someone once catches you lying, how can they know when you're telling the truth? And if you catch them, ditto, in return, how can you trust them again? A banal parable (boy cries wolf), naive of me to have learnt it only now, embarrassing to relate. But it's no use pretending I'm unused to pretending. I've been bad. I've told lies. Late in the day, I'm trying to tell the truth.

I console myself that I've never told lies in public. It isn't much consolation. How can it be better to lie in private, at home, among friends? I console myself that some lies are more acceptable than others – lies told on behalf of others, for their financial benefit (the impoverished friend you buy lunch for but say, to save his pride, you'll claim on expenses), or to spare them pain (the cancer patient you know doesn't want to know she's dying); lies from which I don't gain myself; lies told to help the vulnerable feel stronger. But lies told towards a greater good or greater truth, are not – let's be honest – the lies that most of us tell.

I remember telling lies in primary school, as Robert and Jon did. Every week, for English, we had to write short accounts of how we'd been spending our time – "Then I went home. Then I watched television. Then I went to bed", that sort of thing. To alleviate the boredom, I took to describing birds I'd seen: robins, wrens, thrushes, blackbirds, swallows, rooks, pied wagtails. Soon this became boring, too. I needed more exotic birds, and described in detail the hoopoe I'd seen on holiday in Scotland, trying to persuade myself that a distant flash of black and white through fir trees might have been this striped but rarely spotted bird. Mrs Hartley ticked and VG'd the hoopoe, as she'd done all my other birds. I was shocked. I'd been cheating. Part of me had hoped she'd be able to see through the lie. But I had also learnt an important lesson: that there aren't always consequences – not every lie you tell is punished (or even detected). If you're clever at concealment you can get away with murder.

Not that I'm comparing myself with Robert and Jon. T & V & me: a tricky business. I don't mean to diminish their wrong-doing, or to exaggerate mine. But I do feel I understand their lying. They lied out of make-believe. And they lied to save their skins. The fact that they told lies is unattractive. But it doesn't make them murderers.

Rousseau understood children's lies very well. In *Émile*, he distinguishes between "the *de facto* lie, which is with respect to the past" and "the *de jure*, which is with respect to the future." The *de facto* lie, he says, is "not natural to children:. . . the present interest in avoiding punishment or reproach wins out over the distant interest of revealing the truth". The *de jure* lie, he says, is even less natural to them: "since their limited view cannot extend beyond the present, in committing themselves they do not know what they are doing . . . If Emile [Rousseau's son] could avoid the whip or get a bag of sugared almonds by promising to throw himself out of the window tomorrow, he would make the promise on the spot . . . It follows from this that children's lies are all the work of masters, and that to want to teach them to tell the truth is nothing other than to teach them to lie . . . If in my absence something bad were to happen and I did not know the author of it, I would take care not to accuse Emile and say to him 'Was it you?' – for what else would I be doing by this than teaching him to deny it."

Rousseau is wise, but he would never have got a job as a police interviewer.

Is it possible for a child to be at once clever, combative, adept, and also blind, confused, out of his depth? This is what Robert sounds like on the tapes. Forgetting the earlier allusion to home decorating, he invents a story about walking past a paint factory to explain how he came to have paint on his jacket. Conceding that he did take James up on the railway, he selects a route other than the one actually taken. Realizing that there's forensic evidence against him, he admits that he touched baby James, but only to "get my ears against his belly to see if he was breathing", and then to move him off the railway line, "so he wouldn't get chopped in half. I didn't want to get full of blood. Because blood stains, doesn't it, and then my mother would have to pay more money." Feeling cornered, and remembering the television crew present at the time, he plays his alibi: "You'll find that I took flowers over to the baby. Why would I do that if I killed him?" There is a convoluted brilliance to some of this. Listening to the police explain what the phrase "point of view" means and then shortly after using it himself. Saying he'd moved James off the tracks so he wouldn't get chopped in half when he moved James on to the tracks so he *would* get chopped in half. Trying to score points as the more honest of the boys ("It was Jon denied we went to the Strand, not me") and the more caring ("I was crying . . I was pulling Jon back but he just threw the brick"). Reminding his interrogators that, however hard they press him, his is the stronger position:

A: Were you there, like?

Q: No.

A: And seen me? That's what you're trying to say.

Read the transcripts, and Robert sounds clever, confident, precocious. But listen, and you hear the desperate voice of a little boy slowly being caught in the web of his own lies. The sticking point comes in the sixth interview, when he's told that blood was found on his clothes – and, crucially, inside the toe cap of his shoes (the stitching between upper and lower soles wasn't tight enough to prevent it spurting there). Even here it's Robert in the role of asking questions, not giving answers, though officially he's the A to their Q:

A: Blood's blood.

Q: No, it's different. Everyone's blood is different.

A: How do you know it's baby James's?

Q: They've got the body.

A: Where?

Q: It doesn't matter where. It's probably been to the hospital first.

A: What for?

Q: To take blood out of his arm like they've done to yours.

A: They've taken him to try and get him alive again.

Ann: No.

A: Yeah, well, I was told he got chopped in half. Well, he couldn't come alive again, could he, if he's got chopped in half.

Robert here is at best naive, at worst disturbed – about blood (that there are different blood groups comes as bad news to him), about the damage done to James, about mortality. "Get him alive again" suggests a cartoon understanding of life and death, and would support a plea of *doli incapax*. Robert talks like a child – a child afraid of getting in trouble, more trouble than he's already in.

The tapes run on, nothing new after the eighth: Robert sticks to his story that, yes, he'd been there when James was abducted, but it was Jon who had done the leading (he, Robert, was always either lagging behind or ahead); and yes, an attack took place, but it had been Jon who struck the blows. Robert cries a lot, but towards the end he's less distressed: the worst is over, and he's not going to concede any more. I look at him listening to himself on his headset. He's slumpy and glazed. He has a skincrop now, against his solicitor's advice – there was a barber at the unit over the weekend, and he wanted to feel like Bobby again, natural, to wear his hair as it used to be, before the arrest. The crop makes him look harder, no longer the cherub face but a convict, resigned to a long spell inside. Being this tough-looking kid, or kid who likes to pretend he's tough, he must hate hearing himself cry, however detached he feels, however superior, if only in knowledge, to the boy he was nine months ago. No, I wouldn't call him detached – not to judge from the paper tissue he's shredded, the heaped piles of it under his hands.

*

As If

The first Jon Venables interview, buzzered off five minutes after Robert's. Present at Lower Lane police station: Jon, his mother, solicitor Laurence Lee, DCs Mark Dale and George Scott. The atmosphere seems convivial, though Lee is having to learn fast (he doesn't know the family, and has come in at short notice from the local magistrates' court), and Susan must still be in shock. Jon's innocent, for sure; it's a misunderstanding; if any wrong's been done, it'll be the other boy who did it. Still, it's been a lot to take in.

From the start it's clear that Mark Dale is a hotshot at interviews, the Studs Terkel of Liverpool, drawing his man out, streets ahead of decent, stumbling Phil Roberts. He treats Jon as a scared kid, not a quiz contestant. He puts him at his ease. He tells him to think of the events of last Friday as a film – and let the cameras roll. Jon's not a stonewaller like Robert. Naughty stories pour out of him – school and skipping school, stolen toys and stolen sweeties, a game they play of climbing over people's hedges and walls. He's an old hand at robbing, but he speaks of sagging as an adventure: "I wanted to see what it was like." The stories of a soft-voiced explorer, an experimentalist.

It's nearly an hour, well into the second tape, before he gets on to the events of that day. He hadn't planned to sag but then he met Robert, who bullied him into it. Off they went. It was quite a journey. Multiple sites were visited and extraordinary distances covered: Argos, Rice Lane, Littlewoods, County Road, Stanley Park, Long Lane, Everton, a playground with swings and sandpits, an MFI store where they hid in the showers, even Anfield, home of Liverpool FC, with its memorial to the fans who died at Hillsborough. "Robert said: Let's look at the names, and then he said: Do you want to get that flower? And I said: NO, no, it's people's memories."

There are more memories at a cemetery they visited: "I showed Robert me Nan's and grandad's . . . And then he showed me his uncle's grave and that, his dad's dad's grave and his mum's mum's grave." A pious outing: butter wouldn't melt in Jon's mouth. The story is as much possessed by death as the story Jon isn't telling, which he merges into only at the end of the route, at the video shop, where (as he knows everyone knows) his mum caught him. The route, up till there, is intrepid. Almost the only point in Liverpool it doesn't touch is Bootle Strand.

Two tapes, an hour and a half of invention. Jon sounds five years younger than Robert here, a fabulist, a child enthralled by Thunderbirds and words like "teeny-weeny" and "thingy". From time to time there's a high-pitched desperation in his voice, like a mother lapwing whose cries and mock-tumbles are meant to lead intruders from the nest. The desperation isn't only to throw his interrogators off the trail, but to remake what happened that day in an image he has half-convinced himself is true – if only he can keep talking long enough, maybe it *will* come true. Robert is part of this fantasy world, the most exciting friend a boy could ever have, a good-bad guy with courage and machismo, who used to boast of his exploits up on the railway: "He sleeps there and lights fires . . . He told me he walked to London." Jon, it's noticeable, calls his friend Robert, not, as most acquaintances do, Bobby. You wonder how well he knew him. You wonder if it wasn't the comparative briefness of their relationship that made it so dazzling. You wonder if the friend he describes wasn't half, or more than half, a fantasy .

Jon runs on – and on. His interrogators let him run, giving him enough rope. But by the third interview, they've spoken to their colleagues in Walton Lane. They know Robert has owned up to being at Bootle Strand. It's nearly ten p.m. now, but not too indecently late to confront Jon with it. Just the mention of possible variance is enough to crack him up. He cries, terrible baby-baby wails. This is what we're listening to now, in daylight nine months later, in this austere panelled courtroom, beneath the dead judges: huge baby-baby wails. The policemen calm him down, but then break it to him again: Robert has said they were in Bootle Strand. Now his mother shouts at him, demanding to know the truth. Was he there or wasn't he?

Jon: Yeh, we were . . . But we never saw any kids there. We never got a kid, mum, we never, we never, we never got a kid. You think we did but we never . . . [Huge wails. No child has ever cried its heart out like this.] If you knew that I went to Bootle Strand . . .

Susan: I would have strangled you, yeah.

Jon: And wouldn't have you thought I'd killed a kid? I never . . .

Susan: If I would have known all this now, Jon, I would have had you down the police station right away, instead of them banging on my front door and making a show of me in the street . . .

Jon: But I . . .

Susan: . . . humiliation.

Jon: I thought you'd think that I killed him.

The buzzer sounds, the tape ends. Nine months on, Jon is hunched down inside the lapels of his jacket, hiding from the world. He stands, prompted by his social worker, and files out, below. We all do, file into the street, wrung out.

Please God, never let me hear a child cry like that again. Or rather, let those who think these boys inhuman hear their all-too-human distress. By the bus station arcade, all I hear is toddlers keening in pushchairs and babies wailing in prams. I think how many babies in the world must be crying at this moment, and all the babies in history crying, and of the unborn generations whose crying is to come: the power of such tears would dwarf Niagara. Adults tend to patronize weeping children, as if ours were real griefs and theirs counted for less. There's even the idea that crying does them good, by helping their lungs develop. Those Mabel Lucie Atwell pictures, or the classic Woolworths painting: lovely tear-globes in the corner of infant eyes, an exulting in prettified distress. Children's tears as bubbles, as airy nothings; or as baubles, fanciful and meaningless decoration. Sunshine and showers. Sorrows that quickly pass. But not for Jon, whose griefs run on.

In the newsagents, looking for a birthday card, I open a DEEPEST SYMPATHY, sorry for someone's trouble. Its commiseration is bland, insufficient even for the pain I'm feeling, let alone for anyone bereaved. On grief and children I prefer Francis Thompson: "Children's griefs are little, certainly; but so is the child . . . Pour a puddle into a thimble, or an Atlantic into Etna; both thimble and mountain overflow. Adult fools! would not angels smile at *our* griefs, were not angels too wise to smile at them?" Too true. Try telling a boy, locked in anguish, his tears don't matter: they matter to him. Jon Venables has a right to weep. He weeps as if his world is ending. Which it is.

In my bleak hotel room I phone home, as I do each evening, not out of duty but for the contact – the reminder of a world beyond the courtroom, a world in which I'm a husband and dad. My children haven't much to tell me about their day. I've even less to tell them about mine. But the exchange makes me feel human and *wanted*, as if parenthood were the thing, once you've passed forty, that most matters. "I'd do anything for my kids," people say. Anything? Sacrifice one's own life: that goes without saying. But what if one's child has taken a life and the police are on the trail? Ann Thompson admits she had suspicions about Robert, well before the police arrived. Seeing the stills of the security video and noticing the resemblance, she'd asked her son straight out if it was him. Robert denied it, but when the police came next morning her reaction was: "What took you so long?" Susan Venables, by contrast, denies suspecting Jon. When the police arrived, she thought they'd come about his truanting, a follow-up, a friendly warning to put the wind up him, just as she'd asked. She'd seen the television reports of the hunt for James's killers and had noticed Jon was quiet, but so little connected these things that she'd told a neighbour about the paint on his jacket (it was this neighbour who tipped off the police). That's her story. But didn't she have to wash Jon's blood-stained trousers? Hadn't that given her pause? Not even a bit?

Then again: even if the parents had suspicions, and lied to the police by omission, how far should they be blamed? The first boy to be arrested in connection with James Bulger's death, two days before T & V, was Jonathan Green of Snowdrop Street, Kirkdale. Acting on a tip-off, a host of panda cars swooped on his home, at night. The boy went off in haste, under a blanket. An angry crowd of neighbours gathered – neighbours angry enough to tell the assembled newsmen what a nightmare family the Greens were. But the arrest proved to be a mistake: the boy was innocent; he'd not been near Bootle Strand that day. The reason the police believed he had been there was his father. It was he who had called to tip them off: Jonathan had been shopped by his old man. Is this a better model of parenting? What kind of father grasses on his seed? To go to the police, to tell on your own family, to put the public interest higher than kith and kin: most of us couldn't do it, most of us are with E. M. Forster – we'd sooner betray our country than those we love. Mr Green was an Abraham, prepared to sacrifice Isaac on the stone of greater good. But Ann, Susan and Neil are easier to understand. If you suspect your son might have murdered someone, you just don't ask. If he tells you he has murdered someone, you help him bury the corpse.

Do they use polygraphs any more, lie-detectors, when interrogating suspects? We could have done with one this morning, to sort out Jon's sheep (his bleaty little white fibs) from his horned and hulking goats. How do you tell when children are lying? How do they tell when they are lying, since they have the capacity, not always lost in adulthood, to believe absolutely in their inventions? It was simpler with Pinocchio, whose nose grew each time he lied. At an inch a lie, Jon's nose would now be out the courtroom and halfway to the M6. Woodpeckers couldn't cope with the work of restoring him to normal: it would take whole sawmills. And yet it's hard not to feel sorry for Jon. He lies out of fear and wish-fulfilment and sincere conviction.

Today, on the fourth and fifth tapes, he has resumed his urban pastoral, but admits to being in Bootle Strand. There's barely a shop he doesn't own up to stealing from. But all this self-confessed daylight robbery has a purpose: small crimes to disguise the big. No one is fooled. Laurence Lee, after watching the Bootle Strand video on *Crimewatch* at home, has no doubt it was Jon in the frame. And now, after an hour, Mark Dale turns on the screws: Robert, he says, has admitted he and Jon led little James away. Panic, tantrums, thumps on the furniture, hysteria, huge wails of denial and distress: "I never touched the baby . . . You found his body and you think I done it, don't youse . . . Oh, you're going to put me in jail. For nothing, mum. They are. I want to talk to you, mum, and you."

End of interview. Was this the moment Jon elected to tell? It sounds as if he can't keep mum any more, that he's decided letting it out can be no worse. In the official version of events, the Albert Kirby version, it was thanks to sophisticated police manoeuvres that Jon was persuaded to come clean. Discreetly, after the interview, while Laurence Lee went off to lunch, the police spoke to Susan, and said they thought her presence was inhibiting Jon, that he was scared of telling the truth because of *her* recriminations. Susan talked to Neil about what the police had advised: that if they held Jon, and told him they loved him whatever he'd done and whatever happened, he might feel able to speak. Right enough. They sat on either side of him on a bench in the interview room and said they'd always be there for him and he confessed: "I did kill the baby . . . [Crying] What about his mum? Will you tell her I'm sorry." Jon had wanted to tell, and Susan and Neil (via the police) made it easier: maybe that was the halfway truth. But it doesn't really matter who gets the credit. What the sequence shows is the babiness of Jon, the immaturity. His deepest fear isn't prison and moral opprobrium but telling his mum. More *doli incapax* here.

Once Jon's fantasy world collapsed, his solicitor might have tried to stop further interviews. But Laurence Lee could see

no point in being obstructive: Jon could hardly dig himself a
deeper hole. The rest of the tapes (Susan absent, too upset;
Neil in her place) make easier listening. There is only one
hard bit, describing the attack: Robert telling James to stand
there while they get him a plaster, for where the brick has cut
him, then throwing more bricks and a bar: "I can't speak any
more. I've said it now." He can't speak any more, so he cries
some, cries like there's no tomorrow. After his confession, all
Jon can do is try to make himself seem less culpable than his
partner: he was going to give himself up anyway, in time; he
punched and kicked James "only light"; he threw just little
stones; OK, maybe he did throw two or five bricks as well, but
these landed to the side, or on James's arms, and he missed
with them "by accident, on purpose", "by mistake . . . no,
deliberately"; he had acted under pressure from Robert, who
got angry with him for his bad aim (Jon says he told him it was
because of "double vision") and who was "laughing his head
off" after leaving James for dead. (Robert, on his tapes, accuses
Jon of exactly the same thing; they must each have thought
the evil grin of the killer an authenticating, filmic touch.) In
short, "Robert done all of it, mainly."

I look at sweet-faced Jon listening on the head-set to his
dear little co-operative *alter ego*. The voice is protesting its
innocence, its appalled recognition of the terrible thing, all of
it done mainly by Robert. But the same voice has also said: "I
killed him." And after so many lies, it's impossible to know
which bits are true. Having made a clean breast of it, Jon goes
back under cover – and starts to fabricate again. Whereas
Robert, during his interviews, sits as if over a games board,
engaged in a battle of wits, Jon reruns the tape of an action
film, an awfully big adventure. He knows what he has done,
but doesn't quite believe it: it happened by accident, on

purpose; deliberately, by mistake. He seems weak, impressionable, a natural follower – a more innocent liar than Robert. But his fantasizing is in its way no less disturbing than Robert's cunning. Wouldn't it take a fantasist to dream up the idea of getting a kid lost in the first place?

I wander out into the afternoon, which seems already night, darkness come too early. Is one of these boys more guilty than the other? Could one be found guilty of manslaughter, the other of murder? Until now my sympathies have been with Jon – the bright-eyed hamster, the weak kid in thrall to a strong. He's Paul McCartney, the nice one, to Robert's tragic, bad-boy Lennon. He's shown feelings, remorse. He's been surrounded – his parents there beside him – with support and love. Now I'm not so sure. There's something desperate about the Venables's need to look ordinary. They're like a PR operation, a press release, a self-composed image of averageness. Two weeks after Jon was remanded in custody, they sent a thank-you card to Lower Lane police station, grateful to all concerned:

> A message really can't convey
> The gratitude that's sent your way . . .
> But may these words somehow express
> Warm thanks for all your thoughtfulness

These printed words were followed by some in Susan's handwriting, conveying "kind thoughts and respect . . . Without your help I know we would not have coped, we will never forget you. God bless you all." You can't blame Susan and Neil for their floweriness. How to address those who've charged your son with murder: the etiquette books are silent on this. But the card does seem a little too eager to please.

Normal, well-adjusted, decent boy led astray by vicious thug. That's their version of events. How true is it? I've watched Jon in court: I've seen how often he's looked across at Robert, wanting approval, dreading that he's lost it for good. The question is how far Jon might have gone to win that approval. Why assume he was the less active, the less brutal? He could have been the harder, to prove himself hard. He could have done the leading, in order, for once, not to follow. Culpability is difficult to allocate, and not to be decided by appearances. Isn't Jon, with the love he was given, the advantages, more guilty than Robert, who had less family support? Or is this just appearance, too? What's the truth about the home life of T & V? Might it be another factor? The evidence suggests they killed James Bulger jointly. But that jointness, Jon's chemistry with Robert, the T + V = Y of it, is something I still can't understand.

8

Weekend

> We may be excused for not caring much about other people's children, for there are many who care very little about their own.

DR JOHNSON

I'm home for the weekend, the second home, the adult home, next to Kathy, in my own bed. I need the break. I need the rest, though the dawn chorus of little beaks won't let me sleep. My three fledglings, up with the lark, nesting on my pillow before they're even awake. One by one, they flutter in, as if from battle or a long flight, touching base again, groggily disbelieving this is home and we are us and they are them. On a bad day, they'll want action right away; on a good day, like this, they'll doze again beside us and replay the last few tracks of night's cassette. There are mornings, hungover, that I resent sharing my pillow with several heads. But today, after Preston, after tape-recorded tears and thoughts of death, having children here at all seems a grace, a blessing, a miracle. The luck of Lazarus each morning: against all odds, they wake, come round and start to recognize the place; each day reborn.

The pillow empties. I drift off, and so do they. I find them some time later, downstairs, on the sofa, huddled under a rug in front of the television. On the screen, there's a children's quiz game: a half-naked boy, sitting above water in an ejector-seat, is pelted with slop and gunge each time he answers incorrectly; get three questions wrong, and he'll be dropped into the soup. My kids watch with fascination, willing him in. "How much longer is this on for?" I ask, tempted to use the off button. Silence. I try again, saying their names, but they don't respond. Are they transfixed by the screen, or winding me up? Since the trial began, and I've talked to them about T & V, they'll answer only to their initials: S, A & G. A game, a laugh – though their initials spell "sag", I can't help noticing, and my humour isn't what it was. I've talked to them about sagging. I've told them I think too many hours in front of the television a form of sagging. I'd be happier to see them read-ing Roald Dahl. But what they're watching now seems harmless enough, whereas a story by Dahl called "The Swan", involving a child being tied to a railway track, has been advanced as possible inspiration for T & V. I was brought up to think that books were humanizing, civilizing, "better for you" than television. Now I'm not so sure. There've been too many well-read serial killers, too many Goethe-lovers running death-camps. Books can be dangerous – even classics, even *children's* classics. The Grimm brothers, Hans Christian Andersen, Maurice Sendak: plenty of violence there for a child to cut its teeth on. Little Black Quasha and the self-consum-ing tiger pack, blood all over the jungle floor. Beatrix Potter, too: that image (still haunting me, forty years on) of Squirrel Nutkin inserted in a treehole too small for him, his bum and tail stuck out while his furry brother-enemies push him in. What is it right for a child to read? What is it right for a child to watch? Do mad, bad stories inspire mad, bad feelings? Or defuse them? Maybe not even the right things are the right things. Numbskulled by the safe, a child could be driven to dangerous adventures. Who knows, to someone somewhere even pap and gunge such as this quiz show might hold terrors – and be an occasion for further terrors. The boy on the screen gets a third question wrong and disappears into the drink. "How much longer is this on for?" I ask again. "Not long, Dad." I sit on the sofa arm. I let my children be.

It's difficult, being a parent. No one teaches you how to do it, except your own parents, by example, and often that's an example to avoid. The easiest profession to enter (no certificates necessary), it's also the hardest to leave. Long hours, massive expenses, no fringe benefits or pension scheme: why do it? Because you can work from home, be your own boss, see your product grow before your eyes. But what is the relation between product and manufacturer? Does how your children turn out have much to do with you? Child manuals used to promise malleability: children, the theory went, are the wax we mould; blank sheets of paper on which we write our ideas; plants we tend and nurture; drops of water on a polished table we can push with our finger in this direction or that. I know it can look that way. I remember my daughter just born and hardly breathing in her caul, as if she were clay, the colour of earth, waiting to be shaped. But her older brother came out fighting, at the end of his tether, not about to be pushed around by anyone. Right there, at birth, the conflicting evidence: that children are ours to shape; that they are intractably themselves. Clods or pebbles: which are they? Believe the first, and you feel guilty; believe the other, helpless. There are days I frighten myself thinking of the influence I might be having, and days when I'm frightened of having none at all. I blame my genes, for stacking the cards against my children. I blame the environment, for all the risks it puts their way – the burgers that attack their brains, the coke that rots their teeth, the pollution clogging their lungs. Is it safe for them to cross the road or stay out at night? Am I neglectful? Am I over-protective? Am I barmy? Pass. Another handful of slime hits the hapless quiz contestant.

Bored, my children flip over to *Power Rangers* – blows and explosions and kung fu. Some parents ban their kids from watching programmes like this. I'm with the indulgent majority. I don't believe in censorship. Not that I'd allow them to watch snuff movies or rape flicks, venerations of brutal crime. In my suitcase upstairs is a video of *Child's Play 3*, a horror film which – so several reporters at the trial think – might have influenced T & V. I'm going to test this theory. But not until later, after bathtime, bedtime, the watershed.

Power Rangers breaks – a gap for ads. Off the hook, I wander into the kitchen: pools of milk and scatterings of cereal where the children have helped themselves. I start to shout at them to come and clear the mess, then think the better of it: it's Saturday, relax, take Kathy tea in bed, read the papers, make them do it later. If this were a weekday, we'd be bullying them to get dressed, buffing their shoecaps, stooping over the grainy worktop to butter their bread (or Vitalite their Kingsmill). The packed-lunch box, with its cider-smelling plastic drinks container and the blackened, immovable mould marks; the squishy malt loaf; the sea tang of crisps; the cheese and cucumber sandwiches which return each night minus the cucumber. When I'm here, I resent the work it takes to get three kids out of the house in the morning; away, unburdened, I miss it.

Suffer the little children. Yes, yes, we do. *When I was a child I spake as a child, I understood as a child, I thought as a child; but when I became a man, I put away childish things.* Yes, every night, when I'm here, I put away childish things: the Lego and Sticklebricks, the dented drum and chewed-up drumstick, the plastic phone and metal xylophone; the 51-strong pack of playing cards, the 498-piece jigsaw puzzle, the Monopoly set with 7 houses and 2 hotels; the Teenage Ninja Mutant Turtles, Postman Pat and Thomas the Tank Engine stickers, figures, tapes and stationery; among the books, John Burningham's *Avocado Baby*, page 10 torn out at one corner, so the toddler-hero's most Sisyphean feat, pushing the family car, lacks its main protagonist; the various plastic cuboids and rhomboids that could be counting or spelling, honking or flashing, tinging or tonging, if only they had batteries. The cupboards overflow with stuff that will one day go to car boot sales, charity shops, the Third World. We, too, overflow: it's hard work, a man can only take so much, a woman, too. I dream of a solitary life – unfurnished rooms and empty shelves, reprehensibly perfect. Is that why middle-aged married men have affairs with younger women? Not (or not just) for love of their untenanted bodies, but to be taken back to flats uncluttered by *things*, flats in which the teddybear on the pillow is the sole reminder of childhood, and that not far behind. Maybe my going to Preston is similar: an illusion of owning nothing, living nowhere, a father to no one. And a way of sagging off.

Round ten, I get my youngest dressed. I tell him about some friends from university who also have a little boy, and how we plan to get together one of these weekends.

"Is the boy older than me?" he asks.

"A bit, yes."

"Is he bigger than me?"

"Probably."

"Will he beat me up?"

We walk to the shops. Push and shove, a suburban Saturday morning, among the stressed-out shoppers. PUSHCHAIRS ARE NOT ALLOWED says my friendly neighbourhood greengrocer, expecting younger children to be left outside, in harnesses, among the dogs tied to the railings. The newsagents up the street has a problem with stolen sweets: NO MORE THAN TWO SCHOOLCHILDREN AT A TIME is its rule. I have to explain to my four-year-old that there are places he's not welcome, not just restaurants and shops but whole areas of cities, the business end. He looks bemused. He's never had this trouble in playgrounds and McDonalds. Adults, on the whole, are nice to him, so why, as a whole, is the adult world not nice to him as well? I imagine his bemusement turning to knowledge, then resentment, then protest, he and his classmates marching with placards on Westminster. No more discrimination. No more segregation. Reclaim the streets for play spaces. Human rights for the under-tens.

Today the street is thick with Christmas lights. Soon the papers and magazines will be publishing their Holiday Survival guides: How to Get Through Xmas with Your Kids. There used to be an ironic tone to these pieces. Now they're written in earnest, as if the prospect of being left alone with one's children for a week were on a par with journeying to the heart of Borneo or going over Niagara Falls in a barrel. Christmas: once it meant Dickens; then it meant Disney; now it means home alone stories, the kids whose parents or step-parents can't bear to stay with them, who need to get away, if only to the pub. I have the cuttings. "A five-year-old girl was discovered without sheets on her bed or food, police said . . .",

"As the plight of a ninth child left to fend for itself came to light, Virginia Bottomley . . .", "A mob attempted to stop social workers when they went to rescue three more toddlers found alone without food behind the bolted steel door of a flat, Wolverhampton police said yesterday." For a week the papers are full of this stuff. It's Christmas entertainment, a tale of pathos, no room at the inn, with children the innocent victims of awesome adult selfishness and neglect. Then comes the New Year, problem over, a fresh start.

By the butchers, with its hooked and sundered carcasses, I meet Simon, a friend. We get talking about our children, how knowing they are, yet how little we know of them. He tells me about a scene at his house last Sunday, the family poring over the puzzles page in the newspaper.

- Rachel (his wife): Can anyone think of an anagram of
  lax rose?
- Hannah (12): Oral sex.
Pause.
- Saul (9): What's an anagram?

I buy croissants, fruit and veg, a loaf like an old-fashioned hairdo and wine gums for the kids. That's the morning gone. After lunch, the older two have parties, and need ferrying. That's the afternoon. Evening begins at nightfall, round six: pizza for them, gin and tonics for us, *Baywatch* and *Gladiators* as a backdrop. Another hour, and I can get the babysitter. Relief. Exhaustion. You can tell you're getting old when your babysitters are young enough to be your children – when your babysitters *are* your children. We're not quite there yet. But soon.

Supper is local, eight of us around a table – a barrister, a solicitor, a civil servant, an architect, and their husbands. Everyone's curious about the trial. What do the two boys look like? Are their parents with them? Are the parents of Jamie [James, I'm thinking: should I get pedantic?] in court too? How can I bear to sit there day after day? Don't I find it upsetting? "Oh, I don't know, it's interesting," I say, and the looks in return say: ghoul, sicko. There is a change of subject, to something less awkward, our own children: whose, how and at which point, sat up, walked, talked, learnt long division, slept through the night, came off the breast, asked to wear a bra, stopped wearing nappies, started periods, started nursery, grew a moustache, learnt the ABC, developed acne, played with Lego, played the violin, played loud music in the attic, climbed out of the playpen and left home. I find it hard to contribute to this – it's as if my children's childhood is as much a blank as my own. Funny how vague you can be about the various stages of child development, except the ones your own children have currently reached. And yet – to judge from dinners like this – child development is something people think about a great deal, the English middle classes especially, whose way of thinking about children, as about everything else – food, education, art, houses, cars, furniture – is competitive. But I mustn't (and don't) bang on. Pride in one's children is natural. To overprize them through a fog of love: I'm guilty of it, too.

Driving home, orange light from streetlamps passing across Kathy's face, I think: weekends will never be the same, after James Bulger. I can't pass the old standard retail outlets – Mothercare, Clinton Cards – without thinking of Bootle Strand. Harmless domestic items have a new meaning, too: white socks in a chest of drawers; the detachable, fur-lined hood in the hallway; batteries inside toys; Humbrol model paint; garden bricks; the stack of videos by the television. Even my children's initials: S, A, G.

We pay the babysitter off and find them in the ruined postures of sleep, the scattered limbs and *disjecta membra* of unconsciousness. I have to prise G from his bed, the midnight lift to pre-empt his bedwetting. (We have a daytime peeing ritual, too, but it's different: we join forces at the water, swords crossed, an intimate urinal kiss.) My hands in his armpits, his fingers locked around my neck, his legs about my waist, I set him down by the water, swing him round – still asleep – to face the bowl, pull his pyjama bottoms down and find his little prick in its dream-erection. His legs against the cold of the porcelain detumesce him, and I aim him at the centre, the line of pee hitting its target. Pants up, eyes closed still in a torrent of sleep, he lifts his arms to be carried back, monkey-gripping me again as if I were a fireman bearing him from the blaze. I lay him down in his stormy sheets, and pull his duvet up, thinking how in this duvet age no one tucks up their children any more. I wouldn't want them back, those 1950s childhoods of sneezy blankets, lumpy counterpanes and cold sheets pinning you down without ever reaching your chin. Yet something must have been lost in this flop morality where kids put themselves to bed and the only places with sheets and blankets are hotels.

I lie next to Kathy, unable to sleep. So many sirens calling. The late trains clattering down to Dartford, the sex screams of foxes, the whooshy tides of traffic on the A2: these, the usual night-sounds, are drowned tonight by sirens. I drift off briefly, and dream of a man entering the room, his knife bisecting my torso from neck to navel. I wake in a sweat, and think of my father, and of how, for all his difficulties and contradictions (the bullying, the over-attentiveness, the irascibility), he had one simple faith as a parent: that the world could be made a better place for his children than it had been for him. Whereas the worry now is that it's a worse earth our children will inherit, thanks to us. Parents today haven't my father's cock-eyed optimism. As a child, I trusted absolutely that he could protect me, keep the bad out, make things safe. Do my children have the same confidence in me? They'd be unwise to. The man with the bisecting knife re-enters the room. I lie awake in the cold dawn, the tape of my fear playing over. The screen of the future is locked and frozen, and I'm unable to exit from the file.

Sunday morning, a good time for the Royal Academy. We're on the way by ten, guiltily and no doubt illegally leaving the older two home alone with their suddenly attractive home-work ("Art gallery? Nah"), wondering how long we're out the door before the television goes on. Light rain on Piccadilly. No queue. Kathy has a headset; I have G, or he has me. I expect, from previous experience, that I'll manage no more than five minutes, most of them pointing out the angel Gabriel in swirly quattrocento flesh, before there's a scene, an exit to the Gents, a demand for drinks and biscuits. But we do better today. There are a lot of sacrificial victims in these paintings, a lot of flashing blades: Judith with the head of Holofernes, Abraham offering up Isaac, young women being led serenely towards an elder with a kitchen knife. We move from canvas to canvas, carcass to carcass. I crouch down beside him, kneel at his feet, and – wishing I knew or remembered more of classical mythology – explain as best I can why so many people are being killed and how some of them (being gods and goddesses) don't die even though they look dead. He seems unsurprised by this, unreacting, and I wonder if he's getting bored.

"Shall we try the next room?" I ask.

"Will there be more killing?" he asks.

"Probably."

"Good."

At last art is beginning to mean something to him.

Sunday night, after bedtime, I get out my secreted videos: *Child's Play 1–3*. There've been whispers around court that Neil Venables rented *Child's Play 3* just before the killing; that Jon and Robert were steeped in horror films; that the death of James was a copycat crime. Already, *Child's Play 3* has come up at another trial this week, in Manchester: the murder of a teenager, Susanne Capper, tortured by a group of friends in a squat. Before burning her to death, they kept her strapped to a bed, a refrain from the film spooling in the background: "I'm Chucky: wanna play?" Chucky, the doll-hero of the *Child's Play* films, talks rough and American: "Don't fuck with the Chuck". He's a cult in the north of England. It seems he has a lot to answer for.

I press Play. *3* begins with blood, and a doll coming to life, like Pinocchio. Freckled and yellow-haired, Chucky resembles a three-year-old, a little James. But he's an aggressor, not a victim. Inside him is the soul of an adult psychopath. Strong and malevolent, he likes hurting people. You couldn't take him for a toddler. In one scene, blue paint splashes in his face during an exercise at Kent Military Academy. Blue paint! Humbrol! But the episode passes in a flash. There's a much longer and more disturbing one when somebody tries to put lipstick on Chucky, who, seeing his machismo threatened, squirms and resists.

The tape winds towards its climax, on the tracks of a fairground ghost train, where Chucky is horribly mangled – a possible link to the crime. *Could* the film have been a source for T & V? There must be more promising sources: films, books, comics, television. Even the safe bits of television. Even children's television: that report the other day about the two-year-old who strangled himself with wire as he imitated his hero, a snake-carrying American wrestler. In psychology and media studies libraries are books and articles asking the same questions: if we see a murder on screen, are we more likely to commit murder than we would otherwise have been? Do images have an effect? The experts can't agree. They rubbish each other's findings. Too many variables, they say, too many unknowns.

I don't doubt the screen can make things happen. I remember my annual enthusiasm for playing tennis after Wimbledon had come on. I remember how in *Z Cars*, after a row with the sarge, Lynch had gone outside, drained a milk bottle, then hurled it to smithereens against a wall – feeling better for it, as I did, a few days later, astonishing the brickwork, just the same. Most of all I remember William Tell. A garden in Yorkshire, circa 1958, backed up against a sycamore, an apple on my head. Martin Whittle plucks his string: lute music first, then the shooting. He wears a green tunic and feathered cap, and holds his strongbow vertical, as if he's Robin Hood. I tell him to hold it sideways, like a crossbow. He is the father, I am the son: the future of the world depends on him shooting the apple from my head. But it's not easy for a six-year-old to pierce an apple at ten yards, especially when the arrow has a rubber tip. He tries three times, and each time the arrow veers off in the bushes. Now we remove the rubber tip: the arrow will fly truer. With luck it will pierce the apple to its core, so I can turn once it's pinged past me and find it trembling in the bark, ready to be plucked and eaten, like a toffee apple on a stick. We take our places again. Martin has offered me the chance to shoot, but I refuse: I am older than him, I don't want the responsibility. Besides, in my book the hero is the one being shot at. "Ready?" he asks. "Ready" I say, and hold myself like a wineglass. I close my eyes, as young Tell does on the telly, the son in perfect trust. But my father is Martin Whittle, only six, and I squint my left eye half-open again. Martin has stepped forward, his left eye half-open, too, not wanting to miss. He draws the string from a floppy) to a taut >. The fingers under his chin fly open. I see the arrow leave his hand. I close my eyes again, hoping, praying for the whoosh of it through my hair. It catches my eyebrow instead, sticking for a second or two then falling. I stand there like Rodin's thinker, feeling for blood. "It's all right," I say to Martin, who has run across anxiously to check his arrow isn't broken, "only a scratch." I lie down and wait till the blood stops dripping. Then we play cowboys and indians. My eyebrow doesn't hurt that much, and Martin says it will look normal, washed. But when I'm home, and my mother sees it, and hears what we've been doing, she gets angry. She'll tell my father to go straight down to the Whittles and break that bow over Martin's knee. I could have lost an eye. No more Robin Hood games, she says. No more William Tell on telly, either (though I watch in secret, undeterred).

Child's play, 1958. But it's no use blaming art, or thinking censorship would solve the problem. It's not as if life is so innocent either. That fourteen-year-old from Sheffield, three months after James Bulger: he'd seen his mother murder his father when he was six, and here he was, eight years later, bayoneting a kid to death. Copying what you see adults do: it's how children grow up, it's the basis of their play, the dolls, the

Matchbox cars, the plastic guns. Copycat, copycat, we taunted other kids. We were all copycats. We still are. No one would need *Child's Play 3* to get the idea of hurting people. No boy would need a film to show him that it's fun to beat up other boys. It's there through the culture, in the playground, on the streets. Robert and Jon, so schoolfriends said, boasted they were going to kill a kid. We all, as kids (sometimes as adults, too), say we'll kill each other. If brags were crimes, we'd all be lifers. I remember a boy saying he was going to kill me. Coster, he was called: he had Mick Jagger lips and gappy teeth and sticky-out ears, like Plug in *Beano*, and he came up to the window of a bus I was sitting on and mouthed through the window, just before it pulled away: "I'm going to kill you". I was shocked, at the time, that he wanted to kill me, since we'd never spoken or met. But what had reason to do with it? He had no cause, no box of motivation he could tick, only Other. Nothing personal. Boys beat boys up. Law of nature.

This was the climate I'd grown up in, where aggressors were the hero of every story. *They* weren't the headcases; the headcases were their victims, requiring thirty or more stitches. Thirty years on, Robert and Jon grew up in the same culture. Northern, is it, this need for boys to show themselves hard? Not Northern, not British, not even Western, perhaps not even human: fundamental to young males of most species. The social order, properly run, can help control their aggression. Non-violent role models might in time create a different kind of male. But instinct isn't easily quashed, and it's not the job of movies to defeat it. The credits go up. T & V and *3*? No, I can't believe they worked in concert. This was two boys and some bricks, not two boys and a film.

All the same, I hate the video and it disturbs me. Might it have worked subliminally (or at some level below even that), encouraging Robert and Jon to think small children were indestructible like Chucky, little horrors who can take any amount of damage and bounce back? Did they think that by killing Chucky/James they would be saving the world, doing it good? Chucky despises "kids": he uses the word a lot; there is one particular kid he tries to take from its mother and kill, because he needs to possess its body and soul in order to come alive. All crap, voodoo stuff. I'd like to laugh at it. But I keep seeing Chucky slump into his lifeless doll state. Or the scene where it's discovered that Chucky, unlike other Good Guy Dolls, can run without batteries. James was mistaken for a doll by the train driver who ran over him; batteries were found by his body. The film's too close to the bone. Everything is these days, even the phrase "too close to the bone".

I stay up and fast-forward through the two other *Child's Plays*, pausing at parallels, and drifting in and out of sleep. At one point in *Child's Play 2* Jenny Agutter appears, famous from *The Railway Children*. In my half-sleep a vast conspiracy is spun, art imitating life, life imitating art. In Roald Dahl's re-write of *The Railway Children*, adapted for film by Tarantino, the Thompson brothers, waiting for their father to come back from the war, kidnap a small child in a red *Don't Look Now* plastic mac, and tie him to the rails in an attempt to slow down an express train. Jon, Neil and Terry Venables are standing in the driver's cab. Too late the brakes are applied. Blue oil splashes in their face. Then it's only a toytrain on a loop, which runs out of batteries and stops, just as the videotapes capturing the incident stop and eject . . .

I wake in front of the grey hissing screen, too dopey to judge the copycat theory but feeling some sympathy for Neil Venables. It was in June 1991 that he'd joined the Videoscene film club, membership card no 4548. He'd been separated from his wife for five years then. Out of work, on his own in a crummy flat off Breeze Hill, he hired quite a few films from Videoscene. (There'd been another club, Videogold, but it was dearer, £2 a throw, and he'd used it only half a dozen times.) I've a list of his last fifty borrowings: in reverse order, back from *Child's Play 3*, taken out on January 18 (a month rather than days before the murder): *Hook, Ricochet, People under the Stars, Critters, Kuffs, Past Midnight, Kick Fighter, Freddy 6, Manhunt, Curly Sue, The Visitors, JFK, Jacob's Ladder, Thelma and Louise, Double Crossed, FX2, Time Bomb, Marked for Death, The Godfather 3, Suburban Commando, Predator 2, Teen Agent, Ganglands, On the Block, Stepfather 2, Kickboxer 2, New Jack City, Out for Justice, Seeds of Tragedy, Marked for Murder, Robin Hood, See No Evil, Wedlock, Q & A, Dolly Dearest, Rookie, Highlander 7, Wars of the Roses, Child's Play 2, Desperate Hours, Whispers, Trancers, Once Upon a Time in America, Nightmare on the 13th Floor, Famous Tits and Arses, Rain Killer, The Disturbance, Whore, Bird on a Wire.* An odd but not sinister list: a mix of low erotica, B-movies, classy highbrow and kidflicks for Jon; I've seen a few of these films; most people must have; they're not brown-paper-bag material, just regular stuff from your friendly video corner-shop. But for a time the police had got excited about the video theory. They'd searched Neil's flat, and though nothing incriminating was found people were now calling Neil a pervert, a horror addict, a porno buff, an accessory after the fact. There was a figure of 440 films hired in recent months.

My evidence is different: sixty-four films hired from Videoscene in eighteen months, less than one a week. There may have been hot under-the-counter loans as well, but it doesn't seem a lot, for a guy on his own. How many men (and women) of his age haven't watched porn? Every videostore offers it. Hotels, too, lay it on, all part of the service. They understand what it's like. A guy can get lonely. Even married guys can get lonely, and Neil was separated. Suppose he wanked to the odd movie: was a wank to a video worse than a wank to a mag? Wasn't it just higher-tech wanking? And it wasn't as if there were many porn movies among his sixty-four. A handful of famous tits and arses: not enough to justify pillorying the man, not after what he's been through, not after what he's still to go through in the prints, when his self-professed Barry Norman film-buffery is revealed.

On my way to bed I look in at my older son and think: could he have done what Robert and Jon did? And I look in at my younger and think: if some boys had beckoned, down in Lewisham, would he have gone to them? And I walk to my bedroom and think: the gap between my sons is seven and a half years, just as in the murder; T and V (ten and a half) killing James (a month short of three) is like S killing G.

Monday morning's a scramble. I drive my eldest the 200 yards to his coach, then my daughter and two of her friends the quarter mile to their school. Pampering them. Aged seven, my sister and I walked the half mile to primary school, alone. Most kids got themselves to school then, even if it meant public transport across London. And earlier generations thought nothing of walking, twice a day, the six miles or more to school and back. Now kids are chaperoned and chauffeured. To let them get on with it seems negligent and dangerous. Robert Thompson, walking to school alone and rollerbooting the streets of Walton late at night, is a symbol of the risks of freedom – of the harm a child can suffer or cause. The age of indulgence: instead of walking, the school run. The age of anxiety: having to keep a constant eye on your kids because of all the sick people out there, including other children. But is modern life really more dangerous for kids, traffic accidents aside? The statistics don't suggest it. In the eleven years before James Bulger's death, 57 children in Britain were killed by strangers: an average of five a year. (Between 1930 and 1960, the average was twice as high.) The risk to them in their own homes – and from people they know – is far greater. It's a myth, too, that kids today grow up more quickly than their ancestors. A hundred years ago, children had much shorter childhoods, were more quickly introduced to work, marriage, parenthood and death. In 1860, a ten-year-old could legally have sex. In 1993, ten-year-olds are thought too immature for sex, though mature enough to murder. We've come a long way.

At nine, an hour to spare before the train, I walk with my four-year-old to school. It's blue and clear; apples, cones and chestnuts have gone hard underfoot. Cries come from the playground before we reach it. We pass through the main school and stand outside the nursery, a huddle of weary parents, our children uh-aahing, uh-aahing like police cars. I feel awkward, the only man, a father among mothers, not part of the chat, and watch the children chase each other around the yard. At 9.15 the doors open and we enter the ark, two by two, big creatures hand and hand with little. In the hall there's a row of pegs eighteen inches from the ground, with hanging jackets and kitbags. Beyond is the one-room nursery: a table of sand, a goldfish bowl, books, paints, Lego and Fisher Price. A dozen children are already on the floor in the Reading Corner. G selects a book from the shelf, and sits down, but when I try to leave he protests, plucking at my sleeve. I squat down, open his book and begin reading aloud. It's the story of a battle for the title King of the Woods, fought out between an eagle, wolf, bear, moose and wren; the wren eventually wins – a triumph of the Little over the Big. I hadn't meant to have an audience, but the other children in the circle sit listening, eyes lifted, open-mouthed. I do the animals in different voices, very badly, but it doesn't matter, it's a story, that's enough. I could get addicted to this: power over young minds, narrative. When I finish, my son lets go, consenting to be left, no tantrum today, not the usual gut-wrenching good-bye wave and walkout while a teacher hangs on to him and he stretches his arms out for me like one of the mothers in Poussin's *The Slaughter of the Innocents*. I've reason to be grateful to a picturebook. Art has made something happen. It wasn't a good story, and it wasn't told well, but it worked.

At Euston I catch the train back north, not sure if it's sagging to be in Preston or sagging to come home. No escape from children, either way. Two are there in court all day, and at night I fret about my own.

9

Beatings

JUDY: Where's the baby?

PUNCH (in a lemoncholy tone): I have had a misfortune: the
child was so terrible cross, I throwed it out of the
winder.

JUDY: Waaaah. (Lemontation for the loss of her dear child.)

Preston, a Wednesday, the third week of the trial. I wake at
seven, have a piss and call home. Kathy gets it on the last ring
before the answering machine, groggy and morose. I'm
morose, too. We start rock bottom and go downhill from
there. How is she? Not good. How are the kids? Asleep, just.
Does she realize the time, the school bus in half an hour? Do
I realize what kind of night she has had? Just as well I rang
then. No, not much point in ringing at all, I'm just a long-dis-
tance control freak. I'm only trying to help. The only real
help would be being there with her. Pause. Change of subject.
What work has she got on today? A lot of work, a big day –
what do I care? Deaf ear to that. What I've got on is court, but
there's not much point talking about it, pretty dull at the
moment, nothing new. Anything new her end? Only the
nanny, last night, calling in to say she wasn't feeling well and
might have to cry off, today of all days. Shit, that means she'll

have to stay home and miss . . .? There I go saying *she'll* have
to when they're my kids as much as hers: funny – but not at all
funny – how it always falls on her. How am I supposed to
help, this far away? I promised I would if there was a crisis,
I've said the court's dull at the moment, just tapes, if I skipped
off early and caught a train I could be home to do the pick-up
from school. But there must be someone else we could try, if
need be. Like who? Sally? She's away. Jenny? Not temping
any more. Anna, or one of the other mothers? We owe them
too many favours already. An emergency au pair service? Now
there's a great idea, to get someone we don't know to send
someone we've never seen and who's not met any of the kids
and who has to get to two different schools and who can probably speak about six words of English, while I'm 200 miles
away and she's the other side of London unable to check out
that the arrangement has even fucking worked, let alone if
anyone's happy with it, Jesus, I sit there anguishing about
those two kids and yet I'd hand my own over to a complete
stranger. Pause. Silence. Should I – er – come home then?
Probably no need, she'll sort it out somehow, she's just making a point, how it was all going to be equal once but it's
turned out she's the one who always has to pick up the pieces.
Silence again. Time, we agree, to get going. We'll speak some
more tonight, then: if I can get to a phone; if she's got back
from wherever; if the house hasn't burnt down; if the world
hasn't ended. Bye, love. Ta Ta.

Marital rowing. Are we just like all the others? Ann Frank
in her diary, 1942: "Why do grown-ups quarrel so easily, so
much and over the most idiotic things?" Once, at supper,
some newish friends of ours, about to become ex-friends,
declared they'd *never* once argued. In the car home, we passed
the sick bag: *never* argued, it was indecent, inhuman. Later,

hamming it up, we related this story to some other friends, who became a bit embarrassed, looked at each other and said they weren't sure how to tell us this but, well, actually, *they'd* never . . . We were a bit shaken after that, a bit paranoid. Maybe it *was* just us. You hear the odd couple going it down the supermarket aisle, but who's to say they're not siblings, or drunks, or exes, or mad? Who knows what secret harmonies there may be, in private? And the friends who do bicker in our company: maybe they've heard about us and it's all for our benefit, to make us feel better. Maybe we've reached public-nuisance level, and this is their only way to cope.

I tip my face to the burning rays of shower. What's the right amount of arguing? And what's the effect on our children, the care of whom is what these rows are mostly about? Big questions, which we addressed over a bottle or two the other night. But we couldn't agree on the answers. In fact, we began to argue. We had a row about rowing. And about whether it was the drink making us argue. And about whether a row about rowing was less or more serious than an ordinary row. Then we went to bed.

There's a rule I grew up with, something about never letting the sun set on anger. Rather a cosy rule, and not easily adherable to, but it does seem to prevent prolonged sulking and to complete some process: rowing is one release of tension, making up another, and at least this way when couples get physical it's afterwards and non-violent. South-east London, a few years ago: a man walking after midnight, beating, beating – each time she caught him up – the woman dragging after him along the pavement, his blows and her screams echoing off the houses. The noise of them woke us. We stood at the window in our night-things, and for a while the houses opposite stayed dark and unreacting, as if this were the usual: the old fisticuffs, the old duffing-the-girlfriend- up, *tedium vitae*. Then a light went on, a door opened and people were in the street, and we were in the street, and the man ran off, and the beating stopped, though not the woman's wailing pleas – as bad as her screams – for him to forgive her. Forgive? I wondered how bad a thing she'd done that he could do this to her and she still be pooling herself in his wake, wanting his pardon. Some neighbours took the woman in: tea and Elastoplast. We went back inside, where I stood at the window and saw her, patched up, re-emerge and go off the way he'd gone. The last woman beaten in public, in my street, in my small orbit. You don't see it now in pubs or in films, not as you used to, though it still goes on in private, the screams and then silence, and sometimes the sirens afterwards.

I turn off the shower, towel myself dry and get on the phone to home. This time we're gentle with each other. After the noisy, familiar exhaustion of war, the soft, familiar exhaustion of peace. It isn't ideal, we tell each other, agreeing for once: too much pressure, too many things to think of. But it could be worse. It's hard to say what it is, or why it feels all right, or what keeps it going. It's just . . . it's us . . . it's home.

"Notes taken at a Case Conference held at the NSPCC, 125–127 High Street, Wavertree, Liverpool, on Thursday March 25 at 9.30am. Subject: The Thompson Family. Ian (dob 21.10.77), Philip (2.11.78), Robert (23.08.82), Ryan (10.07.84), Ben (05.06.92). Home address: Walton Village, Liverpool 4. Mother: Ann Thompson (dob 11.12.53). Other Thompson siblings: David (29.11.73), Peter (22.12.75). Present: BLACKED-OUT, ILLEGIBLE. Apologies: Dr Roberts, GP. Reason for Case Conference: Alleged Schedule

One Offence committed by Robert. Discussion notes. It was noted that Mrs Thompson and the children have been excluded from the conference.

"Recommendations: No evidence of abuse is established so Robert's name will not be entered on the Liverpool Child Protection Register. No evidence of abuse is established concerning Robert's siblings and so at this time no Child Protection Conference is to be held . . . No connection has been established between any abuse and the alleged offence."

I'm sitting on the floor with witness statements, interview notes, and two confidential reports given to me by a friend who himself got them from a friendly source (he's not sure who: they were posted through his door late one night). My head's aching from going to bed too late, or getting up too early, or arguing, and though I'm trying to concentrate I'm afraid that if I try too hard I'll throw up. Already I'm on to my third mug of instant coffee and third double-row of paracetamols. They don't seem to be working.

I didn't realize there'd been a case conference. But it's obvious, there would have had to be. In the days after the boys' arrest, the tabloids were busy doorstepping and out came friendly-neighbour tales of broken homes, alcoholism, cruelty and abuse. At the offices of the city council, questions were asked of the Director of Social Services: hadn't we known about these kids? Were there files on them? Was Liverpool City Council going to be in the shit come the trial? A case conference was called, six weeks after the murder – two case conferences, in fact, one for each boy. A crowded room, Mr Pickering of Child Protection in the chair. Also present (the felt-tip blacking their names out on this photocopy hasn't worked, quite), social workers, solicitors, nurses, youth project leaders, child protection officers, education welfare officers and the boys' headteacher, Irene Slack – sixteen in all. A gathering of care professionals anxious to understand how family circumstances might have contributed to the murder. An exercise in self-scrutiny. An internal interrogation. It should have been. It might have been. But snoophounds and scoophounds were baying at the door. The City Council, embarrassed in the recent past by rubbish strikes, Toxteth, Militant, Hillsborough and Derek Hatton, felt to be on the hook again, its reputation on the line. If it was admitted the Council knew these two families had problems, then critics would say it should have seen the murder coming. It was clear to everyone the conference mustn't dig too deep. Its main purpose should be self-exoneration: "No connection has been established between any abuse and the alleged offence."

Only connect. The Thompson report is a series of violent incidents, none of them in itself enough to justify the kids being taken into care but the sum of them appalling. The boys, it's said, grew up "afraid of each other". They bit, hammered, battered, tortured, tied each other up. Seven sons bringing each other up the hard way. Seven samurai inducted in the ancient skills of war. Seven sons of a seventh brother, almost – Robert Thompson Senior had been one of eight. Violence was the family norm, thanks to him. If he hadn't drunk so much, Ann might have held things together. But even newly married, he went off boozing with relations, her left behind at the window. As often as not, when he came back drunk, he'd hit her. One of her two miscarriages had come from being jammed in a door at his mother's during a row. When riled, he had a habit of dragging her by the hair.

The violence percolated down. Though none of the boys was now on the Child Protection Register, David had been placed there at four, after being seen with a cigarette burn and black eye. Much later, as a punishment for smoking, Robert Senior made David eat a packet of cigarettes. He was that kind of patriarch. "See the evil in my eyes, twat," he'd say to scare them when he was angry. Chips off the old block, the boys knocked the shit out of each other. Often it seemed best to let them get on with it: that way, the feuds were soon over. They all felt their father's hand – not single blows but battery. Neighbours said Ann, too, hit the kids. The child health records allege she once banged David's head against a door. She denied all charges, stripping the kids in front of a social worker to show there were no bruises. But so what, she'd say at other times, so what if she did hit them? Maybe she hadn't hit them enough. Short of a good hiding, with their dad gone, they'd turned to bad.

I read on, looking for insights, but all I see are blows. Within two weeks of the family (the single-parent family) moving to Walton in 1988, and of the boys enrolling in the school there, Ian (then eleven) is stealing, and Philip (ten) is seen with bite marks. Ryan complains of bullying by Robert. Philip is seen to punch Robert in the face, outside the school. Philip is taken to Walton Lane police station by his mother, after threatening Ian with a knife. Philip complains of bullying by David. Ian says that "because my mum was out a lot, David was put in charge of us all and he would hit us if we did anything wrong . . . with a pole". His mother, too, so Ian tells social services, had once hit him with a stick. Ian was taken into care after that, at his own request. Philip had already gone into care, after an incident, reported to the police, in which (so he alleged) David had battered him, chained him up, tarred and feathered him, and locked him in a shed. Before this, says the report, Philip "had been questioned over two incidents of inciting gross indecency. Detective Inspector

Hope was unable to give any information with regard to the incident." Presumably because the complaint, brought by a younger child or children, did not lead to charges. Only Peter, the second Thompson son, who left home at fourteen (followed by David two months later), goes unmentioned in the report. Peter did the right thing. As quickly as he could, he got out.

"No connection has been established between any abuse and the alleged offence." On the contrary, says the family social worker, "the period before the recent incident was probably one of the most stabilizing times within the family's history. Mrs Thompson had three children living at home, and was slowly gaining insight into the needs of herself and more importantly her children. She was able to acknowledge problems and demonstrate motivation to address them." Except that, with baby Ben on her hands, she didn't feel she could escort Robert and Ryan the half-mile to school, and, as a result, they often failed to get there. Except that, though now off the bottle, she was desperately poor. Except that Irene Slack had fought "a continual battle to bring to the attention of the Social Services and other agencies the problems surrounding these children in the Thompson family". Except that, a fact unmentioned in the report, while Ian Thompson was in care in early 1993, just weeks before the murder, he tried to kill himself with an overdose. In earlier years, Philip and Ann had taken overdoses, too.

Swigging more coffee and paracetamol, I think I've begun to see why Robert led the attack on James. Then I read the Venables file. Harmless enough, to start with. Here's Jon (dob 13.08.82, which makes him ten days older than Robert), living in Scarsdale Rd, Liverpool 11, with his mum Susan (03.03.57), older brother Mark (06.05.79) and younger sister Michelle

(08.11.83). The tone is upbeat – very Venables. "All three children spend time with their father which is seen as very positive." Unlike Robert's, "Jon's attendance at school had been excellent", and there is no suggestion that he "had been behaving in a sexually inappropriate manner in school". Nor is there any suggestion of abuse.

And yet, and yet . . . There are suspicions about Susan, who's known to have had difficulties settling her children at night and isn't averse to "discipline", or "chastisement", meaning a good slap or belting as required. In January 1987, the police were called to her home because the children (then seven, five and three) had been left alone for three hours. Susan had recently separated from Neil and wasn't coping. These were more than the usual strains of single parenthood. Her "serious depressive problem" eventually resulted in "two traumatic incidents": suicide attempts, it seems (the report skirts around this), in 1990 and 1991. Both Mark and Michelle had learning difficulties and went to special schools. Mark, who'd been born with a cleft palate and was taunted as a "divvie" by other kids, "could not defend himself", and had developed "volatile and unexplained bad behaviour": there is a reference in his medical records of violence towards Jon. The special needs of Mark and Michelle were, Susan and Neil thought, one reason for the break-up of their marriage – that and Neil losing his job and Susan liking to go out at night a lot "with friends". Jon not having special needs was what made him special. He was the (blessed) odd one out. On him alone fell his parents' wish for a bright, "normal", achieving child.

But was Jon this kind of boy? Jealous, attention-seeking and troubled by lack of sleep, he copied Mark's behaviour. He "seemed to defy any school control and there were instances of him reacting very severely in class, standing on desks and throwing chairs". His form teacher at Broad Square (name of Bolger) had "never come across a boy like Jon" in fourteen years, and kept a log of his oddities. He would butt his head against heavy objects and fall to the ground, throwing his arms around. He'd pull artwork off the wall. He would rock back and forth moaning and making strange noises. He'd lie irretrievably inside nests of chairs. He slashed himself on purpose with scissors, cut holes in his socks, stuck paper all over his face. He once hung himself upside down from coat pegs, like a bat. And then the ruler incident: riled, Jon got a child by the throat with a twelve-inch ruler, pinning him to a desk and throttling him before having to be dragged off. A social worker had offered Susan a behavioural chart to control Jon, but the groundings and deprivations seemingly had no effect. A change of schools, to Walton, improved his morale, but not his temper. The day before the murder, said his form teacher, Jon's behaviour was the worst she'd ever known.

"No connection." Only connect two different boys: Robert, fairly quiet and impassive at school – he even gets teased for being a girl – but the fifth of seven brothers who beat the hell out of each other; Jon, the "ordinary" middle child between two special-needs kids who himself shows signs of very disturbed behaviour; both with mothers so unhappy they'd tried to kill themselves, Ann before Robert was born, but Susan when Jon was there to see. It changes everything, reading this stuff. I wonder if the defence barristers have read it (almost certainly not: the social services, as is their right, will have kept it from them). If they have, they could argue that Robert's family made him violent (the child under the rod writing revenge in realms of death) and that he doesn't understand right from wrong. Or that Jon is such a strange, explosive child that at the time of his offence he wasn't responsible for his actions. But the Crown wouldn't let them get away with this. Objection, your honour – inadmissible evidence. Objection sustained. The law is arranged so that this knowledge, this Why, must be repressed. A child has died and become an icon. A nation's conscience must be appeased. The intricacies of responsibility are not at issue. The public mood is bleakly vengeful. The boys must be put away, and quick.

More tapes in court, on and on, no longer relevant, so it seems to me. I walk in broody anger around the streets. Anger at what, with whom? At the social services, for its hushing-up of vital evidence. With the court, ditto. With the police and prosecution, for so vehemently pursuing a murder conviction against two damaged and half-formed boys. With the defence, for not finding a loophole. With myself, for sitting in on a barbaric trial. The law is an ass, an arsehole. I've come to the Eileen Vizard view, that "childhood disorders" and "emotional conflicts, doubtless relating to home and school", brought Robert (and Jon) to kill. If so, it's arguably their parents who should be standing trial. George A. Dickinson, MD, Toronto, 1909, in his study *Your Boy*: "No child is a criminal; all are born mindless and ignorant. If a boy breaks the law he is not responsible; the parent, the guardian or the state is to blame."

And yet, and yet. It wasn't as if the parents hadn't tried, or hadn't their own childhoods to get over. Ann Thompson, beaten by her own father, a lorry driver. The second of three, the gobshite in the middle, she was his favourite for thrashings with an army belt. She came to fear him so much – her own beatings, her mother's beatings – she was still bedwetting at fifteen. If only she'd been cleverer, like her younger brother, who later ran a timber firm. But she was made to feel as thick as two short planks. She escaped by marrying Robert Thompson on her eighteenth birthday, a week after her last thrashing: frying-pan to fire. People joked that he looked like Peter Sutcliffe. He'd had a difficult childhood, too: very young when his father died, brought up strictly by his older brothers – dog-eats (or beats)-dog was the only family model he understood. For years, he and Ann ran a slaphappy ship, then right out of the blue he was gone. The humiliation: he left her for another woman, Barbara, an older woman (a grandmother, fifty-two to his thirty-four!), and a so-called family friend. The shock, too: Ann had been happy, she'd thought he was happy, they had some money at last, he'd bought a caravan, they liked to go camping, they'd got into the habit of going over to Southport for holidays, which was where they met Barbara. Then he was having an affair and was gone, leaving just a £5 note on the kitchen table. A cataclysm. Even the house burnt down, six days after his departure, and she and the boys had to move. Neighbours called her a lazy slag who couldn't be arsed to keep her children under control. But then neighbours often do say such things, and Ann was struggling to survive. There was the Welfare, but try keeping a large family on the Welfare. An old story: poverty, too many mouths to feed, too many feet to shoe. In earlier ages, parents in Ann's position would have quietly lost a son or two, "exposed" them. These days infanticide isn't an option – though infanticide, as it happened, was where the crisis led.

Ann, by these standards, can't be harshly judged. Nor Susan, whose childhood – her father one of four brothers – was no less shadowed by drinking, brawling men. Her mother was a part-time barmaid. Her father, a builder, played in a band at weekends – it could get a bit rough in the clubs. Susan left school at fifteen and, like Ann, married at eighteen: too young, she later felt; she'd expected too much. They had four years on their own, then Mark arrived, who never stopped screaming and drove her berserk. She'd nag Neil when he came home from work. Later he lost his job and couldn't find another. Later still, they separated. The marriage had been no fairytale for Sue but living on her own she found a night-mare: she felt lonely, a prisoner in her own house. Occasionally she bolted for an hour or so and left the kids alone – as a child, she'd been left alone at home, too. Given all this, and the stress of two special-needs kids, it was hardly surprising she suffered from depression. And came close to doing herself in. And sometimes turned violently on Jon.

No, I mustn't vilify Ann or Susan. They, too, felt beaten by life. Who are we to blame for what we are? Ourselves, our parents, their parents, genes, society, history, environment – not any one of these, though maybe a bit of all. How to attribute responsibility? Ann, Susan and Neil may have been less than perfect parents but they weren't murderers or abusers. Many adults are. Each week, the stories of babies abandoned – on doorsteps, in telephone boxes, on rubbish heaps. Each month, some new report on underage labour – of children slaving in mines, and fields, and sweat shops. Each day fresh cuttings from the stem of abuse. The age-old ambivalence of our care. Dandled, coddled, mangled, swad-dled, smothered, buggered, sexually abused. The cases in newspapers, or on social services files. The baby born addicted to heroin. The toddler who, when her stepfather threw her against it, so badly damaged the living-room wall (cracks, indents, leavings of blood and hair) he had to hide the evi-dence with Polyfilla. Parental neglect and cruelty: each day fresh cuttings. Think of the famous whose parenting was infamous. Byron, whose daughter Allegra died at the age of five in the Ravenna convent where, ignoring her mother's warnings, he'd dumped her a year before ("I do not know," he said after, "that I have any thing to reproach in my conduct"). Robert Graves, Lawrence Durrell, Rebecca West: plenty to reproach themselves for. Even Coleridge, who wrote so tenderly about his children. Even Rousseau, who entrusted his five children to a Foundling Hospital. The home lives of Jon and Robert look stable in comparison. Their parents failed, but so do most parents. I, too, have lashed out – have shouted and smacked and been unjust and set the wrong example. Here in the rainy streets, the memories come flooding back.

So much that can go wrong, so many mistakes to live (and die) with. The heart shrinks and my own negligence sings to me. I head for my room, to pick up the phone and dial home.

The night air glistens. I eat alone at an Italian restaurant not far from court: breadsticks, spaghetti carbonara, green salad, a bottle of chardonnay I don't expect to get through but do, easily. My fellow diners are three couples who seem to symbolize the three stages of relationships, rather like one of those Renaissance paintings of different-sized human figures on a bridge, the Ages of Man.

At the far end of the room, a couple who have met only recently. You can tell this because she is staring into his eyes to see how she looks in them. You can tell because he is holding her hand, feeling its contours, reading the lines (and between the lines) for what it will bring. They laugh and whisper a lot. He holds his dessert spoon in front of her, like a palm, and turns her upside down in it; he tips it over, convex, and rights her again. Everything is a secret joke. Anything could happen.

He doesn't know yet what she likes to eat: that she never chooses lasagne on account of being sick the one time she had it at Aunt Sarah's, that she usually plays safe and goes for pizza but sometimes – defiant, gloriously unguilty – plumps for veal. She doesn't know yet that he drinks rather a lot, used to anyway, not just with mates but in front of the telly, alone, and that he's making a special effort tonight: sharing this one bottle, as they do, is tough on him and a sign of how much he wants to impress her, even though, unobtrusively, by topping up her half-full glass and his empty one, he manages five glasses to her two. They are in love – in love with an idea of each other, and what love will make of them. She shows him her charm bracelet, and he puts it under the microscope of his loving attention, hanging on to each of her charms in turn. They lean across the wine and kiss, a little bridge of sighs. It will never be this perfect again.

Two tables from them, next to me, a slightly older pair, thirty, thirty-fiveish, in torment. She has an amber lozenge at her throat. He's saturnine in a charcoal suit. Is it his ring she's wearing? Why doesn't he wear one? Are they married, or lovers? Impossible to tell. No spooning or swooning here but a busy agony. She frowns, not drinking herself, when he orders another Stella. She forgives him when, at exactly the right moment, having put down her napkin, he offers her a tipped cigarette. The mood lightens as she smokes: I can hear her talking about star signs. But then the fag runs out, her voice drops, her eyes lower, there are tears in them now, and when he tries to rest his hand on her hand she snatches it free, like children do playing that pit-a-pat-pile game. I'd guess these two don't have children, though there is plenty else between them, enough of a history – eighteen months, eighteen years – for staying together to have become an issue.

Does he want to be with her? He had better decide if he does. It can't go on like this. He loves her: he tells her he loves her, not mouthing it soppily or as a sop over the candles, but just slipped in, as you do with someone you know as well he knows her, an everyday thing, what she needs to hear every day or she'd begin to doubt it. But her words back to him are that words are not enough. They cannot make things right.

Watching this, watching me watching this, watching everything else in the room – the pastas steaming from the kitchen, the soft sift of parmesan, the giant turbo pepper mill, the head waiter on guard – are the third couple, late-fifties, overweight, silent, resigned. They met and married aeons ago, wake up and go to bed together – two adjoining single divans actually, more comfortable, easier to get a good night on – every day. How could there be anything new between them? What is there they can share, in conversation, when everything in their life is shared, all they do, watch, eat, listen to, read? What they most share, it seems, is disappointment. This is what keeps them silent. She has her back to the wall, big-bosomed in green velvet, her weightless, still beautiful hands basketwoven in front of her. Top fly-button undone, he has half-turned his chair, not rudely away from her but benignly, to see what she sees, something they can turn back from and discuss. Not that they do. They have sat for half an hour over the ruins of their meal, and nothing has stirred, not even their coffee spoons. Having the measure of each other, they see no point in speaking for the sake of speaking, and nothing the one says can ever surprise the other. It is not that there is hate here, or coldness: they have passed beyond those, as also beyond infatuation, desire, doubt, frustration and rage. Once in a while, with friends, at anniversaries, too many drinks, something flickers in the limbo, something of how it was and what brought them together. Something flickers even now, as she slides from under the table: he is watching her bum as she walks to the Ladies, watching it as he watched it before she was his wife, watching it experimentally, with would-be objectivity, as a stranger might, trying it out for size. It is big, too big, no getting round it. But look who's talking (or not talking), him with all that flab, him who was a trim thirty, who used to think he was something. There was a woman at work once, over drinks, away on business, at the annual party, something like that, who by little more than a lift of the eye hinted that he was wasting himself, that she could look after him better than he seemed to be looked after at home. What was her name? All long ago now. He pats and strokes his stomach, like a teddy on a children's cartoon indicating hunger, though he is far from hungry, least of all for his big-bummed wife. Still, she is all he has and ever will have now. Here she comes, back from the Ladies, catching him looking, suddenly self-conscious, her hand flying to her hair.

And me, the miserable git *as if*ing in the corner, where do I fit in? How would I describe my state of mind? Happier than I used to be, though not tonight, at this trial, eating alone. Feeling both how unnatural marriage is – how unenterprising to stick with one person, dead below and above the waist – and how lost I'd be without it, without *her*, how little I'd like to be the person I'm playing at being tonight. Married, I love my inches of solitude. Single, I'd fear the acres. The guy in the corner, whom I envy less for his girl (though she's beautiful) than for being newly in love: how will he behave when the time comes, as it must, for him to choose? Too easy to say love allows no choice. He will have to commit, if only not to commit, and it will feel like a decision. He looks like the non-committal sort to me. But how many times can you start from scratch? How many women can you tell "I've never felt like this" before they stop believing it, before *you* stop believing it? When does *déjà vu* begin? When do you become cynical about yourself? When the nineteenth woman puts on your shirt after you've made love? When you've sat over the twenty-seventh naked breakfast of orange juice, croissants and coffee? When you've sent the fifty-sixth bouquet of white lilies? The hundredth Valentine, "from a secret admirer", in very un-secret writing? The rake's progress, the sinking reputation (from a hunk to a shit to a wanker), the darkening years. Bachelordom: it can look attractive sometimes, from the Blu-tac walls of a child-beleaguered home. But not from where I'm sitting tonight.

Is this the point of children? To avoid the awfulness of being on your own, whether alone or in a marriage? Because otherwise relationships would have nothing to hold them together? Are children less the fruit of love than a substitute for it? No, don't let me fall into that stuff, just because I'm here and feeling mawkish. I know several happy childless couples. And several couples with children who're praying for the day when they'll be childless again. Children as glue, keeping marriages going. It doesn't hold. It doesn't stand up. It stops standing up the minute they start standing up. You want them, or maybe you don't, but either way you get them without really knowing what you're getting, what it will mean, how much will change because of them, and how quickly they change from cartable-about dollies to people in their own right – and it's your job to get them safely through.

But it's not easy. The children you wanted to complete yourselves can make you feel broken, empty, sidelined. They get on your nerves. They cry and fight all the time. The pressures can drive you apart. The pressures can make you brutal.

The bright blade of hope turns dangerous when disappointed. Instilled with violence yourself, chances are you'll instil it in turn. The kids won't stop hitting each other. The only way to stop them is to hit them. The blows are handed down a generation, like silverware. Once beaten, twice a batterer – the cycle of hurt, the wheel of fire. Teachers, social workers, probation officers, prison warders try to put a spoke in it. But it isn't easy to stop. And if you don't see the damage, and what may come . . .

The old couple look across, curious, as if about to speak. Perhaps they've fantasized about me as I have about them. Seeing me flick through *The Language and Lore of Schoolchildren* (on page 372, along with *bobbing, fagging, jigging, jouking, lagging, mitching, plunking, skiving, ticking* and *twagging*, I find "*sagging*, definitely the prevailing term for truancy among delinquents in all parts of Liverpool"), they'll have taken me for a teacher. A teacher away from home in November: why? A job interview maybe, but surely for that I'd not be staying overnight. It could be I've a relation in hospital, but if so would I be tucking in so heartily? I wear a wedding ring, but what does that mean these days? And why am I writing? *What* am I writing? I don't mean to unnerve them, if that is what I'm doing. It's only doodles on my pad, an attempt to look occupied. If they want to talk, I wouldn't mind talking, to any of them, though the young pair at the end have eyes only for each other. Frankly, I would like to talk, though not frankly – the food we've eaten, holidays we've had, religion and politics, safe ground like that. A man can get lonely, at a murder trial. He can go a little mad.

It's late, and the couples leave in turn. Before the froth has settled on my cappuccino, the chef and head waiter disappear, leaving only the younger lad, who now stands by the cash register in his overcoat. I pay my bill. Scatterings of glass on the pavement, scatterings of light above. At the hotel, a brown envelope's been slid under the door and there's a message inside to ring "Andy". I don't know any Andys. In bed, bloated, I fall asleep at once and dream a dream I've often dreamt before. I'm lying beside my wife, and can feel her body, but now it's someone else's body as well, someone I shouldn't be in bed with. The *frisson* of the forbidden: I have to make love to this other woman while not waking my wife, which is difficult, since she occupies the same body. I am making love to two bodies at once, or one body in two different ways: a body to excite, a body to lull. My hands are on the other woman's breasts when they become my wife's breasts and I wake up, as always happens, except that tonight, today, there are no breasts because I'm in bed on my own.

I lie under the dull, constant streetlight, and drift back to sleep again. The images turn harder. I see my father raise his fist, wanting to teach me a lesson. I see the long teeth of Coster as he mouths through the bus window that he's going to kill me. I see myself, out of my skull with rage, smacking and whacking a bewildered child. The child's cries become a row Kathy and I are having, early on in our relationship, at my parents' old house. I've said the wrong thing, done the wrong thing, been inattentive. She hates it there – the room is damp and dusty, she'll be wheezing all night, the place is a madhouse, I promised James Herriott but have brought her to Wuthering Heights. We begin to argue, in whispers. She's had enough, she says, raising her voice. I clamp my hand over her mouth: what if my parents hear us? She unclamps herself: what if they do? She doesn't care, it's over between us, she's off. Her suitcase is open on the bed: the clothes inside it seem to crackle with static. Even the air in the room is electric with violence. We struggle with each other, moving towards the blow that might resolve this. She breaks free and pulls away, walks over to her suitcase and slams the lid down. There's an obstruction, a plastic bottle of suntan oil optimistically packed at the last moment. A loud crack as the lid comes down, and oil explodes on to the grey flock wallpaper. Shocked, silent, we stand and look. The wall is lightly tanned in the shape of a tree: scattered leaf patterns up high, dense foliage in the middle, the drip of a trunk on to the skirting board. Jesus, what a mess. Together again, for this, we work away with tissues, toilet paper, towels, water, the acidic antidote of after-shave. To no effect: the stain can't be removed. We sit on the bed, surveying the damage, then lie down and hold each other and begin to laugh and make love. Downstairs, chastened, we confess there's been a little accident, and offer to pay for new wallpaper. My parents won't hear of it. We sit and eat and drink and laugh together, and Kathy stays. The stain stays, too. There it is, each time we go back, in full bloom behind the bedside cabinet my mother has bought to conceal it: a spot of time, oil and troubled water, a memory of fractiousness.

The stain was papered over when the new owner redecorated the bedroom. Our explosions are gentler, since the children came. But something remains and reaches me here in the insomniac dawn: blows and cries and rows that shake a house, and the stains left on minds and memories.

10

Sex Marks

Infancy, fearless, lustful, happy! nestling for delight
In laps of pleasure . . .

WILLIAM BLAKE, "Visions of the Daughters of Albion"

It's early evening in the bedroom, a sweet breeze through the sash, the heat of honeysuckled July. Skirtless, jumperless, she lies on the floor (I lie her on the floor), her hair settling about her like a silky parachute. She turns away and laughs, stretching her left arm to a book behind her, just beyond reach, stretching further to slide it from the shelf. I unbuckle her shoes and pluck them in turn from each heel: they brush her soles as they pass, tickling, it seems, for she turns her head away from the book and giggles. The tights next. Tights on such a day! It must have been cold this morning when *that* decision was made. Practised, instinctive, not stirring from her page, she lifts her bum to let the seat of the tights pass under, and then I roll them down over her moly thighs and gleaming calves. The tights furl and thicken as they go, closing in on themselves then dropping from her ankles in a figure of eight. I hold her foot in my hand, and run a finger along its length, from the crispy heel, over the film of sweat beads on her arch (like the moist underside of canal bridges), to the caterpillar softness at the back of each toe. I wiggle my fingers, as if to tickle her, an incy-wincy spider, moving up from toe to neck, along the skin of air just above her actual skin. It drives her mad, most nights, but tonight she's too preoccupied to notice, absorbed in her book, maybe, or bored of me. How often in the past she's sat in my lap, drumming those legs against my legs, my face behind her neck, as she sings a jingle to me or I recount some well-worn narrative from my paltry canon. It can't last, I know, the way she hangs on to my words as I hang on to her, the transfixion, the big-eyed trust and reverence. It can't last, her sense of me as someone who can do no wrong, no wrong by her, anyway, which is all of me she knows. I want to savour it while I can: the luck, the idolatry, the responsibility it bestows.

The blouse now, penultimate: I unbutton it from the top, she still distracted in her book. It snags here and there where thread has loosened in the buttonholes, down down to the last button, which as it comes away brings with it the right side of her blouse, exposing her right nipple, shallow navel and the rosepink butterfly hovering on the waistband of her white pants. She sits up now, languorous from evening sun and carpet pile, still no words between us, though she's quietly humming to herself as I slip the right sleeve of her blouse off, then – but first she has to switch her book – peel the last of it away from her left. I expect her to stand now, so I can kneel in front of her (as is our custom) and slide her knickers over her knees and let her, step by step, walk free of them. But she's frolicsome on the shagpile and lies back again, waving her legs in the air as she dips back in her book and waits for me to do it all for her. Between finger and thumb, I take hold of the

waistband by her little hip-juts and pull the knickers off –
upwards, not downwards, for her legs are still pointing at the
ceiling. Finally naked now, she pedals her feet and skirls with
laughter, though whether at the book or at her nudity it's hard
to say. Here am I, kneeling at her feet. And there she lies, a
fizz of cream on the floor. I want to move her to the bed for
the rest of our nightly ritual, but no, she says, no, she's staying
as she is, digging into the pile, riveting her spine to the floor,
leaving me impatient but marvelling at her body – tilty nose,
avalanche of hair, pale nipples, soft stomach, candid slit – and
pondering my part in it. I think of tickling and pinching her to
transcendent helplessness. I think of hoisting her on top of
me, to ride and jockey me, another of our games. I think of
lifting her by the feet and dangling her upside down, like
those abandoned children in medieval paintings, tied by the
ankles from the branches of trees to save them from wild animals. But her languor wins me over: all right, she can have it
her way. I lift the pillow on her bed and from under it her
nightie, which I carry to where she lies, a dairy squiggle, on
the floor.

Time's running out. I hear a shout from below:

"Ready yet?"

"Nearly," I call.

"Shall I come up and do her?"

"No, it's OK, my turn, I'll do her."

Then, quieter, just to her, I say:

"Story now?"

At once she's on her feet, arms raised as the nightie col-
lapses over her head, washing herself at the basin with her
green hippo sponge, taking from me the yellow toothbrush
with its twirl of Macleans Milkteeth, hopping as she does. A
gleamy, gappy grin, a last little spit-out of pink and then she

hurls herself in the gap between the pillows and the duvet, the runkled hollow where half her life is spent. I serve her with a kiss. I stare down into the lair of her infancy. I stand and wait as my wife comes in with *Alice in Wonderland* and the milk.

Is a father allowed to miss his children *physically*? Should I feel guilty that I do? Tactility, skin-joy. A baby's hand around my little finger. The silver seal of a milk-blister on an upper lip – a suck-bruise, a transparent chancre. The rolling Rubens thighs, and yet the navel so flat, neither inkwell nor fluffpool. The legs so pliable that babies can suck their own ankles. The pink implosion of a birthmark. The snake-flick of a tongue. The downy downs of shoulder, back and bum. The damp patch on my cotton T-shirt where a mouth's been nuzzling at my heart. Or whiter, frothier tide-marks – the sick-up from a drained breast. Unbroken threads and plumb-lines of drool. Those reflex smiles and whimperings in sleep, exactly as you see in dreaming dogs. Banana goo darkening in a dish with Peter Rabbits around.

The economy of language when they're babies – no wasted words, no words at all, just these hums and purrs and back-of-the-throat pleasure-sounds. Your own inarticulacy, matching theirs – the silly names you use, no matter what you've called them: babby, bubby, bubsy, gubsy, gubs. Their untroubled brows, like a *tabula rasa*. The puggy plughole of a nostril, struggling to take it all in. The whorled, Danish pastry of an ear, the stretched skin above the lobe so paper-thin the sun shines through. The black eyes you can see yourself come and go in. For six months even their shit smells beautiful – soft fudge and caramel.

A child in my lap, being read to, and I find myself erect.

Love of children. It's not supposed to be to do with sex. It isn't to do with sex. I have no desire to have sex with my child, with any child, but this feeling is something like desire. It would horrify me for this child to touch my erection, or even know I had one, yet it is there. Love of children. No mother would have to defend herself. For fathers it's more difficult. No one trusts a man now, with small kids. The anger I felt, when that woman in the babysitting circle explained with some embarrassment she could not let me sit for her, nothing personal I must understand, but she would not leave her three girls in the custody of a male. No point being angry. We're liabilities. Too many other men have queered the pitch. And how to explain that erection, if you had to? Not desire but love's ecstasy, suffusion, bliss, warmth in your lap, the rub of a little bottom on a prick. A child makes you feel alive, yourself a child. Newness amid so much age and death.

And yet their life eats into yours, takes it away. New-born, they bring you closer to mortality. Their cries are like little ropes, tying you down – Gulliver among the Lilliputians. Children: a vexation to our youth, what's left of it, and no comfort to old age. That great need for them to sleep – for their own good, for ours, too, whose dream is to rest in peace. All those opiates – poppy syrup, Quietness, Mother Siegel's Soothing Syrup, Calpol – to get them off and out of the way. All that cradle-rocking, the gentle push of exasperation. All those fantasies of their death, in songs and paintings: "The sleeping and the dead/Are but as pictures." No child is more perfect than when silent as the grave.

Another memory, from a holiday in North Wales: moon, midnight, the knife-beam of the lighthouse. She has been crying for two hours, inconsolably, from an angry red mouth. I've walked up and down and back and forth with her, feeling the anger rising in me too. But now she's silent at last, rocked asleep on my shoulder, her body against my chest, my right hand cupping the back of her head, my left arm tucked beneath her bum. Slowly, still rocking, I move towards the object of desire. A barred chamber of rest, the cot glows under its night-light like a prison camp. I bend my knees, so that I'm poised above it, old crookback, victim of the ricks. Feeling muscles in my back I didn't know were there, I lower myself further. The white sheet shines from the compound. She stirs, my prisoner stirs. She is now *inside* the cot, but poised nine inches above the mattress, at arm's length, suspended in flight. Slowly, slowly I pilot her to the sheet, and she's down now, a landing so soft the passengers are cheering in my head. One of my hands is still trapped beneath her, the other pressed sooth-ingly above. Rocking with my knee against the bars, I have to slide the lower hand free without disturbing her and before I withdraw the upper hand I slide a cotton duvet over and up to her chin. I raise myself to upright, the pain in my back mak-ing me catch my breath (shhhh). Gently, silently, I walk backwards from the room, remembering to miss the creaky board. Once I'm in the hall, I leap two feet and punch the air. I feel a touch of contempt for her now – that she hadn't seen through my little trick. But my triumph is short-lived. Two minutes later I hear the cries. Livid, with clenched fists, I go back into the room, ready to kill her.

I don't, of course, but not for the first time it strikes me that the term employed for getting babies into their cots and asleep – "putting them down" – is also what we call the mercy killing of sick or injured animals. The need for silence and an end to pain. Most people with children understand that momentary desire. What tiredness can make you do, or think of doing, the taboos it removes, shouldn't be underestimated.

Family life is mostly banality in front of the telly. But loving your children and hurting them, dreading them dying and wanting them never to stir: all that is there, too.

Sexual abuse as the young Rousseau experienced it, 1731: "One of the two cut-throats who called themselves Moors took a fancy to me . . . Frightened though I naturally was by his dusky face, which was beautified by a long scar, and by his passionate glances, which seemed to me more savage than affectionate, I put up with his kisses, saying to myself 'The poor man has conceived a warm friendship for me; it would be wrong to repulse him.' But he passed by degrees to more unseemly conduct, and sometimes made me such strange suggestions that I thought he was wrong in the head. One night he wanted to share my bed, but I objected on the plea that it was too narrow. He then pressed me to come into his. I still refused, however, for the poor devil was so dirty and smelt so strongly of the tobacco he chewed that he made me feel ill.

"Next day, very early in the morning, we were alone together in the assembly-hall. He resumed his caresses, but with such violence that I was frightened. Finally he tried to work up to the most revolting liberties and, by guiding my hand, to make me take the same liberties with him. I broke wildly away with a cry and leaped backwards, but without displaying indignation or anger, for I had not the slightest idea what it was all about . . . As he gave up the struggle I saw something whitish and sticky shoot towards the fireplace and fall on the ground. My stomach turned over, and I rushed on to the balcony, more upset, more troubled and more frightened as well, than ever I had been in my life."

*

A rimy morning, tapes again, and I'm listening to DC Phil Roberts trying to prise something out of the suspect. Robert v Roberts, and as usual the boy is getting the better of the man, stonewalling, fending off, sticking to his song. He's told the police more than enough for them to charge him. He's told them all he's ever going to tell them. But they don't know this. There are aspects to the murder that baffle them still. There's the hope he'll enlighten them. They press on.

Since the fifth interview, they've been nagging away at something that seems almost irrelevant: batteries.

Q: Did either of you take some batteries?
A: No.
Q: Are you sure about that?
A: Yeah.
Q: Can I just point out something for a moment? You went all red in the face there . . .
A: I never took anything . . .
Q: And I could see you went a bit of a colour of embarrassment, do you understand what I mean?
A: No.
Q: You went a bit red in the face as if you knew something about it.
A: Yeah, well I'm hot . . .
Q: Do you understand what I mean when somebody gets embarrassed about something . . .?
A: Yeah, but I never took no batteries. [Crying]
Q: I'm terrible.

Phil Roberts is terrible? Feels terrible? Finds the sound of Robert's distress terrible? The two police officers try to calm the boy down. They get him to admit that Jon might have taken the batteries, that he knows the shop in the Strand where batteries are sold, "like red ones and Duracell", and maybe Jon stuck some in his pocket. But he's getting very upset. The interview is terminated after a mere seven minutes, the shortest by far, with only one subject: batteries.

Batteries were found by James Bulger's body. They matter as circumstantial evidence, like the splashes of Humbrol paint, the boot marks on the cheek, the blood on Robert's shoes. But the batteries preoccupy the police far more than these other clues. Robert, too, perhaps: only about the batteries, they say, has he blushed. Red cheeks, the shade of culpability. But culpability for what? Kids of ten play with batteries every day. The day before the murder Jon and Robert had been using them at school, in an electrical circuit to light a bulb. It was during this experiment that Jon became so difficult the teacher told him to go sit on the floor, and later, as a punishment, moved his desk to the back of the class. (He knew he'd be made to sit there the following day: no doubt it was another reason for bunking off.) Batteries are all part of the story, then. But what's the big deal about them?

Interview six, two hours later. Robert's been wanting to say something.

A: You know you said you found batteries.
Q: Yeah.
A: Well, Jon might have took them for his Game Gear.

Discussion follows about the kind of batteries used in Game Gear, which weren't the sort found near the body, and there's a ploy to confuse Robert with technical details then hit him with a quick one. It doesn't work.

Q: So how did Jon get them?

A: I don't know. I only said he might. He might have took them and they've fell out of his pocket.

Q: What, on the railway line?

A: Wherever you found them.

Q: Well, I tell you that we did find them on the railway line, but that they were scattered . . . not all in the same place . . .

A: Yeah, well they might have been in, like, ones, mightn't they.

It drifts on. The two policemen suggest to Robert he's not levelling with them. He lied about the paint earlier. He's doing the same again.

Q: Bobby, I want the truth, you know. I like the truth . . .

A: Yeah, but other people might have put them in there, mightn't they . . .

Q: I think they were put there by somebody . . . We know things we won't be telling you, do you understand that?

A: Yeah.

Q: We know some things that have gone on that we won't tell you because we want to find out if you're telling us the truth. It's like testing you to see if you're telling the truth, do you understand that?

A: Yeah.

Q: If you tell us lies about little things then there's a chance you might be telling us lies about big things, isn't there . . .?

A: What's a big thing?

Good question. What's a big thing? What's the big thing here? The batteries by the body? Or the batteries in the body? "Yeah, but other people might have put them *in* there, mightn't they?" *In*? Why *in*? The police haven't said anything about *in*. A slip of the tongue or a confession? Maybe the batteries were put in James as he was lying and dying there. Maybe the boys had some weird idea – from the lesson in school the day before, or from watching Chucky Doll in *Child's Play 3* – that with batteries inside him James might come back to life. Inside him where exactly? In his mouth, which was badly damaged. But how would batteries pull away a bottom lip? If not his mouth, it must have been his anus. That's why the police are so interested. That's where they think the batteries were shoved.

I look through the biologist's report: "The following items have been examined for the presence of semen: Anal swab, rectal swab, swab drainage from nose and mouth, swab from teeth and cheeks, swab from buttocks, swab from anorak, tracksuit top, T-shirt and vest. No semen has been found on any of these items. The penile swab has been examined for saliva; none has been found." I look through the pathologist's report. "The foreskin appeared abnormal and had been partly retracted" and "dissection of the pelvis shows a small area of haemorrhage approximately a quarter inch across in the anterior midline, anterior to the rectum, behind the pubis." Then again "detailed examination of the rectum after removal shows no tearing and no evidence of bruising." A pathologist wouldn't lie under oath. So it seems no batteries were found *in* there (bloodstains were found on one battery, but no excrement), and no batteries were inserted forcefully enough to cause a tear. Yet Albert Kirby had told his men, as he later told social services, that he suspected the batteries were "introduced".

Sex abuse had been on Kirby's mind since James went missing, his abductor presumed to be an adult male. Abuse was still on Kirby's mind, even when two ten-year-olds became the suspects. And the chief evidence was this set of batteries.

The police come back to the batteries in interview seven, in the middle of Robert describing Jon's attack on James: a battery, he says, was thrown in James's face. Again, in the next interview, they steer him back to the batteries. This time their purpose is more blatant. They start to ask Robert about the removal of James's clothes:

Q: Now I'm going to tell you a lot of things now . . . You see, when we find James's body, the bottom, the trousers, everything are off, his shoes are off and his underpants are off. Can you tell me why that is?
A: No.
Q: You can't. Did you start playing with him?
A: With who?
Q: With James's bottom.
A: No.
Q: Are you sure?
A: Yeah, I'm not a pervert, you know.

Robert gets a break from this line of questioning in the next interview. But in the tenth, by which time the police are looking less for incriminating evidence (they have all they need of that) than for motives, they tell him Jon's been confessing things:

Q: Jon has said . . .
A: Most probably that I've took everything off him and I've been playing with him.

Q: How do you know that?
A: Cos I know he's going to say that.
Q: Playing with what?
A: The privates, that's what you said before.

Robert denies touching James, except to lay his body down on the rail. Events move on to the video shop, and the incident with Mrs Venables, and the dirty marks – a scratch, coal dust, mud – on his face:

A: What do you mean, dirty marks?
Q: You know what dirty marks are, don't you?
A: Like sex marks.
Q: Like what?
A: Sex marks, dirty.
Q: Sex marks?
A: Like dirty words . . .
Q: Did you play with his bottom?
A: No, I never.
Q: OK. Did you play with his, erm, penis?
A: No.

It's as far as they get. It's as far as we get. In court we don't even get this far: the prosecution decide not to play either this interview or the concluding one, recorded during a drive along the murder route. I have to rely on a transcript instead. I sit up late with it in the hotel bedroom, falling asleep over the Qs and As.

Graham, a friend who works with sex offenders, has sent me his little book, *Unspeakable Crimes*. I wake early and begin it sceptically, unable to ignore the comedy of its social work-erese: "Very little masturbatory reconditioning was undertaken. The core team saw it as a necessary component, but one which may be better facilitated through individual work rather than the group. Unfortunately there were insufficient resources and experience to follow this aspect through." Jargon aside, it's an interesting book, more rewarding than most of the novels I've read lately. His offenders, Mr B and Mr K and Mr S and so on, are mostly married with children – often stepchildren, a particular target for molestation. A list of abusers' excuses is printed, from the predictable "She liked it" and "Someone had to teach her about it" to "He was too young to understand". There is both "It was OK, because she/he was my son/daughter", and "It was OK, because she/he was *not* my son/daughter", proving that you can justify anything to yourself if you want to do it badly enough.

The book quotes specialist Ray Wyre as saying that there's no such thing as a first-time sex offender: by the time he (almost always he) first offends, he will have done it many times in the imagination; and by the time he's been caught, he may have done it many more in reality. I'm also interested to learn that there's a machine called a penile plethysmograph used in the testing of sex offenders, which measures the size of the penis when introduced to different stimuli, some of them "inappropriate". Predictable results: paedophiles show more arousal to children. But it seems the penile plethysmograph isn't infallible: like the polygraph, the lie-detector, it can be outwitted. I'm not sure how many penises are capable of out-witting anything, except their owners. But I do wonder about this matter of appropriateness, in relation to erections: is getting a hard-on from strangers more appropriate than from friends or office colleagues; is fancying royalty appropriate, or one's teachers (or students), or buxom peroxide blondes in suspenders? Arousal can be a lowering business.

I'm about to put the book down when I notice the "norms and values continuum", printed as an appendix, asking you to consider what's normal or acceptable family practice:

– Seven-year-old daughter likes to give a father a wet kiss.
– Father pushes flannel into his four-year-old's vagina to wash her properly.
– Father still wipes bottom of his four-year-old.
– Father watches blue movies.
– Father avoids cuddling daughter when she reaches puberty.
– Thirteen-year-old gets into bed with parents when unable to sleep.
– Father masturbates when wife and children are in bed asleep.
– Father has sex with thirteen-year-old daughter and tells her this is their special secret.
– Mother and father walk around house with no clothes on.
– Father has erection when cuddling his two-year-old.

All children grow up thinking their families normal. Most parents reassure them they're right. But what is normal? Families operate *in camera*. It's hard to know what happens behind closed doors.

Over at Lower Lane, Jon isn't pushed as hard about the batteries as Robert. Partly it's that he takes much longer to admit to abducting James, and there are fewer interviews about the

railway line. It's towards the end of the tapes before the touching is touched on:

Q: When you dragged him across the track, did any of
   his clothes come loose?
A: Yeah, he [Robert], he's pulled his pants off and that.
Q: When did he do that?
A: At the end, when he was knocked out.
Q: What happened to his shoes?
A: Er, I pulled them off...
Q: Why did you pull his shoes off?
A: I don't know why I pulled his shoes off. I keep forget-
   ting. It was last week.
Q: Just try and imagine why.
A: I don't know, just mad . . . just something to do.
Q: So you pulled his pants off.
A: I never. Robert did.
Q: Sorry, I meant that collectively . . . What else gets
   done?
A: Nothing. Just he picked his underpants up again and
   put them on his face and then threw them back again
   where there was all blood on.
Q: So the pants came off after the iron bar had been
   thrown?
A: Yeah.
Q: Why do you think Robert put his underpants on his
   face?
A: I don't know. To cover it, I think . . . I wasn't looking.
   I was crying.

Jon is crying at this point of the interview, too, and it's terminated. But in the next, and last, the police begin with the

suggestion that Jon has missed out "something important" that happened on the railway.

Q: Didn't you push him and didn't you kick him while you were up at the line?
A: No, Robert did.
Q: Did he? Where?
A: Underneath.
Q: Where's underneath?
A: There.
Q: Right, you're pointing between your legs . . . Let's see what you call it.
A: Willy.

They work round to the batteries.

Q: Think. Think what happened with those batteries.
A: I don't know.
Q: We need to know why they are there.
A: I don't know. I never put them there. [Crying]
Q: Tell us what Robert did with them.
A: He threw them at him.
Q: No, it was a little bit more than throwing them. Now tell us what happened to the batteries and it's all over and done with then.
A: I don't know. I don't know, Dad. [Crying]
Q: You're getting upset for a reason, aren't you?
A: I would even though tell you though what happened to them. [Sic. Still crying]
Q: You know you said he kicked him in his willy?
A: Yeah.
Q: Did he do anything else to his willy?

A: Well, I don't know.

Q: Try and think.

A: I don't [crying], I don't know. [Throws a tantrum]

Q: Hey, hey.

A: I don't know.

Q: Don't go to punch your dad.

A: My dad thinks I know and I don't and you're saying I do and I don't . . . I don't know anything else. I've told you all I know . . . I want me mum.

Jon, said his teachers, had the ability to "turn tears on". You'd have to be a genius of tears to know whether Jon is genuinely bewildered here or suppressing something which he thinks more shaming than murder. A psychiatrist could take an educated guess, but in her report on him, for the Crown, Susan Bailey doesn't allude to sexual abuse. Eileen Vizard does, with Robert Thompson, but he won't play the game even when he's made to play, with dolls.

"Dr Vizard asked at what stage clothes from James's lower body had been removed. Bobby said that Jon had done this while James was lying face upwards on the railway track and that Jon had placed the 'under layer' (i.e. the underclothes) on James's mouth. However, when Dr Vizard asked for this to be demonstrated, it soon became clear that the doll's head was dislodged from its position of restraint by the bricks, as soon as the lower part of the doll's body was moved up and down to remove close-fitting undergarments. In other words, it was difficult to see how the child's pants could have been removed at this point without partially pulling the body off the track and away from the bricks . . .

"Dr Vizard asked Bobby if either he or Jon had touched or interfered with James's genitals at any time. Looking away,

Bobby said 'no', sounding defensive and angry . . . Dr Vizard wondered whether it had been the intention of either boy, Jon or Bobby, to sexually abuse the little boy and whether this all went badly wrong (perhaps the child resisted) with the result that Jon and Bobby became angry and tried to silence him. Bobby listened to this suggestion, head down, playing with some toy animals, and seemed unsurprised or unmoved by the idea that there might have been a sexual motive. Looking up directly at Dr Vizard, Bobby said angrily 'I didn't touch him'."

"Unsurprised or unmoved"? Implying that Ms Vizard's notion of a sexual motive in the killing was close to the truth? That she was so obviously right that he didn't bother to protest? There's a duller possibility, that Robert is bored to death with this line of speculation – had it from the police, has since had it from others, thinks it typically adult and off the point: he's not a pervert. Maybe James was stripped for the same reason that the paint was thrown: to be humiliated, to be robbed of dignity and made easier to kill. Or, since Jon and Robert were cunning enough to place the body across the tracks, in order to suggest James had been run over by a train, might they also have calculatedly removed his clothes, to suggest he was the victim of an adult molester? No knowing. But that red face of Robert's (the sex mark of his blush), Jon's hysteria, the yanked-off trousers, the retracted foreskin: all suggest sex abuse is involved.

Over lunch – pizza and frascati – I ask two of the defence lawyers about it. "When we met at the start," they say, "the prosecution was pretty clear with us: 'Those batteries – just don't ask'." But, I persist, didn't the pathologist's report state there was no tear to the anus? Yes, but it's possible, with all the injuries, the tear was missed. There'd been rumours of a second report, even a photo, showing the tear. The problem was the defence couldn't carry out a full post-mortem. There was pressure to allow James Bulger's funeral to go ahead, and time only for a quick confirmation of the Crown pathologist's findings. Besides, if there was clinching evidence that James had been sexually molested, what good would that do T & V? Despised enough already, they'd be dead in the water. There are the Bulgers to think of, too. Ralph, when first told they'd found the body, suspecting an adult killer, asked: "What have they done to him? Has anybody had him?" Albert Kirby is underplaying the abuse because he likes the Bulgers, considers them "a model family" and wants to spare them the worst. There's an understanding on all sides: go easy – the case is bad enough without fondled willies and batteries up the bum.

I talk to the pathologist, Alan Williams. He's indignant. Cock-up? The post-mortem was carried out carefully and properly. Cover-up? He can restate categorically, and does, that "there was no injury to James Bulger's rectum or anal canal". But he also admits that with buggery, or similar brute insertion, bruising around the anus isn't inevitable. There was no physical evidence of abuse, but he can't rule it out.

I try to think it through. Jon and/or Robert stripped James and played with him, before or after the attack. Where did the idea come from? Had someone done something similar to one of them? If so, who? A parent, sibling, relative, babysitter, older kid? Witnesses said Robert had a habit of pulling up girls' skirts, and once cheeked the man at the fish and chip shop by shouting that his wife had "fishy knickers". His understanding of the word "pervert" was precocious. Did he have an early introduction to sex? One of his brothers was questioned by police for allegedly molesting two small children (there was a later incident, too, a girl in a telephone box and a youth who'd exposed himself). Eighty per cent of abusers have themselves been abused. It works like a chain letter. As a kid you're powerless to stop it, though it may be other kids who start you on it, not, as in Rousseau's case, a knowing adult. Another Jean-Jacques – Jean-Jacques Bouchard: "He was scarcely eight years old when he started to clamber up on little girls . . . Instead of sticking little sticks up their rectums, as children do, pretending to give each other enemas, he lustily screwed them without knowing what he was doing." The question is whether Robert and Jon knew what they were doing when playing with James. It could have been instinctive, natural. It could have been something they were copying – from what Robert had been taught at home, or what Jon had learned watching his Dad's occasional dirty videos. It could have been that a sexual motive on Robert's part lay behind the abduction – and that a violent loss of temper from Jon turned it into something else. There's no telling. But no getting around it. Sex abuse seems to be part of the case.

Is sex abuse part of most people's cases? Is it part of mine? Not that my parents abused me, not that other adults did, either, until an assistant librarian at university made a grab for my balls as I passed him in the stacks near Romanticism (I passed him a second time in case I'd imagined it; I hadn't). An unabused childhood: we were warned of strange men with sweets, whose cars we were not to get into, but none came my way. So we abused each other instead. "Sexually explored each other". Played Doctors and Nurses.

Whose idea was it? His and hers and mine and yours and theirs. Who suggested it first? It could have been any of us. It could have been all of us. It was like deciding who moved the glass on the ouija board. "Mummies and Daddies" was another name, but for my sister and me, our parents being doctors, that came to the same thing. We played it with friends. Keeping it in the family, we played it with our cousins. Most incestuous of all, we played it by ourselves. "Oh, please let us," we pleaded with our parents, "we won't make any noise. We won't make any mess." Not knowing what went on, or knowing but believing it educational, they lent us the necessary equipment: plastic medicine spoons, swabs, cotton wool, bandages, a metal kidney dish, safety pins, a stethoscope, a flick-open metal blood-pressure box, syringes with the needles removed, a thermometer in a silver case like a propelling pencil. Not necessary, really: you could play without props. The main point was taking your clothes off.

To be a doctor you had to be a boy, put a stethoscope around your neck, sit down at the table beside the bed, pretend to be writing a prescription, and ask "What seems to be the matter?" To be a nurse you had to be a girl, fetch patients for doctor, hand him his knives and scalpels, and change bandages. To be a patient you had to lie down, open your mouth, say aaah, breathe deeply, sit up, breathe deeply, undo your zip, pull your pants or skirt down, breathe deeply, take the rest of your clothes off, please, the knickers and vest, lie down again, breathe deeply, keep still while we just check your body over, stop wriggling please, the stethoscope may be cold, the thermometer may tickle, but how do you expect to get better if you wriggle about like that, breathe deeply, lift your arm, lift the other arm, your left leg, your right leg, could you spread your legs a little, breathe deeply, a little wider with the legs please, wider and lift a bit, ah nurse, I think we have located the problem, it will be necessary to do some probing about here, a wooden scalpel, please, and then – this may hurt a bit – the injection, a few moments and you'll be feeling better, is that better, better now, good, take this prescription, these pills, and come back and visit me in a month.

This was Doctors and Nurses. The rules were very simple, and everywhere the same. Once a friend called Emma came and played Doctors and Nurses with me in the stables, just the two of us. It was hot and prickly with the straw and I'd forgotten what girls looked like. It was funny how I did always forget and need to see again, even though each time when I saw I thought: Now I know, that'll do me. Showing yourself wasn't wrong at Emma's age (five was she? six?) when you didn't know what it was for. But I was ten now (or eleven, was it? twelve?) and sensed there was something illicit about it, and knowing this when Emma didn't know but *still making her do it* felt (or afterwards felt) wrong.

There had been another incident, Irving's idea, not mine. We'd made this deal with my sister Gillian: she could have a sherbet fountain if she and Christine Rawlinson came into her bedroom and undressed. Irving and I would be hiding under the beds but we'd not say anything and Christine would never know. Gillian wasn't keen: it took the sherbet fountain we had *and* the promise of a Mars bar. We lay in the dust with the bedspread hanging down, where things had slipped down from behind the pillow, pencils, dolls' clothes, a glass rabbit, a book of pony stories, a shiny-brown pheasant's tail-feather. The girls came in and Gill said, How about being dancers, and they got down to their knickers and vests. We saw this through the purple tassels of the bedspread, where we were trying to keep still but had to shuffle a bit so both of us had a view. We didn't think Christine would take the rest off but, no arguing, she did. They were doing high scissor kicks and I could see the scissor snip between their legs. That's how it looked there, on girls, like they were dresses or curtain material or something and their mums or someone had laid them on the table and started cutting them upwards, just the snippy slit left where the design started before they changed their mind. Irving and I were snorting by then, with dust and the giggling out of hand, and the girls stooped and lifted the bedspread and we crawled out. They got back in their knickers and said it wasn't fair, that we must do the same, show them our willies. No chance, I said, we're off now, but Irving thought we ought to, fair's fair, just for a tick, not as long as they'd done, but so they could see, three seconds, that was our final offer. OK, so we dropped our shorts and then our white underpants and our things stuck up at the same angle, the angle of the pole outside the barber's. Could they touch them for a moment, they asked, just to feel what they felt like? No. Please. Well, all right.

Doctors and Nurses, surrogate sex before we knew what sex was. Only Auntie Sheila seemed suspicious:

"Again? You're always playing that."

"Oh, please."

"Where's the harm Sheila, love?" my father said, "it's natural at their age."

"I know what they do, that's all."

"Of course that's what they do. But it could be worse, love: it'll be Postman's Knock in a year or two, snogging in cupboards."

"Please."

"All right. But not too much taking clothes off."

That day we took Gillian's clothes off once, and Edgar's twice, and Jean's (she being the youngest) three times. We were getting bored when Auntie Sheila called "Is there a doctor in the house?" and in she walked without knocking. We were not used to grown-ups in the surgery, and it was a bit of a mess with the wooden tongue-prodder things scattered everywhere and a roll of bandage which we'd used to tie Gillian to the chair with, and Jean naked on her back on the bed starfishing with her arms and legs, and Edgar pumping himself up with the blood pressure gauge, and Robert and me inside the pillowcase fighting to be first with our heads through. Auntie Sheila looked slitty-eyed cross, and said she would speak to my father. I was afraid. Maybe we'd gone too far – like the time I lost the cricket ball at Uncle Gordon's caravan and hacked his gorse bush to bits trying to find it. There was a right way to behave, and most kids knew it, but sometimes you got carried away and could forget.

Anxious, we tidied up extra carefully, then ran out to play tennis on the back lawn, over a strawberry net strung between two poles. The ball pocked back and forth till a smash into the ground sent it flying over the wall, into next door's garden. I was the one dispatched to fetch it – I didn't mind, since my father was due home any minute, and I feared what would happen when he arrived. Next door was the Bearparks. I climbed over. There were peas held up by string between canes with tin bits dangling, and broad beans in old men's furry pockets, and red stick-up stalks of rhubarb under leaves as big as trees. I couldn't find the missing ball, but I found another, black and skinless, which must have bounced out of someone else's game years before, during the war maybe, and had lain here hidden for someone to rescue it, blacker and skinnier each year. I held it, yukky, in my hand. There was a loose thread on the rind, and I unplucked it, so that the ball dangled like a shrunken head. I dithered among the rhubarb leaves, afraid what trouble might be waiting back on my side of the wall.

There can't have been much trouble, because we continued playing Doctors and Nurses for some years after. How many years? Till I was eleven, twelve, thirteen? Did that, does that, make me an abuser? Of my sister, as well as cousins and friends? Ugly to admit to myself, hard to face, like so much in this trial. Merely to touch a boy's penis, or girl's vagina, is not abuse, or wasn't once thought so, even when adults are doing the touching: those mothers and nannies who used to stroke their babies' sexual parts (still do) to soothe them off to sleep. And aren't children naturally immodest, before they're anything else? Which means when they abuse each other, it's consensual, not a matter for censure. All the same . . . It's hard to know what innocence is, and what's left of it when consciousness enters, and if shame is a condition only of being adult. Doctors and Nurses: it was a harmless game, and it was not.

I think of Robert and Jon stripping James and wonder where murder came in, whether it followed as night does day or was unrelated, something else. Did they do it for themselves, because they wanted to – "just mad . . . something to do"? Or is there an adult further back who taught them this? If so, he – yes, he, it's bound to be – can't be sleeping too well. He must feel, as I do now, a little grubby, a little defiled. He must be waiting for the knock on the door.

A gust of rain and grit blows against the theft-proof, fire-proof, smash-proof window. I'm stuck again in my hotel room, trying to attribute responsibility – what adults do to children; what children do to children; what these children did, and what was done to them, and how much they understood of what went on. Passing judgement in court looks easy in comparison. Judging this is like trying to catch the wind in your hands, or to iron out the creases from the sea.

11

No Defence

A prison wall was round us both,
Two outcast men we were:
The world had thrust us from its heart,
And God from out his care:
And the iron gin that waits for Sin
Had caught us in its snare.

OSCAR WILDE, "The Ballad of Reading Gaol"

Q: Are you saying you weren't there?
A: No.
Q: So what are you saying?
A: I was there but I didn't do anything.
Q: You're denying taking part in the crime?
A: Yes.
Q: But we have witnesses who saw you.
A: Saw me what?
Q: We're not saying. That's for you to tell us.
A: Well, they're lying. Were they in there with me?
   They can't know.
Q: So what is your version of events?
A: I admit I was there. I confess I saw certain incidents
   take place. But it wasn't me.
Q: You didn't touch the victim at all?
A: I touched the victim – but I didn't do that.

Q: What did you do?

A: I went in the broom cupboard with her, that's all.

Q: She says you had sex with her.

A: I didn't – I only kissed, touched . . .

Q: Why are you crying then?

A: Because you think I'm guilty but I'm not.

Q: We don't know. We just want to find out. Now are you going to start telling us what happened?

I wake in my cell in a sweat. It was inevitable, sooner or later, that I'd dream like this. I've been telling myself I wouldn't, that the case isn't getting to me, that I'm all right, a pragmatist, unterrorized by *as if*s. But it's a lie. Since the tapes especially, I do have dreams. I dream I'm sleeping on the courtroom steps. I dream I'm Jon Venables's psychiatrist and make a breakthrough when he tells me: "I've made friends with a magic carrot. It can bring dead babies back to life." I dream of a board game, with two or more players, counters, a dice, two piles of cards (Chance and Community Watch), and the object is to get to the Railway (the Finish), without being intercepted by the policeman with the pointing finger: "Go to Jail".

This dream is different, though. This isn't waking and remembering vaguely something bad from the day before. This is waking and remembering exactly the bad thing, even though it happened a quarter of a century ago. Yesterday must have triggered it, and guilt I'd long forgotten. Dust, mice, mothballs, furniture polish, semen, bleach.

It's 1967, and Lucy Kerrigan's parents have gone out for the night – Dusty Springfield is at the Mecca in Burnley, and they're not due back till 11.30. Someone's parents going out for the night is an excuse for a party, and Lucy has something to celebrate, her fourteenth birthday. It's no one's fault that parties like this turn out as they do. The parents depart imagining ten girls, no boys, orangeade, fish paste sandwiches, "nice" music on the tinny record player in the walnut cabinet with sliding glass doors, maybe some teeny game like blindman's buff or apple-bobbing. The reality will be the Rolling Stones, stained carpets, underage sex and fights. Two dozen boys will gatecrash, drink brown ale and get silly. The girls will be less silly, except about boys. You never know exactly what trouble to expect from these parties, only trouble of some kind. That's why you go. And why, if you've any sense, you never hold a party yourself.

Lucy opens the door of her Barnoldswick house, and noise pours over her shoulder. In her short skirt and flowery blouse she seems heady with fear and elation: so many people in her little house, so many guests for her fourteenth birthday, so many friends she didn't know she had. We fight our way to the bottles on the draining board: Pomagne and brown ale. Most of the guests are boys, which may be pleasing to Lucy, but isn't to me and Stephen, who've walked here two miles from Thornton only to find our chances of getting off with someone aren't good. In the bleakly pristine front room, two girls with their handbags laid like offerings on the floor are dancing to 45s, mostly songs about California. They move only from the waist-up, like trees. Hazel, with the blonde hair and Marianne Faithfull mouth, is rumoured to have one large breast and one small. Which is the duff one? Will the imbalance grow out? Or is the theory a nasty male revenge because she won't let any boy near enough to find out? I look at her, and she catches my eye and turns back to her girlfriend with a noise between a contemptuous snort and a pitying giggle. The girls have the floor to themselves and seem to want to keep it that way and, boys being boys, probably will.

It's boring, everyone says so, as all parties are agreed to be while they're happening – only in retrospect are they fun. Back in the kitchen, topping up my cup, I see Mick Turner snogging with Lucy, then breaking off to talk to his mate Pat Conolly about Burnley (the football team), as if the kiss hadn't happened or as if it had happened to someone else. Lucy stands there, beatific with a Babycham bottle. She and Mick kiss some more, by the cupboard under the stairs, then he opens the door and draws her inside: a flash of coat hooks, clothes pegs, brushes, mops, vacuum cleaner implements, and they're gone. Someone turns the music up in the front room. I stand around with Pat and Stephen, drinking beer from paper cups and arguing about football. California seems a long way off.

Then Mick comes out of the broom cupboard, adjusting his clothes, and nods at Pat, who takes his place. Mick tips his head back and glugs a brown ale and explains why Burnley are weak at left-back. Two minutes later, Pat comes out. "Go on, Blake, get in there," he says. Do I want to? Not much. Do I hesitate? No. I close the door behind me, and inhale the smell of dust, mice, perfume, mothballs, cider, furniture polish, semen, bleach. Lucy is moaning against the coat-hooks. She stretches her arms out and draws me into her sourapple kiss. Her eyes are closed, somewhere between sick and ecstasy. Does she know who I am? Her blouse is open and I feel her breasts and slip my hands under her skirt. She isn't wearing knickers or tights: they must be what I'm standing on. She pushes her tongue deeper into me as I push my hand deeper into her. Is the wetness her own desire or the sperm of Mick Turner and Pat Conolly? I know what I'm supposed to do next, but it's only between her and me and the stairs. She'll regret it. I'll regret it. Applesick breath, a quick last tongue, and I go, leaving her against the coat-hooks. I head for the draining board, in search of a drink, and don't look behind me. I don't need to look. I know someone will be taking my place.

Half an hour later, Lucy, crying, is taken off upstairs by three of her friends. The bottles are all empty, and it's quiet, the record off, only a handful of us left. We can hear Lucy's muffled sobs come down. Her friends come down, too, and begin to tidy up. The front door's open: midsummer warmth off the cobbles. Above the hum of Pickles mill, there's the sound of a distant police siren. We slip into the backstreets and are gone.

Later, it seems, sick, sore, crying still, Lucy tells her friends that seven boys had sex with her in the broom cupboard, including me. I learn this from the friends, on the school bus, not from Lucy, who I avoid. They're indignant at what happened to her but not as indignant as I'd expected: a rotten way for her to lose her virginity, they say, but there are no nice ways, and she'd have lost it soon enough. There's a shrug, a worldweariness, seen-it-all-done-it-all at fourteen. The impromptu parties resume. I sometimes see Lucy on the school bus, not outwardly altered. There's no talk of the police. There's no talk of rape charges, or of unlawful sex with a minor. It seems no one's guilty, or should feel guilty, let alone, in court, be found guilty.

Did I lie awake that night? The next night? Any night? I lie awake now (bed, upright chair, sixty watt bulb), a middle-aged man lost in the middle of life, looking for his childhood in a dark wood. I've become my own accuser: police interviews first, then the courtroom, where I cross-examine myself, desperate for exoneration from judge and jury. But I can't get justice. Correction: I can get *only* justice, not mercy.

Q: I put it to you that you took part in the gang rape of a minor.

A: No.

Q: But you admit that gang rape took place.

A: She was not held down or forced. And there was no gang as such.

Q: But she was not fully in control of her actions.

A: She was certainly drunk.

Q: And she was coerced by older men.

A: Scarcely men. Fifteen- and sixteen-year-olds.

Q: But older than her.

A: Yes.

Q: The girl was younger than you, and drunk, and you exploited that.

A: No. I refused to exploit it. I refrained from having intercourse with her, though she was willing.

Q: You deny having intercourse with her, but you admit to touching her intimate parts.

A: Yes.

Q: And you didn't seek to dissuade the other men – or boys – from having sex with her?

A: No.

Q: Why not?

A: I didn't think of it. They'd not have listened anyway.

Q: But is it not the case that there were boys present at the party who did not enter the broom cupboard?

A: Possibly.

Q: So it would have been possible for you to refrain.

A: Yes.

Q: And yet you chose to go ahead. Why?

A: Because I happened to be standing there and was encouraged to go in.

Q: Do you not believe in the exercise of choice and free will?

A: Yes. But I was passive, and immature. Plus, that night, a bit drunk.

Q: Do you think most boys of your age would have done the same?

A: In that era, in that place, yes. You have to remember how young we were, and how repressed the culture was. These chances didn't come often. And there was peer-group pressure. I was afraid of losing face.

Q: Should you not have rescued the victim from the broom cupboard?

A: None of her female friends tried to stop it, either.

Q: But your role was more participatory than theirs.

A: Yes.

Q: Are there any other previous offences you wish to mention now?

A: Nothing serious. I stole the odd thing.

Q: Anything else?

A: I joined in tormenting teachers. I teased and bullied other kids.

Q: Anything else?

A: I told lies.

Q: Are you lying now, about this gang rape?

A: No.

Q: But you admit that, while playing only a small part, you were nonetheless culpable.

A: Technically, no.

Q: Morally, then?

A: Yes.

Q: Morally, you were guilty of the offence?

A: Yes.

*

Court cases are often compared to plays: the drama, the tension, the playing to the public gallery. On the evidence of this trial, they're more like a book you can't put down, a single story told over and over again. Ten times at least.

1 The prosecution outlines its case, the blurb on the dust jacket.
2 The prosecution calls its witnesses, whose fragmented stories add up, it's hoped, to one story, a tale of sin and guilt.
3 The defence cross-examines those witnesses, to suggest they're unreliable narrators.
4 The defence calls its witnesses, who tell a different story, a tale of alibis and innocence.
5 The prosecution cross-examines these witnesses, seeking to restore the ur-text, the original guilt.
6 The prosecution sums up.
7 The defence sums up.
8 The judge sums up, reviewing the evidence and hinting that some stories may have more to recommend them than others.
9 The jury weighs these different narratives and chooses between them, the verdict given, the prize awarded, to the side which has told the best story or, rather, has told its story best.
10 The press tells the story one last time, with detail about the history of the protagonists which has not been available before.

Again and again and again and again . . . No wonder, this morning, listening to the nth policeman confirming some procedure after the arrest, there's a sense of *déjà vu*. I have been here before so often it feels as if I've never been anywhere else.

But there's an air of expectancy, nonetheless. The Crown witnesses have been called, the tapes played, and we've heard the details of the ID parades. The prosecution's almost finished. Any moment now it'll be the turn of the defence.

For days we've been wondering what the boys' defence will be. There are admissions of guilt. There are blood stains and paint stains. There are expert testimonies that T & V knew right from wrong. Some witnesses have been inconsistent, but that's excusable, given their distress about the crime, and may even have endeared them to the jury. It's all gone the way of the Crown.

For David Turner, Robert Thompson's barrister, the experience has been frustrating. His private view is that the trial is "bloody medieval". The kids shouldn't be paraded like circus animals. He can't pretend to warm to Robert, even less so to his mother, but that's beside the point. He's doing the best he can. At the start he thought his side had the better chance, Jon having coughed "I did kill him". But Robert hasn't made a good impression. He's hard to get through to. If he'd been more mature, he might have seen the point of pleading immaturity – of exploiting *doli incapax*. But he's continued to lie even to his helpers. The only other defence line would have been the videos: to have used *Child's Play 3* against Jon. But that route was lurid and sensationalist, with the risk it might rebound. Which left only a damage-limitation exercise – avoid a murder verdict. Now even that looks optimistic.

Frustration, too, in the Venables camp. Any sympathy going in court is all for Jon, but how to exploit it? An offer to the Crown to plead guilty to manslaughter was rejected before the trial began. An argument that Jon has a mental age of less than ten, and shouldn't stand trial, was not firmly enough supported by the psychiatric reports. There's the defence that

Jon was coerced by Robert: a killer under duress. It's what his parents believe. But Jon needs to say it himself. Since the police interviews he's not talked about the killing at all.

Might he now, in the stand? Mary Bell spoke, in her case, a quarter of a century ago; so did her accomplice, Norma. Gitta Sereny, in her book, describes it well: the simple, bewildered Norma, the younger but cleverer Mary in her yellow cotton dress, the long hours in the stand. The two of them had killed two little boys, but Norma was cleared and Mary found guilty only of manslaughter. It seems to have helped their case that they took the stand; it certainly didn't do them any harm. But T & V are suffering from post-traumatic stress disorder (which had no name at the time of Mary Bell). To call them might be cruel and counter-productive: Jon would look furtive, Robert cheeky. Questions might bring out further lies, and there have been lies enough already. Every lie is a victory for the Crown, evidence that the boys are trying to exculpate themselves and thus understand right from wrong. The risk is that by speaking they'd weaken an already flimsy case.

On the other hand, if they stay silent, or are heard only as voices on a tape, they may seem more sinister than they are. To take the stand might move the jury. Never mind the words they speak, there'll also be the words they fail to speak. To stammer, to break down, to show their vulnerability: it might feel bad but do them good. Help the rest of us, too: differences between them would emerge, traits to help us allocate responsibility.

Some thought's been given to this: not in Jon's camp (he bangs the wall hysterically whenever James's killing is even mentioned), but in Robert's. When Ann, on advice, told him he'd have to speak, he said OK – he was frightened, but OK.

They had a dry run, in private. Robert did all right at first, holding eye contact with David Turner and sticking to the story he'd told the police – everything had been done by Jon. But the story had obvious flaws: he was lying, as if by reflex, and began to panic at the questions. "If they put him in that box, they'll bury him," said Ann, backing down. "I'm not going in that box," said Robert, reusing her coffin image. That established, he became cocky again, accusing Turner of asking silly questions and declaring that the shoes in court, with D rings, exhibits 45 and 46, key evidence against him, must belong to someone else. Afterwards, all agreed: it was not in Robert's interest to be called.

That's why, today, it's over in a flash, two men standing up then sitting down again. "We call no defence" says David Turner for Robert. "We call no defence" says Brian Walsh for Jon.

"No defence." But that doesn't mean no answers. I try to set down some of my own:

- Because Jon was disturbed, having grown up in a tense, unhappy home
- Because Robert was brutalized, having grown up in a violent one
- Because of the chemistry: they spurred each other on
- Because of a dare, an incredible plan they never expected to work
- Because no adult they met listened to their appeals to intervene
- Because James became a surrogate for their loathing of their siblings

– Because they didn't know where illusion ended and reality began

– Because they didn't understand death's irrevocability

– Because they were scared of getting into trouble, and silencing James looked like the best way to avoid it.

Tomorrow the prosecution will sum up. The day after, the defence will. The day after that: the judge.

No one doubts T & V killed James Bulger. But there are different kinds of verdict, and now the jury's moment is coming near. What are they like, the jury? They sit to the side, in pews, nine men, three women, middle-aged mostly, middle-class too by the look of it, a dozen earnest burghers, grey, stolid, grave as the dead judges on the wall. From time to time I've felt a pang for them, turning up for jury service perhaps not knowing this was one of the cases and then, sweet Jesus, being chosen for it: four weeks of torment instead of a quickly-over GBH in the next court. The more nervous jurors have looked to be on trial themselves, so much expected of them. One woman, taking her oath, stumbled over her words, like a bride forgetting who she was marrying. There aren't many things in life so serious you have to swear on the Bible. This is one.

Twelve honest citizens determined to be serious. But who can say what they'll decide? It only takes an oddball, a dissenter, a charismatic radical. Maybe they'll be moved by Jon's daily tears. Maybe they'll believe that Robert, one shoe-print aside, was a mere spectator. Maybe they'll choose manslaughter. The dead judges look down from their frames. The door screams at the back of the gallery. The hacks are back, in spades. At last, adrenalin, suspense.

It's getting to the boys, too. What happened to Robert's self-possession? Captain of his own soul, he's hardly flinched for three weeks. When one barrister used the trope of a "broad brush", Robert mouthed to his social worker: "What's a broad brush?" But self-possession (the passage to remorse sealed up) isn't a great asset when you're accused of killing. And I see Robert differently now. I notice how tense he is, and fidgety. I understand, despite his cropped hair, how he might have once been teased for being a girl. "Those who have been dry-eyed may also be feeling pain and misery," says his barrister, David Turner, summing up. Yesterday and today Robert has expressed that misery. "Thratching" my mother would call it, and though some would claim it's behaviour typical of a child who has been sexually abused, I see it as unhappiness and nerves. He rubs a wet finger around his upper lip, pulls out his lower lip (I remember James's injury), strokes his tongue, massages his chin, twiddles his fingers, sucks his clasped hands, chews his neck chain, mock-types on the wooden rail in front of him, rotates the ring on his little finger, nervously dabs his mouth with blue tissue paper, silently coughs into it, folds and refolds the tissue, puts a finger in an ear, screws up his eyes, gazes at the ceiling, fits his fingertips against his teeth, wipes his wet hands on his trousers, licks his fingers one by one. He sucks his thumb, too, not having been warned, as thumb-suckers used to be, that a red-legged scissor man will come and cut it off. And he tears the paper tissue to confetti, bit by shredded bit.

Maybe it's the prosecution summary that upsets him – hearing himself described as the greater and more cunning liar. But he seems just as upset by his own counsel. When David Turner speaks of the terrible sorrow felt for the Bulgers ("The city of Liverpool missed a heartbeat, and the country was shrouded in grief"), and of "a tragedy for three families, not one", Jon starts to blub, and then Robert, too, just a little. There's an awkward moment when Turner discusses the matter of the marks on James's cheek. The Crown has shown conclusively that these marks, looking like staples and horse-hooves, must have come from Robert's shoes: black brogues, traditional uppers coarsely stitched, the laces criss-crossing through D-rings. But doesn't scientific evidence also suggest, Turner asks the jury, quoting from the standard work, *Footwear Impression Evidence*, that bruises like those left on James come from blows of light impact? Could it be that James's cheek, that is to say, impacted on Robert's shoe, not vice versa? That he fell on the shoe, rather than was kicked by it? So it runs. A desperate line of defence. Awkward for all of us. But what is Turner to do? The footprint is the main evidence against his client, who has instructed him to plead not guilty. He has to fight as best he can. His job is to make bricks from straw, or *vice versa*. It doesn't mean he's unfeeling, uninvolved, cab-rank impartial. He has walked from Bootle to Walton with two of his own children, incredulous at the distance. He has been attacked in the papers for upsetting witnesses (particularly female witnesses) with his abrasive questions, and been caricatured as a Georgy-Porgy making them cry. But he can't help his defence sounding desperate – it *is* desperate. Robert knows this. Robert's not stupid. He tears at his tissue. He knows the verdict's coming near.

Maybe it's his mother Robert is worrying about, more than himself. Ann's here every day now, in a brighter, stripier dress, not the sackcloth and ashes she first came in. It hasn't been easy: the other day one of the Bulger relations, passing her in the corridor, called her a twat. She put that down partly to the five-pointed Orange Lodge star she wore on her neck, the denominational jewellery. Typical of Ann to shift the blame from the more obvious source of the Bulgers' anger: her being Robert Thompson's mum. But she does have a point. Liverpool is a sectarian city, and the killing of James had its religious element, its whiff of an ancient feud – like the medieval legend of the Christian boy murdered by Jews, as narrated by Chaucer's Prioress. Tribalism, and the shedding of innocent blood: perhaps Ann is right to feel that, to the Bulgers, Robert and Jon were two Prods (Walton being a strongly Protestant area) slaughtering a little Catholic.

Ann fidgets in her seat as Turner sticks up for Robert. People are staring at her – as if what happened were her fault. I stared at her this way myself at first and loathed the big-eyed self-pitying. But separation, poverty, too many sons to look after and now this – no wonder she feels sorry for herself; I feel sorry for her too. Still in denial, she can't believe Robert guilty of killing. He's too soft for that – the kind of boy who likes to suck his thumb and sit in his mother's lap. She knows when he tells lies and believes him when he says it was Jon. If Robert had planned the killing, why walk back to Walton, where neighbours would recognize him, and why choose the railway, where every kid in the area likes to play? Her boys are always getting the blame. They've been arrested so often, she even asked at Walton Lane for a job, joking she spent more time down the police station than the police did. You have to laugh or you'd kill yourself, as she tried to, with an overdose, after her third child. She'd hoped once for two boys and a girl in the middle (the two boys to protect the girl), and has gone on trying for a girl, without success. Sometimes it feels – here in court especially – that nothing's gone right for her from the beginning, and she'll be struggling still when she goes to her grave.

The counsellors stroke and pet Ann. At the front of the

court, David Turner winds up, reminding the jury of the "petulant" Jon's deceitfulness (that "magical mystery tour" he took the police on for five interviews) and of his own client's denial of the offence. He steps down. We break for coffee. On the pew-rail in front of Robert, like a guinea pig's nest, there's a little mound of paper bits.

Jon's defence takes much longer than Robert's – 160 minutes, rather than 75. It starts before lunch and goes on past knocking-off time. It's not just that Brian Walsh is more fond of peroration, but that he feels he has a better case. He follows much the same line as Turner: the killing of James was a mischievous prank that went horribly wrong when the boys had to rid themselves of their burden. But it's a cut-throat defence, and Walsh's is the sharper blade – a blade he has to bury in Robert. Jon's tears and diffidence, Walsh argues, set him apart: a "brave and truthful little boy", he is "obviously genuine" in his remorse. Any talk of getting a kid lost had been bravado, one of those "dreadfully silly things children say to make themselves look big". Unlike Robert – calm, cunning, arrogant, sophisticated, brazen – Jon was no schemer. He intended to take James to the police station. His lesser part on the railway was "shameful behaviour but not murder". Later, he co-operated with the police. He hadn't tried to absolve himself. He'd come clean. He'd stopped lying. He was *good*.

The jury sit stony-faced. I'd guess Walsh doesn't wash with them. His tone is *de haut en bas*. And there's a fundamental flaw in his defence: Jon may be brave and truthful, but admitting "I did kill him" highlights his active part. Neil and Susan bury their heads. For three weeks they've been icons of ordinariness, guarantors of their offspring's decency. But it's too late for this to have effect any more, if ever it did. They won't have to wait much longer. Walsh winds up. Now only the judge.

How can you tell what a judge thinks? For most of the trial he just sits there, wrapped like a pharaoh and almost as dumb. But what he says at the end can sway the jury. He can steer them gently, or lead them by the nose. He can distil the essence of the case or pour away the lot in favour of a brew of his own. Is this judge, Michael Morland, a distiller or a home-brewer? How will he turn out?

He's been kindly up till now: solicitous towards the jury, patient with witnesses, affable, impeccably liberal, a good egg. But he hasn't looked at T & V much, hasn't been heard to ask: "Do you understand?" It doesn't bode well for them. Nor does his recapitulation of evidence. What the jury has to decide, he says, is not who struck the fatal blow but "were they in it together?" – he makes the analogy of the burglar who nicks a television and his mate who drives the getaway car, both under the law equally guilty. What the jury has to decide is not what T & V planned to do with James along the route, but "were the blows they struck on the railway intended to cause death or serious injury?" What the jury must also decide is whether the boys told lies out of panic, stupidity, confusion and fear – or because they knew what they'd done was wrong and were trying to hide it. Through a long day he goes over what happened, circuitous but also circumspect: "You may think", "It is for you to decide if . . .", "It is a matter for you to . . ." "You may think . . ." They may think. It's up to them to think. He isn't paid to do their thinking for them. Except that he is doing, by thinking aloud himself.

As If

He follows the same line with the taped interviews: by taking them one by one, even-handedly, he implies an equal complicity. I wish I had a tape for his own performance, but tape-recorders are forbidden in court. He repeats the boys' words and mimics their accents: "on me own", "yeah", "cos", "yeah", "If you want, like", "yeah", "God's honest truth", "yeah", "yeah", "yeah". In another context, it might be funny: an impeccably RP judge trying to do Scouse but sounding stage-Cockney instead. The context here is murder, though, and the impersonations, if not malicious, have a sniff of distaste. Middle-class children wouldn't be mimicked like this. T & V are being treated as street urchins (the phrase has occurred more than once during the trial), their dress and accents held against them. There's enough to hold against them without having to refer to their scruffiness and Scouse.

But I don't suppose anyone notices. There's too much else to notice: the pain inflicted on the railway, the pain inflicted still. When the judge recites James's injuries again, Ann Thompson starts crying (she's not heard the kicks and bricks in detail before), and soon Jon and Neil are crying, too; as usual, Susan and Robert are the tougher ones, the non-weepers, though they too have shed tears. This trial is as salt-smeared as the sea.

At 11.45, the jury prepare to go out. T and V face three charges – murder and abduction of James, attempted abduction of another child – and each must be judged on each. It's a lot to think about, all at once. The verdict must be unanimous, the jury is told, "the verdict of each and all of you". It only takes one to be awkward, and, even if all are agreed, after three and half weeks' slow torture it would be indecent to hurry now. Twelve beds have been reserved at a nearby hotel. We expect them to be slept in.

*

The jury out, a barrister for the Mirror Group is petitioning to be allowed to name names. The *Mirror* owns an exclusive on Child X, the child (allegedly) almost abducted before James, and believes that the public has a right to be informed exactly who this four-year-old is. A barrister for Associated Newspapers is making a similar appeal: he, too, talks of "public interest" – if Boy A and Boy B can become Robert Thompson and Jon Venables, the world will be a safer, better place. The arguments have been poorly prepared (there's mention of the precedent of Mary Bell "and her sister" Norma, a schoolboy howler), and I can't imagine them succeeding. We've grown used to the sound of Boy A and Boy B. To name them now will make their eventual rehabilitation more difficult. No public interest is served by naming a child who was *nearly* abducted. To print the names (and photographs) of T & V is mere gawping – and will wreck the lives of their parents and siblings. This is what the defence lawyers are arguing, and I go along with them. T & V should remain initials. I'd want my children to remain initials. I'd want anyone's children to remain initials. Offenders under sixteen are never normally named in public: why should these two be? But there are counter-arguments. That fair, accurate and open reporting is better than sneaky imputation. That disclosing T & V's names and backgrounds will be a deterrent to other potential child child-killers. That murderers shouldn't be granted the privilege of anonymity when it's been denied to the murderee. The debates run on. The judge says he'll announce his decision after the verdicts. But he hints at what it will be: the "bizarre and terrible circumstances" of the killing are an argument for names to be in the public domain; only detailed and open investigation of the boys' backgrounds can help explain the crime.

Later a clerk hands out a hastily typed sheet, "varying the orders". The embargo will be lifted. I look at the judge suspiciously: has he a streak of vindictiveness towards the boys and their parents? Or is he acting from humane and reformist motives, as if he were Dr Barnardo stumbling on the squalor of children's lives and exposing it to public gaze? Either way, it's a confession of failure. The trial has brought us no nearer to understanding the reason that James was killed. It has failed to give us the Why. The *Sun* and *Star* and *Mirror* will have to do the job instead.

As if.

I sit in the corridor, just outside court, afraid to leave in case the jury reach a verdict. To pass the time, I'm reading Liam Hudson's *Contrary Imaginations*, subtitled "A Psychological Study of the English Schoolboy", which cites intelligence tests performed on teenage boys. The boys were asked to write down as many different uses they could think of for certain objects. These were among their answers.

1: The Brick: To throw at someone. To smash my sister's head in. To tie to cats and drown them in ponds. For hitting and killing people. As a weight to remove a pistol after committing suicide.
2: The Barrel. To put spikes round the inside and shove someone in and roll along the ground. For stuffing headless bodies in. To close the lid on someone and roll over a cliff. To put a cat in when half full. To tar and feather in. To fill with stones and roll down a hill and squash somebody.
3: The Paper Clip. As a thumbscrew. To jab an enemy with. For pinching skin. For hurting someone's finger.

4: The Tin of Boot Polish. For suffocating insects. To make people sick with by putting small quantities in their food. To slap in someone's face.
5: The Blanket. To smother my mother. To remove from my baby sister's bed in winter while she's asleep. For suffocating a person to death. To wrap a dead wife in so blood does not stain the car seat when the body's being dumped.

These answers seem as shocking as anything we've heard in court – and shocking for the same reason. There's a peach-glow and vulnerability about children that seems incompatible with their having violent thoughts, or performing violent deeds. We imagine them as milk-white and pure. We imagine them as old words from the *Golden Treasury*: blossom, gossamer, foam flowers, sea-down, dewy eyes. We imagine them as imagining only good. *As if.*

Just after five, there's a rumour the jury is returning. We take our seats. The boys take their seats. The Bulgers take their seats; heavily pregnant, Denise is here for the first time, to see what her son's killers look like. Susan and Neil Venables are here, too, but not Ann Thompson, who has been left below court, downstairs. The jury comes in. Word is, the foreman's going to say they need longer. The bearded, Scottish, rumbling-voiced clerk asks: "On the first count of attempted abduction, have you reached a verdict yet?" "No", says the foreman, brusque, blunt, in broad Lancastrian. As you were. As we thought. Relax.

"On count 2, have you reached a verdict on which you are all agreed?"

"Yes."

Guilty of the abduction of James Bulger, both of them.

"On count 3, have you reached a verdict on which you are all agreed?"

"Yes."

"Do you find the defendant Robert Thompson guilty or not guilty of the murder of James Bulger?"

"Guilty."

"Do you find the defendant Jon Venables guilty or not guilty of the murder of James Bulger?"

"Guilty."

"And is that the verdict of you all?"

"It is."

"Yes," someone shouts from the public gallery, a Bulger relation punching the air. Jon cries. His parents cry. Albert Kirby walks to the gallery, leans over, kisses Denise. Robert doesn't cry but is taking deep breaths, traumatized, hyperventilating. Down below, Ann, asthmatic, her legs buckling under her, hasn't been able to climb the stairs in time for the verdict. Now she's been told and is crying. When Robert's brought down he hugs her and cries too.

Some minutes later the judge calls everyone back to pass sentence on the boys: "The killing of James Bulger was an act of unparalleled evil and barbarity . . . The sentence that I pass upon you is that you shall be detained during Her Majesty's Pleasure, in such a place and under such conditions as the Secretary of State may direct, and that means that you will be securely detained for very, very many years, until the Home Secretary is satisfied that you have matured and are fully rehabilitated and are no longer a danger to others." Her Majesty's Pleasure. HMP, as T & V have already learned to call it. They hang their heads and try not to cry too freely. Her Majesty would not take pleasure in the sight of them now. The Bulgers aside, no one could. The judge says: "Let them be taken down."

The boys are taken down. "How do you feel now, you little bastards?" shouts Ray Matthews, Denise's brother, as they go. The words will look much worse in tomorrow's headlines than they sound here. In Scouse, "little bastards" is how you might address two kids who've kicked a football through your window, not affectionate exactly, but acknowledging that this is what kids are like. Even "evil" has this level of acceptance: you wouldn't have to murder to be called it; you'd only have, occasionally, to be bad.

With the boys out of the way, the judge addresses the court, adult to adult, just as it's been all along. "It is not for me to pass judgement on their upbringing, but I suspect that exposure to violent video films may in part be an explanation. In fairness to Mrs Thompson and Mr and Mrs Venables, it is very much to their credit that during the police interviews they used every effort to get their sons to tell the truth. The people of Bootle and Walton and all involved in this tragic case will never forget the tragic circumstances of James Bulger's murder. The Bulger family have the sympathy of us all, and everyone in court will especially wish Mrs Bulger well in the months ahead and hope that her new baby will bring her peace and happiness. I hope that all closely involved in this case, whether as witnesses or otherwise, will find peace at Christmas time."

We file out a last time from the chamber of dead judges. No sign of Christmas stars overhead, but I see what the judge means, to invoke a message of hope and healing, of good will to all men. His earlier words are hard to fit with this. "Unparalleled evil and barbarity"? Horrendously cruel, certainly, but "unparalleled evil"? For nearly a month, Michael

Morland has seemed kindly, liberal. Now the wolf hiding under his robe has bared its teeth. But it could be that he is coming on strong to keep the tabloids happy, and to appease the relatives of James Bulger. Only the sentence he recommends will show him for what he is. How long does he intend "very very many years" to be?

In a room off the bar, night fallen, a Christmas party's going on. I stand over a whisky, and a girl fresh from dancing steps up to order a glass of water. Her neck and naked back are flushed with rose. In the cleft above her lip are beads of moisture, like dew on a pane. She drinks the glass in one go and wipes the sweat away with her wrist, eager to get back. Does she want a drink with us, one of the hacks asks. She does not want a drink with us. I feel old and pissed. Each time the music starts the dancers sway, in rhythm, and I sway, too, out of it. I've talked all evening, and gone from measured to excessive to gibbering. Now it's worse than that: I know what I want to say but words won't come at all. I nod my silent excuses, and leave. The keyboxes, behind Reception, look like Bentham's Panopticon, a dovecote of little cells. The lift takes years, finding the room decades.

I slump in front of the television. Wall-to-wall Bulger. On the news, Polly Toynbee, the BBC's social affairs correspondent, says: "Plenty of children grow up deprived. There may be no more moral or social lessons in this case than in any other bizarre murder." And on *Newsnight*, Sean Sexton, the Bulgers' solicitor, says: "This was very much a one-off: it's dangerous to extrapolate lessons for society." Some of the policemen involved speak out for the first time. Albert Kirby says he believes the boys planned the murder ahead: "I truly believe they are just evil," he adds, "and there is nothing to provide any excuse for them." Phil Roberts, who interviewed Robert, says the boys are "freaks who just found each other". It's a blessing they were caught so quickly: "You should not compare these two boys with other boys. They were evil. I think they would have killed again. I think they would have become like the Kray twins."

Later Ralph Bulger is quoted: "One day they'll be out of jail and I'll be waiting for them." And James's uncle, Jim, calls a television phone-in and threatens, before his words are faded out: "when we get hold of them, we will fucking kill them." Bloody vengeance, silenced for the past four weeks but now given its voice. The trial was supposed to excise this hurt, to exorcize demons. But the justice meted out doesn't feel like justice even to the Bulgers, whose pain seems to have increased, not eased.

I think of Robert and Jon being driven away – not to a narrow cell, let alone a foetid dungeon, but a lock-up hostel with therapy. Alive, unlike their little victim, what sympathy do they deserve? This much: that they are little, too; that they killed only half-knowing what they were doing; that however wicked they were in those five minutes, it is also wicked to have paraded them, for nearly a month, in an adult court. They'll spend their youth inside now, as they must, punished, psychoanalysed and protected from mob vengeance. But to call these children evil, or to think that they've been given natural justice: that would be unnatural; that would be the greatest childishness of all.

As I lie on the bed, something monstrous swims out of the dark. James, I think, abandoned on the tracks inside his fur-lined hood, the tape reversed so that the bricks fly back to safety and the blood flows back into his veins. But then his head becomes two bigger heads, the Hydra tears of Boy A and Boy B, T & V, black jacket and mustard jacket, smaller and taller, Robert and Jon, battered by what's been done to them today, and through a month's trial and the nine months of their custody – not death-blows such as they inflicted, but big enough to crush them, and with an echoing darkness that sends me under the covers hiding from complicity and shame.

12

As If

youth is . . . not just like being an animal so much as being like one of these malenky toys you viddy being sold in the streets, like little chellovecks made out of tin and with a spring inside and then a winding handle on the outside and you wind it up grrr grrr grr and off it itties, like walking, O my brothers. But it itties in a straight line and bangs straight into things bang bang and it cannot help what it is doing. Being young is like being like one of these malenky machines.

ANTHONY BURGESS, *A Clockwork Orange*

"What will I look like when I die?" my four-year-old asks one morning.

"How do you mean?"

He repeats it, baffled that I'm baffled: "What will I look like when I die?"

"I don't know . . . Like you are now."

"Like now?"

"Much older, I hope, very very old, but like you, yes."

He seems doubtful, but then he's off hoeing and scything like a Power Ranger. What did he mean? Look like at the moment of death? After death, burnt to bits or rotting in the ground? Or in the next life? He speaks of coming back as a leopard. He believes in heaven, too, and I don't disenchant him. Often, he asks when I'm going to die, and gets frustrated when I say I don't know. Not that he wants me to die, but he's bewildered that I can't be precise, can't give him the year, month, day, hour: aren't I big and supposed to know about things, so why don't I know about this big thing? As for his own death, that's easy. He knows he'll live forever. Though there's no human precedent, he's immortal. There is a precedent: every other child feels immortal, too.

At least he didn't ask what James looked like. I know that. I've seen the photographs, as the jurors did, a deck of shiny prints – anorak, upper torso, legs further down the tracks, wounded face, like a doll. Each March I count the birthdays he should have had. Each August I count the birthdays Jon and Robert do have, in confinement. Do I sound obsessed? I am obsessed. There are others no less obsessed. We gather together in twos and threes, a club, the Bulgerites. We notice every headline. We monitor each new development.

Plenty of these. A month after the trial, Justice Morland gives his recommendation for sentence: a minimum of eight years. It is much shorter than expected, and suggests his strong words at the end of the trial must have been that classic ploy of liberal judges, who follow a weighty pronouncement in court with a light sentence. The Lord Chief Justice, in his recommendation, ups the tariff to ten years. The Home Secretary, Michael Howard, six months later, makes it a minimum tariff of fifteen years, citing the weight of "public concern", including Ralph and Denise Bulger's petition – to let a life sentence mean life – which has gathered nearly 300,000 signatures. (The Bulgers' petition is helped by a television phone-in: as the *Sun* reports it, "80,000 call TV to say Bulger killers must rot in jail". The *Sun* lends its own support, urging its readers to fill in a coupon: "Dear Home

Secretary, I agree with Ralph and Denise Bulger that the boys who killed their son James should stay in jail for LIFE".) In the High Court, lawyers for T & V appeal against the fifteen-year tariff. They argue that the Home Secretary passed sentence without seeing social and psychiatric reports on the boys, and failed to have regard for various mitigating circumstances, including their extreme youth. They argue that, as HMP juveniles, the boys should not have been treated like adults with mandatory life sentences. They also argue that the "deterrence" element in the tariff is inappropriate: killings by ten-year-olds are extremely rare – so who exactly is being deterred? Justices Pill and Newman uphold the appeal. They quash Michael Howard's tariff, finding it "unlawful" and inconsistent with the need regularly to review the progress of young offenders detained at HMP. Michael Howard is "outraged". He counter-appeals. The Master of the Rolls, Lord Woolf, along with Lord Justices Hobhouse and Morritt, turn him down. He takes his case to the House of Lords and loses a third and final time, by a majority of three to two. The case passes to the new Labour government's Home Secretary, Jack Straw, who has a reputation for being tough on juvenile crime. How he will treat the tariff remains to be seen.

Other developments. The Association of Video Retailers recommends to members that they withdraw *Child's Play 3* from their shelves. Twentieth-century Fox announces it's postponing the release of *The Good Son*, in which Macaulay Culkin plays an evil child. An exhibition at the Whitechapel Gallery, which includes photographic images of the Bootle Strand abduction by the artist Jamie Wagg, brings protests: newspapers that have endlessly used the same images accuse such "art" of being indecent, disrespectful, profiteering. Denise has her baby, a boy. Ann Thompson has a baby, also a boy, her eighth on the trot, still out of luck. She changes her name and moves with her younger sons to a new town, nearer Robert. Susan and Neil Venables also move towns and change their names. Ralph Bulger and his brother Philip are charged with assault – an affray in a nightclub, a fight with another pair of brothers. Ralph and Denise break up: not so much the stress, the memories of James, the poisoned jar of money from well-wishers, but Ralph going off with a younger woman.

Another development. The foreman of the Bulger jury, Vincent Moss, speaks out on a radio programme. He regrets the unanimous murder verdict – guilty but with diminished responsibility would, he feels, have been more appropriate: "We should have gone back into court and said, yes, we do have a verdict: our verdict is that these young boys are in urgent need of social and psychiatric help." He says the case should have been tried in a special juvenile court. He thinks there was a shared agenda of public retribution, which the jury were unable to escape. He also complains about the curt letter he received from the court, after the trial. It had come to the court's attention that some of the Bulger jurors felt in need of counselling. Well, so be it. But if they did have to talk to a doctor or counsellor (preferably the former), jurors must remember not to disclose confidential details of their deliberations. Moss says he found this letter insulting. If you're traumatized – and his feelings after the trial were like bereavement – you need to talk, don't you? Otherwise, you go on being haunted. The terrible memories come unbidden.

They do, they do. Not only memories, but fantasies, *as if*s. One of mine is that I'm on the railway at Walton. It's dark, an hour or so past lighting up time. Three small shapes ahead of me. Laughter. The chink of something hitting the rail. The cry of a small child, not in pain, just shocked, bewildered, something spilt down its front. Kids playing catch probably. But who knows when a train might come? Isn't that a rumble now, a shiver along the rails? I move forward through the sodium dark, my eyes getting accustomed to the three shapes, one of them smaller. The kids will be angry at me for stopping their game. But I know something's coming, a long goods train, trouble, deep trouble, deep trouble. It's not too late. I start running. It's never too late. Hey . . .

I feel ashamed of my fantasies. They're inappropriate, I know. I'm a bundle of inappropriateness, a night-wandering man pierced with the remembrance of a grievous wrong. There are days I half-escape my broodings and decide Robert Thompson and Jon Venables were oddballs and no more, that nothing's to be gained by raking over the murder: it happened, it's over, no lessons, no looking back, let's get on. But next day I'll be back in my basement, a weak-eyed bat walled up with my sunless obsessions, *as if*ing myself back to the railway, on the track of a vital clue. I imagine truth dropping in my lap, like a late-basking pear. But the answers are elusive: all these Whys, but no Wherefore; Whys, but no wisdom. It's like living out Zeno's Paradox: if two runners set off at different points, the second, no matter how much faster, can never catch the first. There's truth just up ahead, but by the time I've gathered new evidence, truth has moved on. And keeps moving on, just out of reach, uncatchably ahead.

Times change. The bulbous earth lights up with flowers. In spring, my mother sends back her wheelchair and starts to walk. In summer, I retrek the Bootle–Walton trail: it's hot and sunny and nothing like the wasteland I remember. Were these here before? Did I miss them? Tenderly wired saplings; flats pretty with hanging baskets; a woman cradling a cat leaning down to gossip from her sliding window; young mothers with their pushchairs laughing together, happily conjoined in derision of the shittiness of men. Two boys are chucking something, their arms raised like stone-throwers in Belfast or the Gaza Strip; when I get near, I see it's only a tennis ball. There's glass under my feet, bottle glass, windscreen glass, bus shelter glass, but at dusk, the lights coming on, it shines like scattered jewels. For a moment, as the sun goes down pink over the roofs, the heaven this place was supposed to be is there in ghostly silhouette.

There's something else I see in Liverpool: a drawing, with writing, done by Jon. It was found in the wardrobe of his father's flat, and shows someone – a woman it looks like, with breasts – wielding a pair of knives; two victims entombed in blood-globs lie dead or dying on the ground, one with an arm like an erection. Jon drew this after watching a film called *Hallowe'en*, as he explains, or tries to (is this the writing of a nine- or ten-year-old of "average intelligence"?): "In My DaDs I saw hawowen is when you a girl and this man and he killed people EspECIAl girls and he has got a mask on that he robed knifes out the shop and the police that it was plce [illegible] but it was not it was the Man." The film *Hallowe'en* begins with a six-year-old boy committing murder. Years later, as an adult, he escapes from mental asylum and returns home to commit more murders. The kids call him a bogeyman, or boogieman. He won't stay down, he just keeps getting back up . . . Jon's drawing is dated Tuesday January 28, which means it was done in 1992 – unless he made a slip, and meant Thursday, which would date it a year later, just two weeks before the murder. Either way, the drawing suggests how seeing *Hallowe'en* deeply disturbed an already disturbed little boy. Did something else happen at home to disturb Jon? Was he frightened by Susan's physical chastisings? The knife-wielder in his drawing has breasts. Plenty of material for psychiatrists here. And cause for reflecting that videos may after all have had an influence. Judge Morland, when he suggested it, was mocked. He goes against the liberal grain. But he mightn't be altogether wrong.

Another Why, another motive. Why does Why matter so much? *Tout comprendre, c'est tout pardonner*, that's why. To understand is to forgive. Or maybe not. In the preface to her book *The Drama of Being a Child*, the psychoanalyst and child abuse expert Alice Miller writes: "My own experience has taught me that the enactment of *forgiveness* – which, sixteen years ago, I still believed to be right – brings the therapeutic process to a halt." Her words bring me to a halt. I see what she means: in therapy it's important not to block out feelings of anger. But what kind of model is this for a whole society? No forgiveness for parents who abuse, even if they were them-selves abused. No forgiveness for Susan and Neil Venables, or Ann Thompson, because of who their sons are. No forgive-ness – since they've been judged to be adult abusers and murderers – for Robert and Jon.

No forgiveness. It chimes with the mood of the *People*, the people, and the government of the people – the tabloids, the nation, Westminster. John Major, on juvenile crime, in the wake of the Bulger case: "We must condemn a little more, and understand a little less." Understand, meaning forgive as well as comprehend. A terrible motto, either way: *rien comprendre, c'est rien pardonner*. Epitaph to a weak-minded government. Epitaph to a brute culture. A plea to know less. A plea for ignorance. Forget the Why. Don't make the effort to grasp or know. Never forgive, even when they're adult, even when they're old, an act once committed by two children. The mother of Silje Marie Redegaard, a five-year-old Norwegian girl killed by schoolfriends, said she could forgive: "I cannot hate or bear a grudge against small children. They can't have understood what they did." Not every parent, in such circumstances, could find it in themselves to feel the same. For Ralph and Denise not to forgive is human. But for a whole nation not to, inhuman.

Inhuman and despairing. Only a culture without hope cannot forgive – a culture that doesn't believe in progress or redemption. Have we so little faith in ourselves we can't accept the possibility of maturation, change, cure? Have we so little faith in children? Fifty years ago, children with leukemia had almost no chance of survival. Today 90 per cent of them, the disease seared from their system, survive, prosper, grow up to tell the tale. Children can be restored socially and psychologically as well as medically. Robert and Jon could be rehabilitated, remorseful as they are. Prison shouldn't just be incarceration, but incarceration with therapeutic aspirations. It's inhuman not to forgive damaged children, and despairing not to try to save them. As if kids who kill come from another planet, and don't deserve the chance to be human, to atone, to repair. The future won't forgive us for this – won't forgive us for our lack of forgiveness. The future will think us childish for how we thought about children.

Not that children can't be dangerous. The little horrors run on. In Liverpool, a thirteen-year-old is charged with the murder of a nine-year-old girl, whose body is found on the railway line in Bootle. In Leeds, a ten-year-old, playing with two friends on top of a twelve-storey tower block, tips over a concrete slab, which kills a woman below. But perhaps the moral panic felt about episodes of child violence has begun to pass. At his trial, the boy in Leeds – chubby and crewcut like Robert Thompson – is convicted of manslaughter, but the judge, passing sentence, decides to give him a "fresh start", under a supervision order, rather than detain him. The police, and the woman's relatives, approve.

Between the ages of eight and fourteen, most of us do something terrible – something serious and adult, but performed in a childish, first-time daze. With luck, it isn't rape or murder, and no one gets badly hurt. Robert Thompson and Jon Venables weren't lucky (nor was their victim). They did something horrendous, were caught, put on trial and locked away. But this doesn't make them evil. Childhood is a separate place. You shouldn't punish adults for something they did as ten-year-olds. You can't lock up for life those whose lives have barely begun.

Yes, yes, people say, but those boys *knew* what they were doing. That old calumny, intention. Who are these people, who've never acted unwittingly, or self-transcendingly, or effected consequences they didn't foresee? For *doing* what they did, T & V must be confined for several years, and rightly. For *knowing*, if the media have their way, they may never be released. But they were children. To know, and yet not know – the condition of being ten.

I imagine a passionate advocate who could alter people's minds about this, who could get beyond our baby notions of justice, our eye-for-an-eye kindergarten philosophy, and help forgiveness find its nerve. I imagine books, articles, pamphlets, television programmes effecting a sea-change in our thinking, and Robert and Jon – at eighteen, maybe, or twenty-one – re-entering the world. Not that they crave release. They know the world outside is hostile and retributive. Even their closed units do not at times feel closed enough: they worry whose shift it is, fearing what might be done to them by unsupervised fellow inmates. More comfortable in some ways to know they'll always live behind locked doors. But suppose, after a decade or so of treatment, they were ready to come out. Suppose it was accepted that to have lost their names and homes, their childhood and adolescence was punishment enough. Suppose experts agreed they posed no threat to others. Suppose they walked free from prison, and there wasn't even a lurking photographer, let alone a Bulger relation with a gun. Suppose they were allowed to lead a normal life, to work, marry, have children . . .

As if.

Stranger things have happened. The Home Secretary could exercise his discretion. It depends on British public opinion changing – on Robert and Jon coming to be seen as children when they killed, not as Peter Sutcliffes and Myra Hindleys in miniature. It depends on the boys themselves making good progress. Are they making good progress? What is their health like, their state of mind? How much therapy are they getting, and what kind? What is life like for them in their units? I can't tell you. I haven't seen them in person. Even if I had seen them in person, I wouldn't be able to tell you. Under a court order, no reference can be made to the boys' treatment and place of residence. This order was intended to protect T & V from tabloid intrusion. But the public has a right to know that the boys are receiving proper treatment, that their lives are being rehabilitated, that the story hasn't ended.

I tap this out on to the screen while sitting in my basement. Around me are books about children – crumbling anthologies of parental love, dusty histories of Boy Life in Britain, psycho-socio analyses of delinquency. The older these books are, the more hopeful and sentimental. I don't mind this. What will become of us if we don't in some way venerate children? What will become of *them*? Thumbing through one of these books, I come across W. B. Yeats's "A Prayer for my Daughter". I've read the poem many times before, and have wished my own daughter, as Yeats does his, beauty and kindness. But I've somehow missed the last line of the second stanza, where he speaks of "the murderous innocence of the sea". Murderous innocence. A common enough idea, the sea as unknowingly destructive. A more troubling idea, applied to the human. The little hands of T and V, the little faces and voices, and the damage they did. The boys weren't innocent. But they weren't murderous either. Murderous innocence: something in-between.

I tap this out, and think of my children, and of my own childhood, and what we have in common, with each other and with T & V. There's an idea that some children are uniquely damaged, a race apart. I understand this idea, but I don't like it. There's too much Us and Them in it, a denial of shared humanity. I prefer to look at Robert and Jon in another way: as children I recognize from my own childhood, and as children I recognize from being a parent. There are dangers in this approach, too: liberal goo, moral relativism. But I don't think we can understand these boys and what they did unless we look within, at our own lives.

I tap this out, then turn off the screen and go out into the garden. At the far end, there's a patch of evening sunlight, and foxes are moving through the long grass. It's kindly, warm, bluebells and borage pushing through, as if the world might have some good in it after all. I walk down to the old shed, in search of something, I'm not sure what. Among the rakes, spades, watering cans, compost bags and coils of plastic hose, I find a packet of grass seed on a high shelf. I tear a corner off and let the seeds spill in my hand. They mill in my palm, hundreds and thousands, waiting to be born. I roll and shuffle them under my thumb, and let some fall, then spill them with more design, in a long trail across the earth. My hand's low to the ground, and I'm spilling seeds as I walk backwards, and the seeds are like a march in my wake, a line of marchers, a crusade. I think of hands being taken, and of a journey beginning in hope, and ending not in tragedy but miracles. I think of sunlight falling through the stained-glass Resurrection of a parish church, and of sins I've committed and people I've hurt, and of words from the Bible I'd forgotten: penance, shrift, expiation, propitiation, atonement. The seeds run out, and I wonder if I've wasted them in the hard and shadowed ground. But the evening's gentle, and I imagine grass, or even wheat, long silver-green blades growing and ripening, and the wind passing through them like a blessing.

As if.

Acknowledgements

At the trial of Robert Thompson and Jon Venables, I met Gitta Sereny and David James Smith, and spent many hours, then and later, talking to them: their own accounts of the case – Gitta Sereny's in the afterword to her reissued study *The Case of Mary Bell* (Pimlico, 1995), David James Smith's in *The Sleep of Reason* (Century, 1994) – are invaluable. Among others who helped in various ways are Frances Coady, Ursula Doyle, Richard Isaacson, Ian Jack, Pat Kavanagh, Laurence Lee, Elizabeth Levy, Dominic Lloyd, David Turner, Alan Williams and Graham Willis. One of my largest debts is to Paula Rego, who passed on material about The Children's Crusade and whose own paintings of children are a source of inspiration. Above all, I'm grateful, once again, to my own family.